Elizabeth Carmichael

Chloë Sayer

The Skeleton at the Feast
The Day of the Dead in Mexico

Published for the Trustees of the British Museum
by British Museum Press

This book is dedicated
with affection and grateful thanks
to all our Totonac friends
and colleagues in the town of Papantla
and surrounding communities

Frontispiece: Detail of a lifesize
papier mâché figure of a skeleton with flowering branches
made by Felipe Linares, Mexico
City. See plate *16.*

The cover shows: (*front, centre*)
Offerings for the souls of the
dead. Chicontepec, Veracruz.
(*Left*) Papier mâché figure
of a skeleton selling bread.
Mexico City. H *69*cms
(*Back*) Woman selling *cempa-
súchil* flowers for the Day of the
Dead. Acaxochitlán, Hidalgo.

© 1991 Trustees of the British Museum

The list of illustrations on p. 156 gives
copyright details of illustrations.

Published by British Museum Press
A division of British Museum Publications Ltd
46 Bloomsbury Street, London WC1B 3QQ

British Library Cataloguing in Publication Data

Carmichael, Elizabeth
    The skeleton at the feast: the Day of the Dead
      in Mexico.
    I. Title II. Sayer, Chloë
    394.2683

ISBN 0-7141-2503 2

Designed by Tony Kitzinger
Set in Monotype Plantin
and printed in Great Britain
by The Bath Press, Avon

Contents

Acknowledgements

The authors offer their thanks to all those who have assisted them during their work in the field and in the preparation of this publication and the exhibition that it accompanies.

We are indebted to the Trustees of the British Museum for enabling us to pursue our research in Mexico as part of the Ethnography Department's programme of Latin American Research and Collection and to the Director, Sir David Wilson, for his support. We also thank all British Museum staff, in all departments concerned, for their contributions. The realisation of ventures such as this is the work of many hands and minds.

In Mexico, we thank Jorge Angulo and his wife Chappie, the late Hedwig Yampolsky, Mariana Yampolsky and Arjen van der Sluis. These two families permitted us to fill their homes with our skulls and skeletons and endured the packing operations that concluded each visit. For that and much more besides we are most grateful. We also thank Ruth D. Lechuga for generously sharing her knowledge of Mexican popular culture. Over the years we have received much help from staff in the British Embassy and the British Council in Mexico City, particularly Marcela Ramírez, who has helped us above and beyond the call of duty.

Our appreciation goes to those artists and craftworkers whose words form part of the present text and to the many other people who generously gave information and unstinting hospitality. Among those who assisted us were: Roberto Ruiz; Louisa Reynoso; Marta Turok; Roberto Williams García; Mª del Refugio Cabrera Vargas; Simón Gómez Atzín; José Becerra O'Leary; Fabián Oviedo Mendiola; Nestor Aguirre Espinosa; the late Raúl Kamffer; Elia Gutiérrez; Lucila and Rafael Múzquiz; David, Felipe and Leonardo Linares and Tiburcio Soteno. The Totonac anthropologists Domingo García García and Áurea Vásquez Olmos greatly facilitated our work in the communities near Papantla; we thank them, Carlos Márquez Hernández and other staff of both the Instituto Nacional Indigenista and the regional office of Culturas Populares for their assistance. Our collection would have been the poorer but for the excellent recordings of music made in Veracruz by Eduardo Llerenas and Enrique Ramírez de Arellano.

In London, we thank the Mexican Ambassador, HE Bernardo Sepúlveda GCMG, for his interest in our endeavours and the several members of his mission who have worked on our behalf, especially Raúl Ortiz y Ortiz, Minister for Cultural Affairs. Sir John and Lady Morgan who share our love for Mexico have been constant in their support. We offer gratitude to John Lonsdale, Jenny Evans and other staff of the Technical Section at the Royal Botanic Gardens, Kew; also to Robert Allkin.

Thanks are also due to Simon Terry, Alicia Cazorla, Coryn Greatorex-Bell, David Phillipson and his staff, Seamus Murphy, Kristen Norget and all who have shared our enthusiasm and given us aid.

We would finally like to call attention to the generosity of the photographers who have allowed us to use their work and who are named in the list of illustrations.

Mexico

The names of States appear in the key below in *italic*

Distrito Federal
1 Mexico City
2 Mixquic
Veracruz
3 Tantoyuca
4 Chicontepec
5 Papantla, El Tajín, etc.
6 Zozocolco
7 Jalapa
8 Veracruz
Hidalgo
9 Huejutla de Reyes, Chililico, etc.
Guanajuato
10 San Miguel de Allende
Michoacán
11 Ocumicho
12 Morelia
13 Pátzcuaro, Janitzio, etc.

Estado de México
14 Toluca, Metepec
Puebla
15 Atla, San Pablito
16 Puebla City
17 San Salvador Huixcolotla
18 Atlixco
19 Huaquechula
20 Izúcar de Matamoros
21 San Gabriel Chilac
Guerrero
22 Iguala
Oaxaca
23 Oaxaca City
Yucatán
24 Chichén Itzá
25 Kabáh

USA

GULF OF MEXICO

PACIFIC OCEAN

Foreword

In one sense death is not an event which has to do with life for by definition it is something beyond the experience of living. Yet how individual cultures treat this circumstance is variable. In many, death is certainly not regarded as a termination but as an elevation to another level of existing. It is an event initially tinged with uncertain emotion, but ultimately one to be celebrated as the dead are reaccommodated as ancestors. Mortuary rites, in the classic analysis of the French anthropologist Marcel Mauss, separate out these elements. Actual burial has one set of characteristics and emotional content, subsequent ritual quite another. This book is concerned with the second set of circumstances – the Day of the Dead as it is celebrated in Mexico each year around All Saints' Day (1 November). Though associated with the dead, indeed dedicated to their remembrance, it is quite the reverse of morbid; it is a period full of life, colour and festival.

Some aspects of this contemporary annual celebration are presented by Mexicans themselves as 'traditional', some as unashamedly modern. Yet, in practice, there is no real disjunction: all is interwoven together. How such a range of reference came to be incorporated into a single contemporary event is by no means simple. Such is already implied in the fact that Mexicans of whatever background celebrate the event – indeed, even those who choose not to do so must make a definite decision to the contrary for its observance is a part of what constitutes engaging in popular Mexican culture. Clearly a whole series of accommodations are involved in giving the events the character they have today. The authors of this work, Elizabeth Carmichael and Chloë Sayer, have been especially concerned to give appropriate weight to both historical and present perception of the significance of the Day of the Dead. Rather than suppress, or interpret in a remote theoretical way, their aim has been direct and documentary. Such an approach is all the more necessary in a field where studies in English are few, and none seeks to reflect the variety of Day of the Dead celebrations whether across time or in its contemporary regional differences.

To that end there are at least three voices

which they have sought to articulate. The 'Skeleton' observed at 'the Feast' of the title might in its most immediate sense be taken to refer to the dead themselves called back at the appropriate season of the year; in a further sense it is also perhaps the spectre of past history and of the complexity of cultural tradition as seen in the Day of the Dead. It is especially timely to stress this link when the whole conspectus of relations of Europe to the Americas are beginning to be re-examined in the wake of another historical co-incidence – the quincentenial of Columbus' voyage of discovery. The present cultural significance of that voyage can readily escape consideration; yet it is incarnate in the form of the Day of the Dead festival. One voice, then, is of the past, both the pre-Hispanic conception of the relations of the living to the dead and the Christian-inspired view of such essentially Indian forms of celebration. The second is a contemporary voice literally recorded by the authors and offered here in the form of translated interviews for the insight it provides into the more personal and intimate aspects of the contemporary celebration. Many of the interviews are with the artists who make the variety of objects and decoration which are incorporated into the set-piece displays, the *ofrendas* (offerings), that are created in family homes.

A third voice that is present is the personal observation of the authors themselves, for this publication is at once the outcome of historical research and of direct participation in the events described. Elizabeth Carmichael and Chloë Sayer both have long experience of Latin American studies. Elizabeth Carmichael has had curatorial responsibility for the British Museum holdings from Middle, Central and South America for many years, a responsibility demanding an expertise that ranges across the fields of archaeology and ethnography. Chloë Sayer has undertaken original research on aspects of Mexican culture over a period of nearly two decades and has both organised exhibitions of Mexican popular arts and published extensively in the field. They began their collaboration in Mexico in 1985 as part of a deliberate programme of field research and collecting generously supported by the Trustees of the British Museum. In succeeding years this work extended over the States of Puebla, Mexico and Veracruz gradually focusing in on the events surrounding Day of the Dead celebrations.

Yet the book is also designed to provide an

evocation of another kind. The occasion for its publication is an exhibition of the same title opened on the Day of the Dead 1991 at the British Museum's Museum of Mankind, London. Many of the objects displayed are also illustrated here and the fieldwork which lends the authority of personal witness to this publication also included the study of associated artistic creations and acquisition of appropriate materials for the permanent collections of the Museum. The creation of such varied objects and the manner of their display in Mexican homes provides a further, visual commentary on the context within which the events take place.

John Mack
Keeper
Department of Ethnography

1. **The Day of the Dead in urban Mexico is a time when social comment is expressed in a wry and humorous way, often by means of skeleton figures engaged in everyday activities. Here, a complaints' clerk of the Mexican telephone service appears unable to place his own telephone call. Mexico City. H 34 cms**

Introduction

Mexicans often say: *somos muy fiesteros*, 'we enjoy a good celebration', an opinion that is abundantly evident in the large number of festivals and ceremonies that crowd their calendar. To these public events must be added the private family celebrations in which the same zestful relish for life finds further expression.

The famous author Octavio Paz has, as so often, placed a knowing finger on the Mexican national pulse when he writes:

Fiestas are our sole luxury. They are a substitute for, and perhaps have the advantage over theatre and vacations, Anglo Saxon 'weekends' and cocktail parties, bourgeois receptions and the Mediterranean café . . .

What is important is to go out, open up a way, get drunk on noise, people, colours. Mexico is in fiesta. And this fiesta, shot through with lightning and delirium, is the brilliant opposite of our silence and apathy, our reticence and gloom. (Paz: 1959)

That a festival to do with the dead should be a joyous occasion perhaps strikes those of us from other cultures with our different perceptions as something hard to come to terms with. The Day of the Dead is just that: a festival of welcome for the souls of the dead which the living prepare and delight in. The souls return each year to enjoy for a few brief hours the pleasures they once knew in life.

In the urban setting of Mexico City and other large towns the celebration is seen at its most exuberant, with figures of skulls and skeletons everywhere. These mimic the living and disport themselves in a mocking modern dance of death. It is not surprising that so colourful an occasion should have become a tourist event. Another celebrated Mexican author, Carlos Monsiváis tells us that in Mixquic, a town close to Mexico City, and at Pátzcuaro in the State of Michoacán, both famous for their celebrations of the Day of the Dead, the cameras have come to outnumber the candles in the cemeteries: 'Kodak takes possession', and 'Mexico has sold its cult of death and the tourists smile anthropologically satiated' (Monsiváis: 1970). The dead move with the times in Mexico.

Not far away from the tourist routes there is, however, another Mexico. In the rural areas, in every village or small town, the Day of the Dead

2. **Two traditional paper puppets of skeletal musicians as sold in urban markets in central Mexico for the Day of the Dead. Purchased in Toluca, State of Mexico. H (approx.) 49 cms**

witches and plastic pumpkins of Halloween are making their appearance alongside the traditional puppets and toy coffins; the great museums and galleries mount set-piece *ofrendas* (offerings) for the Day of the Dead, designed by artists and curators.

A short step away, one seems to be in the midst of something that has endured through centuries, some parts of it perhaps from pre-Hispanic times. In the countryside there are few if any skulls or skeletons; the images of the Christian saints who replaced the old gods stand on the household altars surrounded by the same offerings of food and flowers as were prepared for ancient feasts. The yellow marigolds – the *cempasúchil*[1] or 'flower of the dead' – give off their aromatic scent to attract the souls and draw them to the offering prepared in their honour.

Among the Mexicans themselves there is much debate upon the subject of death and the dead. Is there in Mexico a special attitude towards death that differs from that of other nations? Again, Octavio Paz in a passage from *The Labyrinth of Solitude* (1959), describes the so-called 'special relationship' with death:

To the modern Mexican death doesn't have any meaning. It has ceased to be the transition, the access to the other life which is more authentic than this one. But the unimportance of death has not taken it away from us and eliminated it from our daily lives. To the inhabitant of New York, Paris, or London death is a word that is never uttered because it burns the lips. The Mexican, on the other hand, frequents it, mocks it, caresses it, sleeps with it, entertains it; it is one of his favourite playthings and his most enduring love. It is true that in his attitude there is perhaps the same fear that others also have, but at least he does not hide this fear nor does he hide death; he contemplates her face to face with impatience, with contempt, with irony: 'If they're going to kill me tomorrow, let them kill me for once and for all'.[2]

There are many who dissent from the view that the special relationship exists. Scholars such as Carlos Navarrete (1982) scrupulously seek to avoid being drawn into what he sees as the undisciplined morass of description and the 'long list of generalisations which have been written on the theme of Death in Mexico'. These feed 'the myth of Death and the Mexican being . . . It is necessary to take in hand the task of demystifying the myth, to question it, and demonstrate its fragility as a component of a premeditated national prototype.'

He makes an important distinction between

is celebrated beyond the glare of flash-bulbs and noise of whirring video cameras. Each household prepares its offering of food and drink for the dead to be set out on a table among flowers and candles. The blue smoke of burning *copal* incense sanctifies the ceremony, just as it has done for centuries. Outside, the peace is shattered by the explosions of the rockets set off to mark the fulfilment of an obligation deeply felt. The whole company of the living and the dead share in the flowering and fruiting of the land which both have cultivated.

Whatever distractions tourism brings – the competitions for the best offering, the 'discos' for the dead with all their sequins and grotesqueries – there is at the core of it all an old tradition which informs and invigorates every kind of manifestation of the event and which has so far defied debasement. What is astonishing to the visitor is that so many different styles of celebration can co-exist under one sky. Today draculas, demons and Batman mingle with the skeletons and sugar skulls; the cardboard death cults and cults of the dead. The death cults, of which Mexico has its share, centre upon the image of Death as the 'Grim-Reaper', the *Santísima Muerte* (Most Holy Death) associated with the practice of witchcraft. From at least the eighteenth century, and perhaps before then, wooden images of Death personified as a skeleton were carried in procession through the streets, riding triumphant in carts and carriages. These took their descent from the images of Death of medieval Europe, brought to the New World from Spain in the early sixteenth century. Painted on the tiered catafalques associated with funerary rites in Colonial Mexico, the same skeletons ride and prance. They appeared on playing cards, in books and tracts and in the nineteenth century were triumphantly transmuted by the hand of the famous engraver of popular prints, José Guadalupe Posada. By this time, they were less the mocking harbingers of death, but rather wry commentators upon the vanities of life.

As toys, with nodding heads and dangling limbs, they have danced their way into the modern world, where they have not entirely lost their function as vehicles for satire. More often, they are simply amusing playthings which may sometimes produce a slight *frisson*, as felt for a Halloween witch, but never a grim and ghoulish shudder. In the modern world, Carlos Monsiváis suggests, 'death is still the terrible yet amusing entity that establishes a compromise between memory and the sense of humour, and between the sense of humour and the irremediable' (Monsiváis: 1987).

3. Sixteenth-century wooden figure of Death seated on a throne on a dais with wheels. He is shown wearing a crown and holding a scythe and sceptre. Yanhuitlán, Oaxaca.

4. 'The Cry' ('*El Grito*'): performer wearing a skull mask. Mexico City.

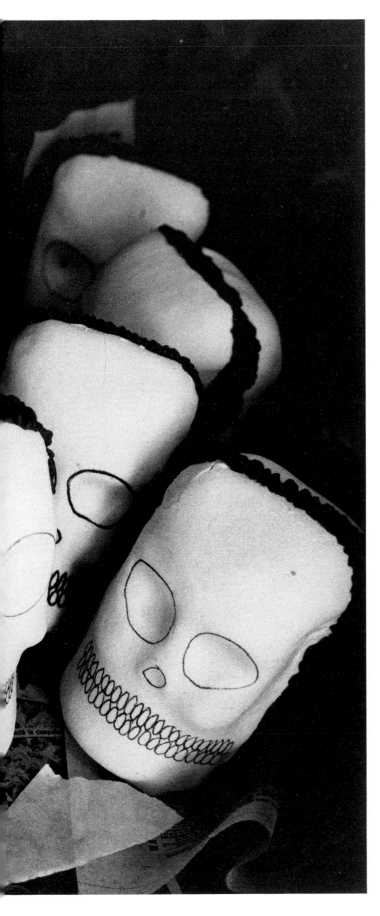

Part I

5. Hollow sugar skulls on sale for the Day of the Dead in San Miguel de Allende, Guanajuato.

The Day of the Dead

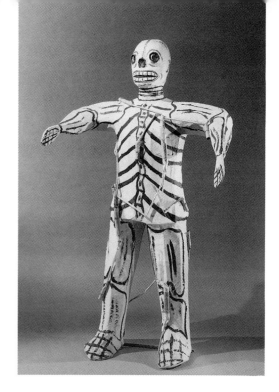

... death revenges us against life, stripping it of all its vanities and pretensions and showing it for what it is: some bare bones and a dreadful grimace ... Skulls made of sugar or tissue paper, painted skeletons hung with fireworks, our popular representations of death always mock at life; they are the affirmation of the nothingness and insignificance of human existence. We decorate our houses with skulls and on the Day of the Dead we eat bread in the form of bones and enjoy the songs and jokes in which bald death has the laughs; but all this swaggering familiarity does nothing to rid us of the question we all have to ask: 'what is death?' (Paz: 1959)

6. Hollow papier mâché figure of a skeleton (*'Judas'*) hung with fireworks. Mexico City. H 180 cms

For the first two days of November a sweet-smelling cloud of copal[1] incense hangs over most of Mexico. The Day of the Dead is being celebrated. Nominally this is the Christian feast of All Saints' and All Souls', but it is celebrated in Mexico as nowhere else in the Catholic world. The Mexican festival of *Todos Santos*[2] (All Saints'), also called *Día* or *Días de Muertos* (Day, or Days of the Dead), is the most important celebration in the yearly cycle. This is especially so in rural areas, where the preparations in anticipation of the event are a major preoccupation for much of the year.

Celebrations at Christmas and Eastertide are also of note but less distinctive in form. Only the festivals celebrated in honour of local patron saints display some of the same intensity and devotion evident on the Day of the Dead, perhaps because the saints themselves are regarded rather as lesser deities who intercede with God. The dead too ultimately achieve this semi-divine status in the folk-Catholicism of Mexico. As intermediaries they can intervene on behalf of the living, either with the Christian God or, as among some Indian groups, with divinities that have their origin in pre-Hispanic religion.[3]

The Day of the Dead in Mexico is essentially a private or family feast. It has a public aspect at community level, but the core of the celebration takes place within the family home. It is a time of family reunion not only for the living but also the dead who, for a few brief hours each year, return to be with their relatives in this world.

As a time of reunion, there is nothing sombre or macabre about the event: the returning souls do not bring the odour of death and the grave with them, but come as spirits who have returned from another world, which for many Mexican Indians is very like this one.[4] These worlds of the living and the dead exist in a state of permanent interaction.

As celebrated today, *Todos Santos* incorporates elements of pre-Hispanic religious belief and practice, which differentiate it from the orthodox Catholic feast of All Saints' and All Souls'. The origin of the Catholic feasts is obscure. All Saints' (All-Hallows' or Hallow-mas), 1 November, is the commemorative festival of all Christian saints and martyrs known or unknown. Some sources indicate that it was introduced into the festival cycle by Pope Boniface IV in the seventh century in substitution for a pagan festival of the dead. Originally observed in May, it was moved to November by Gregory III in the eighth century.

Amalarius of Metz (*c.* AD 780-850) in his treatise *On the Offices of the Church* included an 'Office for the Dead' on 2 November because 'many pass out of this world without at once being admitted to the company of the blessed' (Metford: 1991). In the year 998, Odilo, Abbot of Cluny, decreed that all Cluniac monasteries should celebrate an office for the dead, following the feast of All Saints'.

14

The Day of the Dead

By the end of the thirteenth century, All Souls' was almost universally accepted in western Christendom as a liturgical day commemorating all the faithful departed, despite the reluctance of the church to establish a specific day for propitiating and honouring the dead. 'The reason for this reluctance was apparently the desire to dissociate the church from the persistent and tenacious pre-Christian rites and ceremonies of the cult of the dead and ancestor worship ... which from the beginning the church regarded as "superstitious"' (Nutini: 1988).

It was, however, found expedient to incorporate the practice of feasting, often associated with the commemoration of the dead in pagan custom, into Christian ritual. Peter Brown, in his excellent account of the way in which the family-centred feasts of the ancient world were transmuted in early Christianity into the 'Cult of the Saints', writes that:

For one generation, a lively debate on 'superstition' within the Christian church flickered around the cemeteries of the Mediterranean. In the 380s, Ambrose at Milan and in the 390s, Augustine at Hippo, attempted to restrict among their Christian congregations certain funerary customs, most notably the habit of feasting at the graves of the dead, either at the family tombs or in the *memoriae* of the martyrs. In Augustine's explicit opinion, these practices were a contaminating legacy of the pagan beliefs: 'When peace came to the church, a mass of pagans who wished to come to Christianity were held back because their feast days with their idols used to be spent in an abundance of eating and drinking.' (Brown: 1981)

The Christian church sought to re-focus the pagan feasting for the dead and establish celebrations for the saints. But family-centred practices associated with the dead showed great strength and persistence and survived for many centuries. When the Spaniards conquered the New World, they brought with them not only the official Catholic religion, but also some of the more popular or folk-religious practices of early sixteenth-century Spain.[5] The European customs of making food-offerings and feasting with the dead found fertile ground in Mexico where superficially similar ceremonies were an important aspect of pre-Hispanic religious ritual.

Because of this and other apparent similarities between the two religions, it is often extremely difficult to determine the origins of particular aspects of celebrations such as the Day of the Dead. It is nonetheless quite clear that in Mexico, the observation of this feast is a deeply rooted and complex event that continues to be of great significance for many people.

7. Food and drink set out on a tomb as an offering for the souls of the dead. Tancoco cemetery, Veracruz.

The Celebration of Todos Santos

Everywhere in Mexico, the days between the evenings of 31 October and 2 November are central to the celebration of *Todos Santos*. These are the days upon which the household offerings of foods and drinks are made to the dead. Other dates which may be included vary from region to region. Among the Totonac of Veracruz State for example, the period for the

8. Traditional *ofrenda* (offering) for the souls of the dead in the house of Pedro Laja, in the Otomí village of San Pablito, Puebla. The candles are set into sections cut from the stem of a banana plant; the *ofrenda* is framed with an arch of sugar canes hung with bread figures, bananas, and citrus fruits. The flowers which form part of the offering are the yellow *cempasúchil* ('flower of the dead') and magenta *mano de león* (cockscomb).

commemoration of the dead begins on the Day of San Lucas (18 October) and continues until the Day of San Andrés (30 November). In many places there are further celebrations including household offerings, or feasting in the cemeteries (or both), at the *octava*, on 9 November. The Totonac also celebrate an *octava* for the souls of dead children on 8 November.

Days are set aside for the remembrance of particular categories of the dead. Quite commonly, those who have died in accidents (*los accidentados*) are remembered on 28 November but there is considerable variation concerning these special categories which seem to be largely a matter of local custom. Galinier, writing of the Otomí of the Sierra Madre, suggests that the dates are hierarchical, with the ancient and therefore 'deified' dead and prominent forbears having their cult celebrated in October. Victims of violent death are remembered on the Day of San Lucas in a ritual performed outside the house (because such souls are feared), and the family dead on 1 and 2 November (Galinier: 1987).

The cleaning and dressing of graves in the cemeteries is most typically carried out within the days of *Todos Santos*. Decoration of tombs takes many forms and the nature of the activities in the cemetery again varies a great deal regionally and locally. At Chilac, in the State of Puebla, it is on 2 November that the community goes in procession to the cemetery, carrying armfuls of flowers, candles, incense and new or refurbished crosses to place upon the tombs. There is much music-making of all kinds, but no conspicuous feasting.

In Tancoco, Veracruz, the decoration, offering and feasting in the cemetery takes place upon the *octava*. *Rezanderos* (professional prayer-makers) chant at the gravesides, there is music and masked dancing,[6] and the singing of improvised songs which poke fun at local figures. Both here and in Chilac these are daytime celebrations. In other areas, the visits to the cemetery take the form of a nightlong candlelit vigil, as for example at many places in the State of Michoacán such as on the island of Janitzio on Lake Pátzcuaro and in the nearby town of Tzintzuntzan.[7]

16

At San Pablito in the state of Puebla the date of the visit to the cemetery as observed in 1985, was adjusted to take account of the availability of the local priest. There the whole community went in solemn procession to the cemetery after a mass in the church, taking flowers and candles. The graves were dressed in a quiet and subdued atmosphere, with no feasting. As often happens, the decoration of the graves was left largely to the women and the older men; the young men were present, but hung back on the fringes of the proceedings. The atmosphere here was markedly different from the examples cited above, all of which were occasions of cheerful enjoyment.

The organised religious content of the fiesta is variable. Where a priest is available special masses will be said and he may, as at San Pablito, lead the activities which take place in the cemeteries but his presence is not essential. It is often among the Mestizo[8] population that the Catholic rites are of greatest importance, while the Indian population may carry out their own observances. Among the Cora Indians of western Mexico, Herrasti and Vargas (1985)

9. **Villagers entering the cemetery at San Gabriel Chilac, Puebla. They carry vases filled with flowers to decorate the graves and baskets containing food to offer to the dead. They also bring from home small chairs to use whilst watching beside the tombs.**

10. **Nahua men cleaning and decorating graves for *Todos Santos* in Xochitlán, Puebla. The tombs are adorned with palm leaves and *cempasúchil* flowers.**

describe the curate as being 'a few metres away [from the Indians making their offerings in the church], kneeling before the central altar, trying to recite the rosary but failing to attract much attention for his orations.'

The Offering or 'ofrenda'

11. Domestic pottery in the market for *Todos Santos* at Yecapixtla, Morelos.

12. Banner of tissue paper for the Day of the Dead. The design is punched out using chisels. Animals, a chicken and a snake are shown as skeletons. San Salvador Huixcolotla, Puebla. W 69 cms

Many preparations for the Day of the Dead take place much earlier in the year. In areas where pottery is made, the production of large cooking vessels (*ollas*), incense burners and other necessary items starts in September or even earlier. Traditionally, everything should be new for the offering, even down to the clothes the family wear; in practice, this cannot always be adhered to. But when needed, this is the time to consider replacing household items such as the enormous round-bellied cooking-

pots used in rural areas to prepare *tamales* (see below) and other festival dishes that are consumed in large quantities.

Goods for the offering to the dead may be gradually acquired throughout the year, but the period of intense preparation begins in the period immediately preceding *Todos Santos*. The rural markets in the week or so before the critical date are the finest of the year, humming with colour and excitement. Everything essential for the offering is on sale: the flowers, breads, fruits and vegetables, candles, sugar sweets, pottery dishes and toys and many grades of incense. Traders come from afar to the larger markets, bringing goods not available locally – pottery from other centres, factory-made ceramics, baskets, wooden cooking utensils, tissue-papers with punched or cut-out decorative designs, paper puppets, and so on. While many of these things are quite common in urban markets, they are exotic in many rural areas, as are the plastic toys and masks representing the pumpkins and witches of Halloween, although even these make an occasional appearance. The sense of anticipation and exhilaration is infectious, and excited family groups stand before the stalls debating their choice of plastic sheeting for the offering table or a new vase or pottery candlestick.

The flowers form brilliant mounds of colour. Predominant is the vivid orange and yellow of the *cempasúchil*, the 'flower of the dead', which has been associated with festivals for the dead since pre-Hispanic times. Both its colour and aromatic scent are important for they are thought to attract the souls towards the offering. 'Paths' of marigold petals are strewn from the *ofrenda* to the door of the house to guide the souls to their feast. Sometimes the flower-path also leads from the door of the house out into the roadway in the direction of the cemetery. This is to ensure that the souls will not only find their way to the offering, but also back to the cemetery; should they lose their way, they might remain in this world to trouble the living.

The other most common flower is the brilliant magenta cockscomb, or *mano de león*[9] (lion's paw). Although this and, above all, the *cempasúchil* are the most important flowers for the decoration of offerings, many others are used including a gypsophila-like white flower, *nube*, gladioli and carnations. All purchases are ideally completed before 28 October and the final preparations in the houses will by then be well underway.

The Day of the Dead

When a family has a bread oven, the baking of the bread for the dead will begin before 30 October; it is a duty always carried out by men, either the head of the family or a close relative. Otherwise, a wide variety of breads in many different forms[10] will be purchased from bakeries or the market. The cooking of the special dishes for the offering, and the making of such items as chocolate figures in many forms, is also begun well in advance.

On 30 or 31 October, according to local custom, if not begun before, the *ofrenda* itself will be constructed. The whole family will probably play some part in this. A table is set up (or, as with the Totonac, a platform suspended from the roof-beams of the house), covered with a white or embroidered cloth or perhaps decorative plastic sheeting. It is usually set close to the permanent household altar for the saints.

Above the table, framing the front of the offering, an arch is constructed using supple canes which is then decorated with palm or other green leaves and sometimes sugar canes. This is then embellished with an arrangement of flowers, fruits and other ornaments. Additional ornaments may be added which will vary from region to region. A cloth or plastic sheet can be draped above the arch to form a 'sky' (*cielo*) over the offering. There may be tissue paper tied into decorative forms adorning the arch and table, or *papeles picados* (sheets of multi-coloured tissue paper with punched or cut-out designs) or *papeles recortados* (layered sheets of coloured paper with cut designs of saints, virgins, churches, birds and flowers). These are hung in front of and behind the offering table.

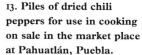

13. Piles of dried chili peppers for use in cooking on sale in the market place at Pahuatlán, Puebla.

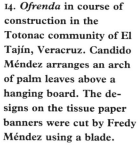

14. *Ofrenda* in course of construction in the Totonac community of El Tajín, Veracruz. Candido Méndez arranges an arch of palm leaves above a hanging board. The designs on the tissue paper banners were cut by Fredy Méndez using a blade.

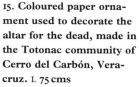

15. Coloured paper ornament used to decorate the altar for the dead, made in the Totonac community of Cerro del Carbón, Veracruz. L 75 cms

16. Altar for the dead with an arch of palm leaves and *cempasúchil* flowers. The photographs of the family dead are shown among a profusion of crêpe paper flowers. The offering table is covered with decorative plastic sheeting. Ixhuatlán de Madero, Veracruz.

On the table are placed pictures or figures of particular saints, a Virgin or a Christ, of importance to the family. Candles of various types[11] and candlesticks are placed both on and before the offering; the candles are sometimes set into a section of the stem of a banana plant set up on wooden trestles. Before the table will be a new *petate*, a rush or palm-leaf mat upon which the incense burners are placed ready for use.

If the family have portraits or photographs of the deceased, these will be given a central position on the offering, although this is not common in Indian households. More vases of flowers will complete the decorations, leaving only space for the food offerings which will follow.

The Return of the Souls

The most widely held belief is that the souls of children return first, and food and gifts appropriate to their age and tastes will be set out for them. When the children withdraw, the souls of the adult dead are in turn offered the foods and

drinks that they preferred in life. The child souls are sometimes divided into two categories, those who die before baptism, *los niños limbos* (infants in limbo) who return on 30 October (Nutini: 1988), and the souls of other children who return on 31 October.[12] The foods for children will on the whole be simpler and less highly seasoned than for adults. Breads and water are always included, sweets of various kinds, fruits and perhaps milk or soft drinks. It is sometimes the custom to set out a special offering table especially for children alongside that for the adults, with everything in miniature: cups, plates, and miniature breads and sugar animals.

The adult dead return on 1 November and are, in their turn, given the most splendid offering of foods and drinks the family can afford. In addition to the breads there may be biscuits of various types, sugar figures, fresh and candied fruits, especially *dulce de calabaza* (candied pumpkin) and fruit pastes. Cooked dishes might include chicken or turkey in *mole*,[13] and certainly various forms of *tamales*, the maize dough 'cakes', with various fillings

both savoury and sweet, which are wrapped in maize husks and steamed. These and other dishes such as *enchiladas* (*tortillas*[14] with red chili sauce) and *chalupas* (fried *tortillas* with meat or cheese) are made ready in abundance, and brought in succession to be placed steaming upon the offering table. The beverages offered in addition to water, range from coffee, chocolate and *atole*, (a drink of maize meal with various flavourings) to whatever form of alcohol the deceased favoured when alive: beer, tequila, mescal, or *aguardiente* (cane spirit).

When the offering table is fully decorated and provisioned it can be a magnificent sight. Everything is very carefully arranged; boxes and packing cases covered with paper or cloth will perhaps have been arranged to form several 'tiers' above the surface of the table for the better display of the goods offered. Some dishes will be covered with brightly embroidered cloths, or piled into painted wooden dishes.

Clothing and personal goods, either favourite possessions of the deceased when alive, or new items specially made or purchased for the occasion, are added to some offerings. These will be placed to the side of the table. For a man, these might include a sombrero, carrying bag (*moral*), *machete*, or *sarape* (blanket); for a woman, possibly a woven belt (*faja*), embroidered blouse or cloth. As with the food offering, these items will eventually be used by the living.

The souls are not usually seen but their presence is sensed. They do not physically consume the foods and drinks, but rather absorb their essence. When the souls have had their fill, it will be the turn of the living members of the family to take their share of the *ofrenda*. Some part of the offering will also be distributed among relatives, godparents, friends and neighbours and some part will be taken to the cemetery to be placed upon the graves of the deceased. The community-wide sharing of the offerings is an important social occasion during which relationships of all kinds are reaffirmed. When all is over, the community settles back into its normal routines; the members of the family who have come from afar leave to take up their lives elsewhere; the dead have already returned to the other world.

In rural communities with a generally more wealthy Mestizo population, the style of offerings may closely resemble the local Indian *ofrendas*, but will include a higher proportion of 'exotic' goods. There may be some commercially produced chocolate instead of the home-made variety, or packets of biscuits, tinned foods, or other expensive goods. One offering for a child seen in the town of Huaquechula consisted entirely of 'junk' foods. The principal is the same: whatever pleased the dead in life they are to have again. There is also an element in this of impressing one's neighbours – the ability to make an elaborate and expensive offering confers status upon the family.

In larger villages and small towns, Mestizo offerings can differ greatly from those of the surrounding villages. The origins of the style of offerings in centres such as Iguala and Huaquechula (see pp. 66 and 68) are not known but seem to derive from Spanish Colonial traditions. Mestizo families sometimes call upon the help of specialist builders in the construction of their *ofrendas*, especially in those communities where very elaborate offerings are made for people who have died within the preceding year.

In truly urban contexts, the offerings may also resemble those of the surrounding villages but occasionally vestiges of older urban customs are found. This is the case in Puebla where a few people still continue the almost obsolete custom of setting the family dining-room table with a place for each dead relative. On the chairs, or nearby are placed some favourite possessions or clothing of the deceased (see fig. 119).

Mexico City

In Mexico City there are no limits. People often build an offering in the regional style of the place they originally come from. In quite wealthy middle-class homes there may well be an *ofrenda*, perhaps traditional in form, perhaps consisting merely of a few photographs, flowers

17. *Ofrenda* for *angelitos* (souls of dead children) at La Venta, near Huaquechula, Puebla. Everything is in miniature, including the breads and the vessels in which the foods and drinks are served. This small altar for children was set up alongside an altar for the adult dead in the Huaquechula style.

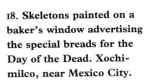

18. Skeletons painted on a baker's window advertising the special breads for the Day of the Dead. Xochimilco, near Mexico City.

19. Detail from a papier mâché tableau made by the Linares family in 1989. The work, a homage to the artist José Guadalupe Posada, was commissioned by the Museum of Modern Art, Chapultepec Park, Mexico City.

and candles. There are *ofrendas* that are highly idiosyncratic in style, with perhaps coloured neon lights bathing the assemblage of objects, or indeed whatever the ingenuity of the individual suggests in the way of unusual decoration. Food, apart perhaps from some token gesture – an *hojaldra* (bread of the dead) and some fruit – may not feature at all.

And here the skulls and skeletons which only rarely make their appearance in rural areas hold sway. They belong in the urban context: not only in Mexico City but at other major centres (notably Oaxaca City, famous for its craftsmen) every material is pressed into skeleton form, and the grinning skulls, who bear no malice or trace of malevolence, cheerily rattle their bones in the markets and ape the antics of the living.

Today, an addition to the Mexico City repertoire are the dances and discos for *Día de Muertos*; these are now a fixture something like a 'Chelsea Arts Ball' in terms of elaborate costumes – all associated with death, though in this case its more bizarre and macabre aspects.

Many public buildings, museums and galleries, hotels and even shops will set up an *ofrenda*. In the museums, these may be carefully copied versions of rural offerings, or generalised versions of them, or elaborate 'set-pieces', sometimes of great size.[15] Some museums and galleries commission works on a particular theme from artists and craftsmen, particularly from the celebrated Linares family of Mexico

The Day of the Dead

City who make large skeleton figures in papier mâché. In homage to the artist Posada, the Modern Art Museum made an *ofrenda* in 1989 in which, beneath a giant *hojaldra*, the papier mâché figures of Posada and some of his most famous creations were placed.

It is traditional for bread-shop windows to be painted with scenes of skeletons hugging, munching and savouring *hojaldras*. Beyond this the window displays of many other shops now sport skulls, skeletons and grotesque masks whatever the goods on sale inside. It is a strange notion to us perhaps that skulls and grotesqueries might be a help in selling the latest in menswear, ladies underwear or electrical goods, but at this time of year it is part of the general exhilaration in the City air. And that exhilaration is one of the unifying factors that draws together all the manifest expressions of the Day of the Dead. Whether in rural villages or in towns, there is excitement abroad, and everywhere activity devoted to the preparations and ultimately the celebration of the fiesta.

Competition Offerings

There are now official competitions (*concursos*) for the 'best' *ofrenda*, both in Mexico City and in other towns large and small throughout Mexico. *Ofrendas* will be built, usually in a civic building, and will be judged for their quality; prizes are awarded by prominent citizens, or members of the government organisations who foster arts and crafts.

In Atlixco, a town in the State of Puebla, the participants in 1989 were mostly schools. Each had prepared an offering, either in a traditional regional style, or upon a particular theme. One was a homage to Mexico's pre-Hispanic past; another commemorated revolutionary heroes. Also present were representatives of nearby Indian communities who had set up offerings in their own styles. For the children this was as amusing as any competition but still they took pride in what they were doing. The Indian participants went about a time-honoured task with loving reverence, as if they were in their own homes.

In the same year, in the city of Puebla, the *concurso* was even more diverse in content, including rural and urban styles of offering, some with atmospheric background music. In seeking to capture attention, some examples had perhaps become a little pretentious, and even obscure, but local enthusiasm was unbounded.

At the University of Puebla, the theme for the Day of the Dead in 1989 was *La Última Movida*,[16] a phrase difficult to translate, encompassing ideas of the 'last dance', but with reference too, to great upheaval, as at the time of earthquakes. Dominated by a large female figure of death in skeleton form and a papier mâché juke-box that Claes Oldenburg might have been proud to have made, costumes of various kinds were set out: an Indian costume, a city-businessman's suit, jeans and other currently fashionable student gear – all left as if

20. Decorative skulls of papier mâché with painted designs and spangles of glitter. Mexico City. H (both) 24 cms

21. Traditional Indian *ofrenda* for the Day of the Dead, erected as an entry in a competition (*concurso*) in the town of Atlixco, Puebla. *Cempasúchil* petals spell out the name of the makers' village: San Juan Tianguismanalco.

23

22. Detail of an installation for the Day of the Dead in a Colonial building in Puebla City. Entitled *La Última Movida* (The Final Shake-up), the display showed Death presiding over a modern 'Dance of Death'. Organised by Rufo Alberto Morales Pérez.

in offering to the souls. They looked like the cast-off garments of participants in a modern 'Dance of Death'.[17]

All this diversity is part of the present-day celebration of the Day of the Dead, and the examples cited do not begin to encompass the variety of forms. If in the cities the impulse that prompts the desire to make an offering to the dead is becoming customary rather than obligatory, and is often far divorced from any religious significance the event still holds, in rural areas, especially among Indian peoples, the sense of obligation is still very deeply felt. In substantiation of this, there are the stories told almost everywhere, although with many vari-

ations upon the theme, of the dire consequences of not fulfilling the necessary rites in honour of the dead. In most versions the outcome of failure to conform is sickness or death. In every story someone, who has either through disbelief or sheer neglectfulness failed to prepare a suitable offering, sees the dead returning to their graves (usually only people with special powers can see the dead), delightedly bearing the goods from the *ofrendas*. His or her own dead kin come last, weeping and in distress. Even remorse, in the form of a hasty rush home to make an offering, fails to save the recalcitrant. The making of the offering is then an obligation, a vital part of maintaining good relations with the dead.

The Pre-Hispanic Background

Are flowers carried to the kingdom of death?
It is true that we go, it is true that we go!
Where do we go? Where do we go?
Are we dead there or do we still live?
Do we exist there again?[1]

23. **Stone figure of a male deity with a crested headdress and skull face, possibly Mictlantecuhtli the Death god. Aztec, c. AD 1300–1521. H 61 cms**

Human mortality is the result of an accident. Had Quetzalcoatl, the 'Plumed Serpent', the great Mesoamerican creator god, not stumbled and dropped the bones of our predecessors on earth, we might all be immortal. So tells a Náhuatl[2] creation myth. It was on a journey to Mictlan, the ninth and deepest level of the underworld that misfortune befell Quetzalcoatl. This was the realm of the Lord of Death, Mictlantecuhtli and his consort, Mictlancíhuatl. There the precious bones were kept, the remains of the previous beings who had inhabited the earth before its destruction. This was the fourth time that the earth or 'sun' had been destroyed by cataclysmic events.[3]

Poised at that moment after the end of the fourth sun, the gods were troubled for now there was no-one to live on earth. Quetzalcoatl therefore undertook to make this journey, telling the Lord of Mictlan that he had come to collect and take away the precious bones: 'What will you do with them, Quetzalcoatl?' asked Mictlantecuhtli and Quetzalcoatl told him of the gods' predicament. Mictlantecuhtli set seemingly impossible conditions for the removal of the bones which Quetzalcoatl overcame by magical means. Finally, gathering up the bones of man and woman, he left the Dead Land; but he stumbled, startled by birds (quail). The precious bones fell and were scattered and damaged by the quail who 'bit into them and nibbled them.'[4]

Bundling up the bones once more, Quetzalcoatl finally reached Tamoanchan, the 'paradise' of the Aztecs. There the bones were ground up by the Earth Goddess, Cihuacoatl and fertilised with Quetzalcoatl's own blood. From them there arose a new race of human beings, who were however, fatally flawed: because of the damage the bones had suffered the inhabitants of the earth were mortal. All the gods did penance, and since that time, humankind has owed the gods a reciprocal debt of penance.

In this myth, recorded after the Spanish Conquest when, for the first time, the oral narratives of the Aztecs could be written down,[5] the pre-Hispanic idea of life arising out of death is very clear. It also, as Bierhorst says in his translation, has the theme of 'life's uncertainty.'[6] In Aztec religion (and indeed all Mesoamerican religions) this is the recurrent theme: the interdependency and interaction between humanity and the gods.

The polytheistic religions of pre-Hispanic

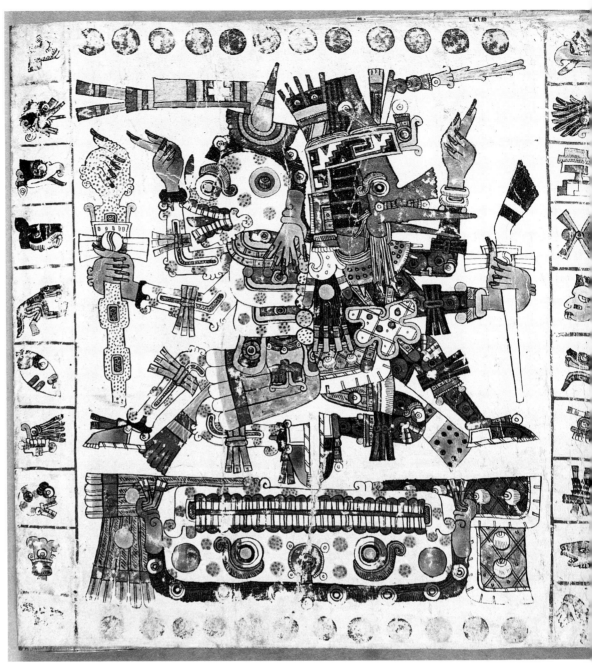

24. Page from *Codex Borgia* showing two deities back to back. One in skeletal form is probably Mictlantecuhtli, the Death god, the other is Quetzalcoatl, the Creator god. H 26.5 cms

Mesoamerica are labyrinthine in their complexity. Cosmogonic and cosmological concepts have to be reconstructed from a variety of sources which often give differing accounts,[7] presumably reflecting regional and perhaps temporal variations in belief. For the Aztecs, the world in which they lived was conceived as a flat disk of earth, surrounded by water that stretched out to the horizons where it met the sky. This world was set at the centre of the four great cardinal regions of the universe. Sometimes the earth was conceived as a great crocodile-like creature, floating in a sea filled with water-lilies; sometimes as a great toad.

The four world directions, north, south, east and west, each had an associated sacred colour, a sacred tree, bird and in some sources, an animal. Particular gods were also associated with each sector. Some of these anthropomorphised deities were conceived as having four aspects, each again identified with one of the cardinal world directions and its special colour. A fifth manifestation of some gods was associated with the centre point of the world. In the case of Tlaloc, the god of rain, four *tlaloque*, 'conceived as dwarfish assistants to a pre-eminent Tlaloc, were individualized and known by proper names' (Nicholson: 1971).

Above the earth rose the thirteen layers of the heavens,[8] and below the earth were the nine levels of the underworld. After death, the souls of the deceased had to pass through each of

26

these nine levels before reaching Mictlan, the realm of the Death god.

As the last in line of a long succession of great cultures that had waxed and waned in what we now call Mesoamerica,[9] the Aztec had inherited much from the civilisations that had preceded them. Their religion and philosophy reflected this cultural complexity. As they themselves rose to become the dominant power in the central regions of Mexico, with an influence which extended over the major part of Mesoamerica, they often found it expedient to adopt the gods of other peoples into their own already elaborate pantheon. At the heart of the Aztec city of Tenochtitlán, these regional gods of peoples subject to the Aztec, even had their own place of worship. Their cults were celebrated in the *Coateocalli*, a place within the Temple of Huitzilopochtli, the Aztec tribal god.[10]

Our knowledge of the Aztec gods of death and beliefs concerning death and the afterlife is derived from the archaeological record, the pre-Hispanic codices (painted screen-fold books) and from the early Colonial manuscripts which contain a great wealth of information recorded by the early Spanish chroniclers, notably Fray Bernardino de Sahagún.[11] In addition, there are the works of native authors who also wrote of the customs of their ancestors following the Spanish Conquest.

The belief in an afterlife was present in Mesoamerica from early times as the presence of grave-goods attests. For the Aztec, the destiny of a soul after death was decreed by the manner of death rather than conduct during life. A person's destiny was decreed by the gods at the moment of birth; it might however be somewhat modified by fulfilment of certain rites divined by the priests.

In Náhuatl poetry there is much speculation concerning the nature of the afterlife; it abounds in references to life's uncertainty and what might be in the hereafter. Miguel León-Portilla, the eminent translator and interpreter of Aztec philosophy and religious belief, remarks upon the frequency of references in Náhuatl literature to life as a dream, and to the question of the nature of 'the beyond, the region of the dead,' the 'place of the fleshless,' the 'region of mystery' (León-Portilla: 1963).

The souls of those who died normal deaths went to Mictlan, the 'place of the dead,' a shadowy underworld ruled over by Mictlantecuhtli. The journey to reach Mictlan was lengthy and difficult. For four years the soul travelled the hazardous path to the 'place of the

ordinary dead', which was beset with perils to be overcome:

[it took the wanderer] through places where mountains crashed together and could crush him, where the winds were so icy they were [as if] edged with obsidian knives, where arrows flew out at the traveller, across a succession of eight deserts, and finally to a great river which he had to cross.[12]

Here the soul met with dogs who would help him cross the river. According to Sahagún, only yellow dogs would serve this purpose, although in some accounts, black dogs were the helpers. This belief has survived into recent times (see p. 104 and Madsen: 1960). In Mictlan the dead lived as they had upon earth, and for this reason were buried with the things which had served them in life. The four year period during which the soul wandered coincides with the period during which special rites were performed after a death.

Warriors who died in battle went to a region in the sky (*Tonatiuh ichan*) where they accompanied the Sun God, Tonatiuh, on his daily journey to the zenith. After four years, they were transformed into humming-birds. Also to the celestial region went the women who died in childbirth. These spirits, the *cihuateteo*, were considered to have died just as honourable a death as the warriors and they accompanied

25. Detail from a page of *Codex Laud*, showing a male deity in partially skeletonised form, probably Mictlantecuhtli, the Death god.

the sun down to the western horizon. Depicted as skull-faced creatures, these 'Divine women' might reappear on earth at certain times and were much feared (Pasztory: 1983).

Those who died by drowning, by being struck by lightning, or of certain diseases such as dropsy or gout, went to Tlalocan, the 'paradise' of the rain gods (Tlalocs), a place where 'all is ever green, always in growth, always spring,' and suffering was unknown (Sahagún: 1952).

The infant dead went to a place near to Tlalocan, Chichihuacuauhco, where a tree dripped milk from its branches to feed them. There they would wait for the inevitable destruction of the present world and its inhabitants, following which they would be reincarnated as the new human beings (Madsen: 1960). Among the Indian peoples of modern Mexico there are still some remnants of belief in the various pre-Hispanic afterworlds.[13]

Human destiny might not depend upon conduct in life, but the nature of life was strictly governed by the need to propitiate the gods. An elaborate cycle of festivals matched the plethora of deities. 'The active ritual component of the religious system ... was enormously complex. A prodigious amount of time, energy, and wealth was expended in ceremonial activities' (Nicholson: 1971). Among these religious celebrations, the chroniclers of the Conquest period have described the rites concerned with the dead and the gods of death.

The Aztec solar year consisted of eighteen 'months' each of twenty days, and ended with a final five day period, the 'Extra' or 'Useless' days, or *Nemontemi*, which was considered a dangerous and unfortunate time (see Durán: 1971). Each month saw the celebration of festivals, the *veintenas*, in honour of the appropriate gods. Included in this cycle of festivals were several that were associated with cults of the dead.

Two of these are most widely recorded under the titles *Miccailhuitontli* and *Miccailhuitl*.[14] These names may be translated as either the 'Little Feast of the Dead' and the 'Great Feast of the Dead' or, as is sometimes the case, the 'Feast of the Little Dead Ones' and the 'Feast of the Adult Dead.' According to Sahagún in the *Florentine Codex*, the two feasts concerned were also known as the *Tlaxochimaco*, 'The Offering of Flowers' and the *Xocotl uetzi*, 'The Xocotl Falls' (or 'Fruit Falls'). All these variant names help elucidate

the meanings of the ceremonies held in these, the ninth and tenth months of the Aztec year.

The two feasts seem to form one major ritual festival of offering to the dead (Graulich: 1989). Of the first part, Sahagún tells us that in the ninth month, flowers were sought of many kinds, which were then strung together. *Tamales* were made, and turkeys and dogs plucked and singed for the feasts which were to follow. 'All were busy. All went without sleep ... in festive mood ... making preparations.' The garlands of flowers were used to adorn a figure of the Aztec tribal god, Huitzilopochtli, and were strewn before him and before the figures of other gods. This was followed by feasting and dancing.

From Fray Diego Durán, a Dominican friar writing in the late sixteenth century, we learn that for the Aztec, this was the Feast of the Little Dead: 'According to my information, it was the commemoration of innocent [unbaptised] dead children, and that is why the diminutive [*Miccailhuitontli*] was used. In the solemn ceremonies of this day offerings were made to honour and venerate these children' (Durán: 1971). He goes on to remark that he had himself observed offerings being made on the 'Day of Allhallows' and the 'Day of the Faithful Departed' (All Saints' and All Souls') in the Catholic calendar, and been told that these were in honour of the children and the adult dead respectively. This caused him sorrow since he saw that an Aztec significance was being given to the Christian festivals: 'I suspect that if it is an evil simulation ... the feast has been passed to the Feast of Allhallows in order to cover up the ancient ceremony.' This reference is of importance in associating the transferal of a pre-Hispanic festival to match a feast day of the Catholic Church. He mentions offerings of 'chocolate, candles, fowl, fruit, great quantities of seed, and food' on both days.

Continuing with his description of the Aztec ceremony, Durán recorded that an 'enormous thick tree' was felled and its bark stripped away. It was carried to the entrance 'of the city or town', where it was greeted by the Aztec priests with much singing and dancing. Food offerings were made to this 'pole' which was called *xocotl*, meaning 'fruit' (Graulich: 1989); the ceremonies continued for twenty days and included rituals conducted by a male god-impersonator, in the regalia of Toci-Teteo innan (Our Grandmother, Mother of the Gods).[15]

In the second part of the ritual, in the tenth

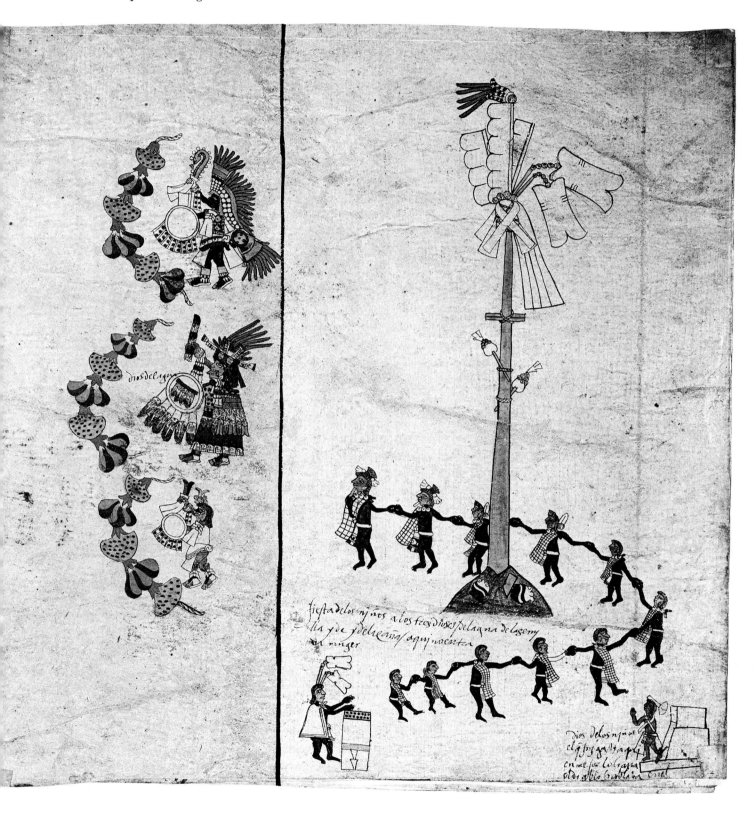

26. Page from *Codex Borbonicus*. On the left is shown a goddess with skull-like face and two attendants; in front of each figure is a chain of yellow *cempasúchil* and other flowers. On the right are figures dancing around a *xocotl* pole with decorations of bark-paper banners at its top. The dancers are accompanied by a drummer (lower left-hand corner). H 38.5 cms

27. Detail of a stone sculpture representing a *tzompantli* (skull-rack). From the Maya site of Chichén Itzá, Yucatán, *c.* AD 1200.

Aztec month, the *xocotl* pole having been raised into a vertical position and decorated by the priests 'with papers', an image was made of a dough of amaranth seeds and maize meal, which was set at the top of the pole. According to some sources, the figure was in the form of a bird, and to others, in the form of a man with wings, dressed in white paper ornaments: 'he had "wings" painted with falcons and held a shield. Three wooden sticks from which hung three tamales of amaranth seeds were set up over the image' (Graulich: 1989; Sahagún: 1951). Dances were held before it and, on the twentieth day, captives were led to the *tzompantli* (skull-rack, where the skulls of sacrificial victims were displayed). When their paper costumes had been burned and other rites performed, they were taken to the top of the temple to be sacrificed. First they were cast into a fire; then their hearts were removed with a knife.

The ceremonies which followed the sacrifice were of feasting and dancing 'the serpent dance' (Sahagún: 1951). The young men climbed up the ropes securing the *xocotl* pole to reach the *xocotl* image and *tamales*, which were

thrown to the ground where the pieces of the image were scrambled for. Offerings were made to the image and then the great tree was pulled down. Whereas before there had been noise and jostling, now there was quiet in the precinct of the Great Temple. The captor of the *xocotl* image was arrayed in special garments and the ceremony was at an end.

Durán records that the dances at the foot of the pole were performed by nobles 'covered with feathers and jewels' and with painted bodies, carrying images and balls of dough. Food and drink were abundant and it was a day of indulgence.[16]

Other sources help clarify the association of these feasts with the dead. In the *Codex Telleriano-Remensis* there is the following description for the feast of *Miccailhuitl*:

The feast of all the dead begins on the third of August. During this feast they made offerings to the dead, placing food and drink on the tombs; this they did for four years because they believed that in all that time the souls did not reach their place of rest. Thus, the dead were buried with all their clothing, because they believed that by the end of the four years, the souls would have suffered much toil, cold, and fatigue and passed through places where there was much snow and thorns.[17]

From the same source comes the description of the larger feast for the dead which began on 23 August:

... they have another feast of the dead which is much larger than the previous one ... for the last three days of this month the living fasted for the dead and went to disport themselves in the countryside by way of recreation ... Every year at the time of the festival for the dead, while the priests carried out the sacrifices, each person climbed up onto the roof of his own house and turning towards the north, recited long prayers to the dead, – to each dead member of his family, and called out to them: 'Come quickly for we are waiting for you.'

Sahagún also mentions offerings to the dead in the thirteenth, fourteenth and eighteenth months of the Aztec year. In the thirteenth month, *Tepeilhuitl*, he describes the making of images of wood which were then covered with a dough 'which they call *tzoal*.' These images were made in memory of those who had drowned or had died in such ways that they had been buried rather than cremated. 'After having placed these images on their altars with many ceremonies they offered them *tamales* and other foods, and sang songs of praise and drank wine in their honour.' He also describes other activities associated with the dead at this time:

They also placed these images of the dead on these wreaths of grass (*zacate*), and then at dawn placed these images in their oratories, on beds of grass, rush or reed; having placed them there they offered them food, *tamales* and *mazamorra* (a maize gruel), or stew made of fowl or dog meat, and later burned incense to them in a pottery incense burner like a big cup filled with coals, and they called this ceremony *calonoac*.
And the rich sang and drank pulque in the honour of these gods and their dead: the poor only offer them food as has been mentioned.

In the fourteenth month, *Quecholli*, he recorded that 'upon the fifth day, one was concerned only with the dead. For them they made small arrows ... they bound four arrows and four pine torches ... and laid them where the dead lay buried. And they placed there two sweet *tamales*. They remained there all day. And at sundown they burned them for the dead in the same place.'
In the eighteenth and final month of the year,

Izcalli, was a feast when *tamales* 'stuffed with greens' were eaten.

Whoever first cooked her *tamal* of greens then went to offer it to her kin. Thus she showed her self-esteem. [When this was done and] she had offered it everywhere to others, [to her neighbours] ... they all sat down to eat their *tamales* ... They were arranged in a circle; they brought ... their children, forming family groups.
And first they made an offering to the fire; they offered five *tamales* ... before the hearth. These were in a wooden vessel. Then they each set in place and made offering for their dead, where they laid buried ... And only during one day were they eaten. By night they were done; all finished. They left nothing for the next day.

This last description seems not dissimilar to the modern *Todos Santos*: a family-based feast that also involves exchange of foodstuffs in the wider community, offerings first in the house and then elsewhere 'where [the dead] laid buried.' Common to both ancient and modern ceremonial connected with the propitiation of the dead are the flowers, food, incense, paper ornaments, dancing and music. These were not officially elements in the Spanish Catholicism introduced to Mexico in the sixteenth century. The Indians were condemned for continuing their 'pagan' customs of offering food, drink, and candles to the dead in their homes during nightlong feasts (Serna: 1892).

Many of the artefacts included in the descriptions of the *veintenas* were obviously ephemeral: the images of maize or amaranth dough and the paper costumes, etc. Incense burners are found in archaeological contexts and are also a category of object still made and used today, but otherwise we are dependant for information concerning the appearance of the ceremonies upon the codices and other manuscripts.

While not suggesting that any direct descent can be claimed for the tissue paper ornaments of today from the paper of pre-Hispanic religious festivals, there are in present-day Mexico Indian groups to whom the use of bark- and tissue-paper figures remains an important part of religious ceremonial. Notably among the Otomí and the Nahua of the Sierra de Puebla and Huasteca, tissue and bark-paper images of pre-Christian deities are still a focus of ritual activity. Cut-out figures of these gods are offered and displayed during ceremonies that are carried out to ensure success in agriculture. They are also used in healing ceremonies conducted by the local *brujos* ('witches' both male

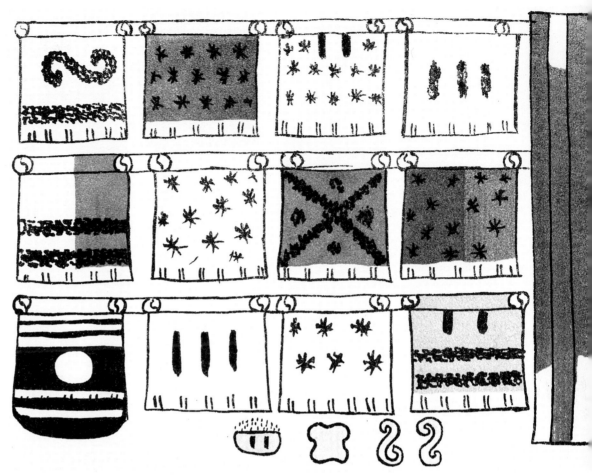

28. Page from *Codex Magliabecchiano* showing painted paper banners with decorative designs. Paper banners, painted and splashed with rubber (*amatetehuitl*), were common ceremonial offerings in pre-Hispanic times (Nicholson: 1971; Johnson: 1971).
H (approx.) 17 cms

and female with shamanic powers) and, among some groups, still play an important part in death rituals and the ceremonies for the Day of the Dead. Among the Nahua, for example, paper shawls are placed upon the graves of female relatives 'to keep them warm in the underworld.'[18]

Another practice which is carried out among contemporary Indian groups may have its origin in the pre-Hispanic festival of the eleventh month, *Ochpaniztli*. In this month the feast of 'The Sweeping of the Way' was celebrated with the 'hand-waving' dance (Sahagún: 1951) honouring the goddess Toci, the 'Mother of the Gods.' 'This was the first act of the day: everyone had to sweep his possessions, his house, and all its corners, leaving nothing without diligent sweeping and cleaning. Besides this, all the streets of the town were swept before dawn. This custom has remained in the country ... [and this practice is followed] because it is such an ancient rite' (Durán: 1971). Durán goes on to state how fiercely he has opposed this, explaining that it is 'a superstition, a pagan custom, but I do not know whether this has done any good.'

In the ethnographic literature describing the

Day of the Dead, there are many references to the sweeping and cleaning of streets and houses, as well as the universal cleaning of graves and cemeteries (Cortés Ruiz, et al.: 1988; García García, García Ramos: 1985; Sartorius: 1858). In the literature concerning the Totonac of Veracruz, the point is made that this is also a time for cleaning fields before a new season of planting.

In the festival of the fifteenth month, *Panquetzaliztli*, there is reference to the making of amaranth seed *tamales* and an image of the tribal god, Huitzilopochtli, also of amaranth seeds, which was 'captured' and eaten after being shared between kinsmen and neighbours. (Sahagún: 1951; Durán: 1971). Leyenaar writes of the suppression of the use of amaranth seed for the making of images precisely because it was used for making images of the deities which were an important part of religious ritual (Leyenaar: 1987). The breads of wheat-flour in many shapes and forms used in *ofrendas* of Colonial times and still today, may perhaps have replaced the amaranth-dough 'idols'; perhaps too, the figures of sugar and *dulce de pepita* (pumpkin seeds) absorbed part of this ceremonial.[19]

32

PLATE I   Stone sculpture of a woman with a skull face; this represents one of the *cihuateteo*, the malevolent spirits of women who died in childbirth. Aztec, AD 1300–1521. H 72 cms

Dawn view of the Purépecha Indian cemetery on the island of Janitzio, Michoacán. During the night-long vigil for the dead on 1 November the graves are illuminated with candles.   PLATE 2

a. Pottery tableau of feasting skeletons seated at a table set with a food offering. Made by Adrián Luis González. Metepec, State of Mexico. H (approx.) 8 cms

b. Household *ofrenda* (offering) for the Day of the Dead in the Nahua village of Atla, Puebla. Felix and Cecilia Vargas are shown putting the final touches to their offering of fruits, flowers, breads and candles for the dead.

PLATE 3

Polychrome painted pottery scene showing two devils and a skeletonised corpse beneath a cross of flowers. They are watched over by a skull and the figures of several *ánimas* (souls). Ocumicho, Michoacán. H 27 cms

Suspended altar with food offering for the dead in the Totonac village of Cazuelas, Veracruz. The altar is decorated with coloured tissue paper and bunches of fruit. The handtowels and cloths are for the use of the returning souls. On the floor, in front of the offering, is a locally made pottery incense burner.

PLATE 4

PLATE 5

Papier mâché figure of a bride with two
male attendants, presumably the groom
and best man. Mexico City. H 62 cms

PLATE 6

PLATE 7

Pottery 'Tree of Life' with figures of Adam and Eve (top); at the centre is the
planet Earth, surrounded by figures representing the evolution of man. The
scenes forming the outer circle (reading anti-clockwise) show the life cycle from
birth to death including baptism, courtship and marriage; an offering for the
Day of the Dead is included (top right). Made by Tiburcio Soteno. Metepec,
State of Mexico. H 105 cms

Scene in the cemetery at San Gabriel Chilac, Puebla. On 2 November, families tend the graves of their loved ones, decorating them with flowers, candles and photographs of the dead and renewing the wooden or metal crosses. Some families construct shelters of leaves and reeds above the tombs to give privacy and shelter from the sun.

PLATE 8

Michel Graulich, discussing the Central Mexican feasts for the dead, also considers the possible association of the *xocotl* pole, and the present-day ceremonies of the *voladores* – the 'flying dancers' who swing down on ropes from the top of high poles. That the *volador* 'dance' is pre-Hispanic in origin there is no doubt: it is described for example by Durán. Graulich finds that: 'The meanings given to the [modern *volador*] rituals correspond well to the meaning of the *xocotl* rite.'[20]

To what extent these pre-Hispanic festivals and their associated rituals were transmuted into the Christian festivals remains a matter of keen debate. Before the Spanish priests learned the indigenous languages, and Indians came to understand some Spanish, Christian rituals were poorly understood by the Indians. They sought to interpret them in terms of their own religious beliefs and practices. Later, there were certainly conscious efforts to incorporate the remnants of native religion, and 'hide' them beneath the cloak of Christian practice.

There were of course some attempts to maintain the native religions in secret, suppressing only those parts that revolved around warfare and sacrifice which had been so crucial a part of Central Mexican religion. But having no priesthood to conduct the ceremonies, such secret survivals were themselves only partial and reflective images of pre-Hispanic religion.[21] Nonetheless, even in Mexico today, there are areas where religious beliefs of pre-Hispanic origin survive quite strongly alongside Catholic religion; sometimes tolerated, sometimes under attack from the Catholic priesthood.[22]

In addition to the accounts of pre-Hispanic religion at the time of the Conquest, archaeological finds provide much information concerning the iconography of death before the

arrival of the Spaniards. Following the Conquest, the sculptures of the native gods were overturned and smashed; the temples were destroyed and the painted manuscripts were burned. Such few objects as survived the zeal of the Spanish Conquistadors to destroy what they saw as idolatrous, were hidden from view, or had already been safely buried in the graves and ruins of earlier times. Sometimes the remains of the smashed 'idols' were concealed within the buildings and monuments that the Indians were required to construct for the new (Christian) religion.

From the archaeological record we find concern with death and belief in an afterlife expressed centuries before the Aztecs rose to power. The dead were accompanied in the grave by goods, and sometimes, in the case of nobles, by people who had been sacrificed to sustain and attend them in another world.

In the pre-Classic period (*c.* 2000–200 BC) when the successful exploitation of plants permitted a settled village life based on agriculture, the use of pottery expanded and decorative wares and small figurines give the first indications of an interest in the relationship between life and death. From Tlatilco for example, a rich pre-Classic site in the Valley of Mexico, comes a figurine head showing a face half fleshed and half bare skull.

The Olmec, the first of the major civilisations which arose in the Gulf Coast region (*c.* 1000–400 BC), set the cultural patterns for all the succession of great cultures that were to follow.

29. Stone with low relief carving of skeletal death deity. Izapa, Chiapas, *c.* 300 BC

30. Pottery figurine head showing a face half fleshed and half as a skull: the duality of life and death. *c.* AD 800–1000. Soyaltepec, Oaxaca.

Imagery associated with death does not feature in their sculpture and pottery. But from Izapa, a site in Chiapas which flourished at this same early period (*c.* 800 BC), comes a fine low relief sculpture of a skeletal figure.

Early in the Classic period (*c.* AD 200–900), the major site of Teotihuacan, just north of present-day Mexico City, again has few representations of death among its frescoes and sculptures. The notable exception is a circular stone carved on both sides with the representation of a skull with protruding tongue, set at the centre of a fluted disc.

Among the Maya of southern Mexico, Guatemala and adjacent territories, there are many representations of skulls, often forming parts of architectural decoration, or seen as ornaments adorning the elaborate costumes in representations of rulers.

The major Classic period sites of the Gulf Coast, also show skulls and skeletonised figures, good examples being from the reliefs in the Ball Court at Tajín, and from the same site, a fine column with a death god.

Some of these figures are associated with sacrificial scenes, others, like the Late Classic pottery head from Soyaltepec in Oaxaca, which

31. Detail from a stone frieze from a ball-court at El Tajín, Veracruz, showing a death god. The ball-courts of pre-Hispanic Mesoamerica are often decorated with images associated with death and sacrifice. Totonac, *c.* AD 600–1000.

32. Stone carving of a skull. Aztec, *c.* AD 1300–1521. H 17 cms

again shows a head half living and half skull, have no such direct association. But where, as for example in the ball-court scenes such as those at Tajín and Chichén Itzá, sacrifice is shown, it is associated with symbols of new life. At Chichén Itzá, from the neck of the sacrificial victim, whose severed head is shown in the hand of his opponent, spring six serpents, and a plant, with flowers and fruit.

It is in the civilisations of the post-Classic period (*c.* AD 900–1520) that imagery of death proliferates, and examples become too numerous to count.[23] In Central Mexico, the Maya area and on the Gulf Coast, there are everywhere scenes of sacrifice, gods of death, skull-racks (*tzompantli*) for the display of the skulls of sacrificial victims, and innumerable pottery vessels in the form of skulls and skeletons. The equation of death and renewal has taken on a new urgency. Mankind must make recompense to the gods for the sacrifice that brought them into being. The life-force must be offered sacrifice – blood and the human heart are the supreme sacrifice – vitally necessary to keep the sun moving in the heavens.

There is not space here to enlarge upon the subject of death and the dead as represented in pre-Hispanic art.[24] Fortunately, there is an extensive literature on the subject.

33. **Stone panel with low-relief carving of a skeletal figure. Benque Viejo, Belize. Maya, *c.* 600–900(?). H 46 cms**

34. **Stone low-relief carving of a skull (detail from a larger sculpture). Aztec, *c.* AD 1300–1521.**

35

The Spanish Conquest

Broken spears lie in the roads;
we have torn our hair in our grief.
The houses are roofless now, and their walls
are red with blood.

Worms are swarming in the streets and plazas.
and the walls are spattered with gore.
The water has turned red, as if it were dyed,
And when we drink it,
it has the taste of brine.

We have pounded our hands in despair
against the adobe walls,
for our inheritance, our city, is lost and dead.
The shields of our warriors were its defence,
but they could not save it.

We have chewed dry twigs and salt grasses;
we have filled our mouths with dust and
*   bits of adobe;*
we have eaten lizards, rats and worms . . .[1]

The horrors of the Spanish Conquest of Mexico in the early sixteenth century have been described many times. There are the vivid accounts of the Conquistadors themselves – those of Hernán Cortés and Bernal Díaz del Castillo[2] being perhaps the best known. Less familiar are the Aztec's own accounts of the Conquest in which the sense of tragedy and loss are expressed most poignantly.[3]

Cortés marched beneath a banner that proclaimed: 'We shall conquer under the sign of the cross.' Many authors have sought to discover what part religious conviction played in Cortés' belief in his right to conquer. Robert Ricard (1966) writes: 'He was greedy, debauched, a politician without scruples, but he had his quixotic moments, for, despite his weaknesses, of which he later humbly repented, he had deep Christian convictions.'

When finally in Tenochtitlán, Cortés sought to convert the great Aztec ruler Moctezuma II, hoping that the people would follow him. 'Beginning with the first day, he summarized Christian doctrine to the "emperor", pronounced against human sacrifices, and told him of the coming of the missionaries. Moctezuma firmly refused to accept [any of this], resisted all his arguments, all the sermons' (Ricard: 1966). Finally, with great misgiving, Mocte-

35 & 36. Lifesize painted pottery figures of a skeletonised bishop (left) and king (right). The representation of figures symbolising religious and political power in skeleton form remains important in the repertoire of modern Mexican craftworkers. Made by Tiburcio Soteno. Metepec, State of Mexico. H (approx.) 168 cms

zuma allowed a Christian cross to be erected in the shrine of the Great Temple of Tenochtitlán, and an image of the Virgin Mary to be placed there.

Cortés persisted in his attempts to convert Moctezuma to the idea that 'their [the Mexicans'] man-made idols were not worthy of the worship due to the one true God of the Christians . . .' He wrote to Charles V:

... And everyone, especially the said Moctezuma, replied that ... owing to the very long time that had passed since the arrival of their ancestors to these lands, it was perfectly possible that they could be mistaken in their beliefs ... and that I, as a recent arrival, should know better the things that they should hold and believe.[4]

Moctezuma and Cortés were locked in a battle of words, and language became an ever present dilemma in the ensuing religious conquest. Cortés was insistent in his letters to his king of the need for missionaries to assist with the conversion of the Indians:

Each time I have written to Your Majesty I have told Your Highness of the readiness displayed by some of the natives of these parts to be converted to Our Holy Catholic Faith and to become Christians; and for this purpose I have begged Your Caesarian Majesty to send religious persons of a goodly life and character.[5]

The first Catholic missionaries to set foot in New Spain were three Flemish monks who arrived in 1522. Their immediate task was to learn Náhuatl, the language of the Aztecs. From the first, there were difficulties. The friar Pedro de Gante wrote:

The common people were like animals without reason. We could not bring them into the pale or congregation of the church, nor to the doctrine classes, nor to the sermons without their fleeing from these things like the devil flees from the cross. For more than three years they fled like wild things from the priests.

It was for this reason that the first Christian churches had large enclosed areas where the Indians could gather in the open air as they were accustomed to do for their own religious ceremonies, and external pulpits were built for the priest to preach from. Until the friars learned Náhuatl, they had to use sign language and Madsen (1967) cites a report that seeing a priest waving his arms and preaching loudly in an unintelligible tongue, the Indians concluded that he must be crazed.

In 1524, twelve Franciscan friars arrived in Mexico City, having walked barefoot from the

37

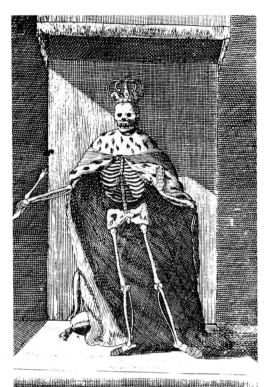

37. **Image of Death dressed as a king from the book** *La Portentosa Vida de la Muerte ...* **by Fray Joaquín Bolaños, printed in Mexico City in 1792.**

port of Vera Cruz. Cortés knelt before them as they arrived, and 'the respect they commanded from the conquerors created among the Aztec a favorable impression which endured and became a powerful influence in the conversion' (Madsen: 1967). They learnt Náhuatl and established schools in which to teach Christian doctrine. As the first steps towards conversion 'the friars taught their Indian pupils how to kneel, make the sign of the cross, and recite Latin prayers' (Mendieta: 1870).

In the schools of doctrine, young men were kept apart from their families and not allowed to converse. 'This rule was made so they would forget their bloody idolatries and excessive sacrifices,' recorded Gante. 'When there is a fiesta or dedication for the demons [native gods] the most able students are sent to forbid it,' and the perpetrators were called to Mexico City to be reprimanded and threatened with punishment.

Language continued to present a formidable problem. Although Náhuatl served as something of a *lingua franca*, there were many other native languages, and many areas where knowledge of Náhuatl was slight, and it took some years to establish it as the official language of conversion. By 1550, thirty years after the Conquest, the Franciscan friar Rodrigo de la Cruz

was still fighting this battle; he wrote to Charles V:

It seems to me that Your Majesty should order that all the Indians learn the Mexican language, for in every village today there are many Indians who know it and learn it easily ... It is an extremely elegant language, as elegant as any in the world. A grammar and dictionary of it have been written, and many parts of the Holy Scripture have been translated into it.

His plea was born of the discovery that so many of the apparent conversions to Christianity had more form than substance. As the friars themselves became increasingly skilled in their mastery of the Indian languages, many of their apparent triumphs seemed to slip away and dissolve before their eyes. They grappled with the problem of presenting the terms of Christian doctrine. Was it better for God to be named in Spanish as *Dios*, or rendered *Teotl* so that the Indians could understand the concept in their own language? The issue was fraught with possible misunderstandings.

The superficial and unassimilated nature of the native understanding of Christian teaching could only be combatted by 'a delicate understanding of Náhuatl and the native mentality, a mastery of the many metaphors. Those who urged the Náhuatl equivalent for such terms argued that it made Christianity more intelligible to the native, whereas those who opposed it argued that it tended to maintain idolatrous pagan concepts' (Dibble: 1974).

The distress of the Catholic friars became greater as it was found that native religious practices were continuing, whether overtly or under the guise of Christian ritual. Compounding their unease was the discovery that as they learned more of native religions, they found many concepts that seemed close to Christianity and many rituals that were apparently similar to those of the Christian church. There were infant bathing ceremonies not unlike baptism; there was the eating of fragments of the amaranth-dough figures of the gods that seemed like communion; there were ideas that seemed close to those of confession. Motolinía[6] was inclined to think this was God's work, to have predisposed the Indian in so many ways to the Church before the event of the Conquest. Of this dilemma Fernando Cervantes writes:

The intellectual difficulties that such similarities provoked among the mendicants would be difficult to exaggerate. For even more important than their belief in the universality of European cultural values was the missionaries' faith in the

38. In Colonial period Mexico, it was customary among certain orders of nuns to have paintings made after death. In this eighteenth-century example the nun is shown in the habit and crown of flowers she first wore as a Bride of Christ.

39. Masked figures representing Death and the Devil. During religious festivals Náhuatl-speaking villagers take these roles during *La Danza de los Diablos* (The Dance of the Devils) in the village of Petlacala, Guerrero.

unique and universal vocation of the Christian church. Any attempt to relativise these similarities through an exercise in what we might call 'comparative religion' would have seemed to them not merely unthinkable but positively sacrilegious. If the Christian sacraments were believed to have been established by Christ himself as material channels of supernatural grace, how could they possibly find such striking parallels in the idolatrous rites of remote pagans? At best the phenomenon could be explained as the result of a mysterious initiative on the part of God to prepare the Indians for the reception of the Gospel: a kind of prelude to what was to come ... But such hopes were not easy to hold in face of the more frequent orgiastic ceremonies that were encountered and which seemed to the friars to represent a form of pseudo-sacramentalism imbued with Satanic inversion. (Cervantes: 1991)

The debate continued through two centuries, perhaps culminating in the sermon of Fray Servando Teresa de Mier, a Dominican friar from northern Mexico. He caused:

a furor such as had never before shaken the religious life of New Spain with his memorable sermon of December 12, 1794. In the Shrine of Guadalupe he revealed to his astonished listeners that the Aztecs had actually been a Christian people, though their Christianity had been deformed. They had worshipped God the Father under the name of Tezcatlipoca, the Son as Huitzilopochtli, and venerated the Virgin Mary as

40. **Performers from the Dance of the Moors and Christians in Tepoztlán, Morelos. This dance, introduced by the Spaniards into Mexico, is still widely performed in many regions.**

41. **The Virgin of Guadalupe, Patron Saint of Mexico. Her image appears everywhere, reproduced in all media; here it is printed upon a cloth.**

hammocks from seven and eight leagues' distance.

In this way they first came to show obedience to the church and from then on the churches and patios were full of people.

The friars had some success with their religious dramas, dances and processions. The content of the dramas was carefully selected; the texts were in the native languages, and the male performers all Indian. In more secular dance dramas imported from Spain, such as the 'Moors and Christians', the Indians found an immediate parallel to their own Conquest by the Spaniards and readily adopted the theme, which survives as a 'Conquest Dance' to the present day. And secular themes gave rise to splendid pageants in which the Indian skill at making costumes and figures was given expression, and which even provided opportunities for them to represent the glories of their own past.[7]

In the previous chapter it has been seen that where there was some possibility of combining an Aztec fiesta with a feast day in the Catholic calendar, this was done. Madsen records that 'the Indians frequently made offerings to images of Catholic saints and pagan gods placed side by side on their home altars' (Madsen: 1960a). The saints were quickly adopted and replaced the gods of the polytheistic religion of pre-Hispanic times. The best-documented example of this syncretism was the identification of the Virgin Mary with the goddess Tonantzin. In 1531, in a miraculous apparition at the site of Tonantzin's temple, the dark-skinned Virgin of Guadalupe, who was to become the patron saint of all Mexico, made herself known to the Indian Juan Diego. The Virgin is still referred to as Tonantzin in some Indian

Coatlicue. He went one step further: no apparition of the Virgin Mary had occurred in 1531 since none had been needed. Saint Thomas the Apostle (Quetzalcoatl) had already revealed all Christian truths to the natives many centuries before. In sum, aside from an unwelcome conquest and odious oppression, what did Mexico owe Spain? Needless to say, Father Mier soon found himself behind bars after the delivery of his momentous, if somewhat fantastic, sermon of 1794. (Horcasitas: 1979)

There were also attempts to exploit the nature of pre-Hispanic religious celebrations to promote better understanding of Christianity. Having observed the singing and dancing that accompanied Aztec religious festivals, Pedro de Gante was quick to respond. He wrote in 1558:

By the grace of God I began to know them and understand their conditions . . . and what I should do with them. In all their adorations of their gods they sang and danced before the gods. When they had to sacrifice some victims for some purpose such as obtaining victory over their enemies or for temporal necessities, before they killed the victim they had to dance and sing before the idol.

Since I had seen this and that all their songs were dedicated to their gods I composed a very solemn song about the law of God and the faith and how God made man to save the human race and how he was born of the Virgin Mary leaving her pure and entire. This was done two months before Christmas.

I also gave them patterns to paint their mantles so they could dance with them because this was the way the patterns had been used by the Indians. The patterns conformed to the dances and the songs they sang. Thus they were dressed gayly or in mourning or for victory . . . then we invited the people within ten leagues of Mexico City to come to the fiesta of the Nativity of Christ Our Redeemer and so many came that they could not get into the patio . . . Some sick people came in

villages of today (Madsen: 1960). Quetzalcoatl was identified with Saint Thomas the Apostle; Tlaloc with Saint John the Baptist. The local patron deities of pre-Hispanic times were each replaced by a Catholic Saint, and the worship of the community's patron Saint is today still the most important religious festival of the year in many rural areas.

The religious zeal with which the friars caused the Aztec idols to be destroyed,[8] was sometimes circumvented. Some images of pre-Hispanic gods were removed to caves or other places of safety. Sometimes the smashed fragments were buried beneath the stone crosses of the Spaniards, or in the foundations of the new churches. In 1929, Anita Brenner[9] published her book entitled *Idols Behind Altars*, a phrase which captured the literary imagination. She describes how the Spaniards sometimes inadvertently assisted in the preservation of the old gods. She quotes from Fray Jacinto de la Serna:

And in all their idolatries, they were greatly helped by the fact that many of the idols were placed as foundation stones, cornerstones and pillars of the Church, and in other houses, and to adorn the streets ... The demon took advantage of [them], to greater deceive them, so that they could say, that their gods were so strong, that they were put as foundations and cornerstones of the temples.

The figures of the gods they destroyed must have seemed demonic indeed to the Spaniards, and the symbols with which they were decorated totally incomprehensible. Among these symbols there were however at least a few that were recognizable: the skulls and bones, the universal symbols of death. In the charnel-houses of Spain there were piles of skulls and bones, decoratively arranged; even so, the piled up skulls of the *tzompantli* and the stone sculptures representing these structures horrified the Spaniards. The charnel-houses held the remains of those who had died a Christian death, the Aztec *tzompantli* held the remains of victims of dreadful sacrifice. The skull as *memento mori* was the reminder that this life is just a preparation for the true life with God after death.

The Christian God did not demand human sacrifice, rather He forbade it. In His one world, that had had no preceding creations, a person's actions and conduct determined his fate in the afterworld. For the Aztec, the pattern of life was determined by the gods at the time of birth, though one might modify this destiny somewhat by making the right offerings and sacrifices under the guidance of the priests. The

42. Colonial period stone cross with a carving of the body of Christ. It is set upon a pre-Hispanic stone sphere. In post-Conquest Mexico the Christian cross was sometimes regarded as a living intermediary between God and man. The incorporation of pre-Hispanic elements was therefore a means of retaining contact with the native deities. Huaquechula, Puebla.

43. Human skull decorated with a mosaic of lignite, turquoise and shell and with eyes of iron pyrites. This skull representing the god Tezcatlipoca would have been worn as a back ornament and still retains the long leather straps that held it in place. H 20 cms

destiny of the soul in the afterlife was according to the manner of death. There was no Purgatory or Hell in the religion of the Aztec; for them the afterlife held no threat of eternal damnation, which made the task of teaching salvation of the soul by means of a life lived according to Christian ethic extremely difficult.

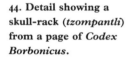

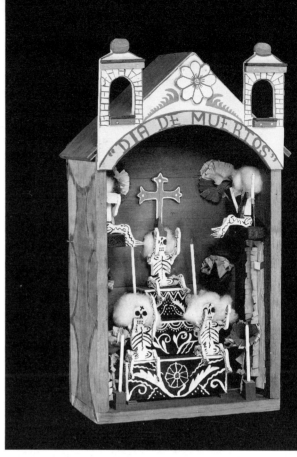

44. Detail showing a skull-rack (*tzompantli*) from a page of *Codex Borbonicus*.

45. Toy church of painted wood with a scene of skeletons and a catafalque. The limbs of the skeletons can be moved by turning a handle at the side. H 44.5 cms

If the friars sought to bring to the New World a version of Catholic faith purged of practices that were disapproved of by the Church in Spain, it was impossible to prevent other Spanish settlers from bringing deeply-rooted customs with them. From the villages of Spain came the elements of pre-Christian ritual that the Church had often sought to eliminate.

William Christian, Jr, writing of local religions in sixteenth-century Spain, notes that 'The church in Spain had long waged a frustrating battle against "pagan" customs and institutions, which it often characterized as traffic with the devil' (Christian: 1981a).

Some insight into the Spanish attitudes towards the commemoration of the dead are afforded in the same author's studies of apparitions in late medieval and Renaissance Spain (1981b), which include visions that make reference to the offerings to the dead in the late fifteenth century. One such, the vision of María Torrent of Sant Aniol, Catalonia, 'occurred on All Saints Day, and draws attention to the people's anxieties about their obligations to the dead.' Unable to deliver the money she carried to the church to pay for the responses for the souls of her dead parents and 'for those for whom she had obligations,' because the priest was busy, she returned home in an unhappy state, and commenced prayer to the Virgin of

the Arches. The Virgin gave her instructions to wear only white clothing for a year and to fulfil certain religious promises she had made; also to instruct the local people in their comportment.

For the people in the villages where they occurred, such visions implied questions concerning the situation of their dead. In answer they were exhorted to fulfill the last wishes of their family dead, to have masses said, to honour dead martyrs, to have psalms sung. Other visions have as part of their underlying theme the very prevalent fear of death coming suddenly when a person was not in a state of grace.

In more recent times, the Spanish forms of celebration for the days of All Saints' and All Souls' have been described by Foster (1960) who visited Spanish villages upon several occasions between 1944 and 1950 and found that the feasts were celebrated in much the same way throughout the country. Both days had special offices at the morning masses, and on one of the two days, visits were made to the cemeteries to pay homage to the dead. He notes that in the larger cities, these visits had become festive and social occasions: 'but in smaller villages the visits are still impressively marked by solemnity and signs of piety.' Flowers were taken to decorate the graves and oil-lamps and candles to light them. Only in a few places was there still the belief that the dead returned to earth to partake of offerings of food and wine. As part of his observations of the festival in the village of Hoyos del Espino in Avila he notes that on 2 November, a catafalque was erected in the church, 'a large black cloth-covered bier on one end of which rested a bleached human skull. This *tumba*, we were told, would remain during the octave, to be removed a week hence.' He adds in a note that this custom was also common in Mexico. It does indeed still occur in Mexico, and in some towns and villages has greatly influenced the style of domestic offerings for *Todos Santos* (see Huaquechula, p. 66 and Iguala, p. 68).

From Colonial Mexico there are still a few survivals of the splendid funerary catafalques decorated with paintings of skeletons and skulls and verses on the subject of death. In eighteenth-century Mexico, some truly splendid catafalques were built upon special occasions, such as that for Carlos II at Coatepec, with the crowned figure of Death triumphant at its apex. It seems likely that the form of these catafalques gives rise to the tiered form of the *ofrendas* especially in Mestizo homes. And perhaps too, the lively skeleton figures on the humbler painted versions (such as that preserved in the Museum at Toluca) are one of the sources that may have inspired the work of artists such as José Guadalupe Posada in the nineteenth century.

In the late Colonial period, celebrations and fiestas reached a peak of riotous display in the cities, so much so that the civil authorities sought to repress them. An account of the Day of the Dead at this time is given by Juan-Pedro Viqueira:

This festival, which was deeply rooted among the inhabitants of New Spain, was also a ritual of inversion of the social and natural order. The complex relationship between life and death in the belief of the indigenous population, castes and poor Mestizos, was made manifest on this day. The night-time visit to the cemeteries made by men, women and children of the town, the festivities and drunkenness that took place there, could not have seemed more scandalous and above all, horrifying to the illustrious elite, who sought to expel death from social life. This fiesta which blurred the boundaries between the living and the dead and partly inverted their roles, sought to make manifest the presence of death in the bosom of life, at a time when the new Spanish elite, always seeking to avoid rites and beliefs which allowed [death] to confront them, were seeking to forget its existence. (Viqueira: 1984)

He goes on to describe the attempts to keep the Indians and poorer people out of the cemeteries. In 1766, the Royal Office of Crime prohibited gatherings in the cemeteries at the time of *Todos Santos* and decreed that intoxicating drinks might not be sold after nine o'clock in the evening. Viqueira suspects that the ban did not have great force in the outskirts of the city, but in some cemeteries, for example that attached to the *Hospital Real de Naturales*, there was a ban upon admittance for several years. 'The dead were usually buried in the burial ground of the hospital so that there were few indigenous families in the Valley of Mexico who did not have a dead relative or friend in this cemetery.' The refusal of access to the burial ground 'totally disregarded the beliefs and feelings of the indigenous people . . . thousands of families were separated from their dead; they could not make contact with them upon the Day of the Dead. The Indians showed their profound discontent with the measure, ceasing to give donations to the chaplain charged with praying for the souls.'

The clerics made complaint to the viceroy about this serious loss of income, but their petition to have a gate into the cemetery opened met with no success. So far as officialdom was concerned, the Indians could say their responses for the dead souls in the church of the hospital. What was distasteful to the civil authorities representing the elite of the city was

46. Death triumphant above a catafalque designed for Carlos II, Coatepec, Puebla, AD 1700.

the 'mixture which existed between the adoration of the sacred mysteries and the diversions and pleasures.' For the intellectuals of the Age of Enlightenment, who saw a profound division between the earth and the heavens, this mixture seemed sacrilegious. In the combat of the vice-regal authorities against the 'disorders and excesses' of the popular religious festivals, they were met with the resistance of the ordinary people

who to defend their interests, became entrenched behind their traditions, many of them of a religious nature. To evaluate the importance of this phenomenon, it must be remembered that it was a mass uprising, led by a curate – Hidalgo – which proudly boasted on its standard a popular religious image – the Virgin of Guadalupe –, which was the point of departure for the struggles which resulted in the ending of Spanish domination in Mexico. (Viqueira: 1984)

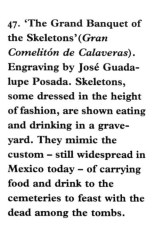

47. 'The Grand Banquet of the Skeletons'(*Gran Comelitón de Calaveras*). Engraving by José Guadalupe Posada. Skeletons, some dressed in the height of fashion, are shown eating and drinking in a grave-yard. They mimic the custom – still widespread in Mexico today – of carrying food and drink to the cemeteries to feast with the dead among the tombs.

Travellers' Tales

48. **Frieze of skulls and bones (detail). José Guadalupe Posada.**

The wealth of literature describing life in later Colonial times in Mexico and in the early decades following the long fought for Independence from Spain (1821), offers at least a few glimpses of events on the Day of the Dead.[1]

Thomas Gage was a Dominican friar[2] who lived and travelled in the New World between 1625 and 1637. His lively account of his travels[3] is a work delightful both for its vigorous descriptions of life in seventeenth-century Mexico and Guatemala and for what it reveals of the character of Gage himself. He gives, for example, many descriptions of the foods and sweets consumed in Mexico at that time. Several paragraphs are devoted to descriptions of the preparation of the drinks, chocolate and *atole* – both of which are important in offerings to the dead at *Todos Santos*:

Here [Oaxaca City] there are two cloisters of nuns, which are talked of far and near, not for their religious practices, but for their skill in making two drinks, which are used in these parts, the one called chocolate and the other *atole*, which is like unto our almond milk, but much thicker, and is made of the juice of the young maize or Indian wheat, which they so confection with spices, musk, and sugar that it is not only admirable in the sweetness of the smell, but much more nourishing and comforting to the stomach.

Many convents also specialised in the making of sweetmeats and preserved fruits which were widely available and which Gage mentions with relish several times. Before the Conquest, only honey and plant and fruit juices provided sweetening. Sugar cane was introduced shortly after the arrival of the Spaniards and quickly became important in the economy. Typically, these preserves and sweets, candied squash (*dulce de calabaza*) for example, are much associated with the Day of the Dead.[4]

Gage was writing to impress a Puritan readership and is often vituperative in his comments on the behaviour of the clergy of New Spain. In one such attack he describes a Guatemalan priest's portion of the offerings made to the dead at *Todos Santos*:

So upon the second day of November, which they call All Souls' Day, they are extraordinary foolish and superstitious in offering moneys, fowls, eggs, and maize, and other commodities for the soul's good. But it proves for the profit of the priest, who after Mass wipes away to his chamber all that which the poor Indians had offered to those souls, who needed neither money, food, nor any other provision.

A friar who lived in Petapa boasted unto me once that upon their All Souls' Day his offerings had been about a hundred *reals* [money], two hundred chickens and fowls, half a dozen turkeys, eight bushels of maize, three hundred eggs, four *zontles* of cacao (every *zontle* being four hundred [cacao] beans), twenty bunches of plantains, above a hundred wax candles, besides some loaves of bread, and other trifles of fruits. If all this summed up according to the price of the things there, and with consideration of the coin of money there . . . it amounts to above eight pounds of our money. This is a fair and goodly stipend for a Mass, brave wages for half an hour's work, and a politic ground for that error of Purgatory, if the dead bring to the living priest such wealth in one day only.

Setting aside Gage's bias, in Mexico as in Guatemala the usual practice was to give part of the food-offering to the priest in return for the recital of masses for the souls. The passage shows that the *ofrenda* in the early seventeenth century was much as in later times, including bread and candles as well as abundant quantities of foodstuffs.

Some 125 years later, another clerical

49. Group of sugar animals
including lambs, a dog and
a donkey, as sold in markets
for the Day of the Dead.
Surviving nineteenth-
century examples suggest
that many forms and styles
have a tradition extending
back over at least one
hundred years and probably
far longer. Toluca, State of
Mexico; Huaquechula and
Atlixco, Puebla.
H 4–12 cms

traveller mentions small figures being sold at
the time of the Day of the Dead. Francisco de
Ajofrín,[5] a Capuchin friar, wrote a diary of his
travels, the *Diario del Viaje a la Nueva España*
(Diary of a Voyage to New Spain). Ajofrín
entered Mexico City on 23 December 1763. He
writes that:

Before the Day of the Dead they sell a thousand
figures of little sheep and *carneros*,[6] etc. of sugar
[*alfeñique*], which they call *ofrenda* (offering), and
it is a gift which must perforce be given to girls and
boys of the houses where one has acquaintance.
They also sell coffins, tombs and a thousand
figures of the dead, clerics, monks and nuns of all
denominations, bishops, horsemen, for which
there is a great market and a colourful fair in the
portals of the merchants, where it is incredible [to
see] the crowd of men and women from Mexico
City on the evening before and on the day of
Todos Santos.

This is perhaps the earliest reference to sugar
figures being sold for the Day of the Dead. The
origin of offering sugar figures at the time of the
Day of the Dead remains obscure but Zolla
(1988) writes that in Naples in the twelfth
century sugar bones (*ossi di zuchero*) 'were an
affectionate present for the Day of the Dead
which were offered to family and friends.' The
custom of making sugar figures for the Day of
the Dead has certainly survived in Palermo in
Sicily to the present day and the custom seems

therefore to be of European origin. Further
confirmation of this comes from María Teresa
de Sepúlveda (1973) who, drawing upon information published by Luis de Hoyos Sáinz
(1947), notes that sweets were included in offerings for the dead in Spain.

The subject matter chosen by modern sugar-
figure makers in Mexico is very much as described by Ajofrín, although he makes no mention
of sugar skulls. The figures of clerics, monks
and nuns are not now made in sugar, but survive as miniature pottery toys.

The sugar sheep and lambs possibly make reference to the 'Lamb of God'. One of the contemporary sugar-makers of Toluca so described
them, and an explanation for this choice of subject in association with the Day of the Dead is
suggested by the lesson for the Feast of All
Saints' Day in the Roman Missal. John M.
Ingham, in his study of folk-Catholicism in
Central Mexico (1986), tells that the designated
lesson is from The Revelation of St John the
Divine (7:1–17).[7]

The passage describes John's vision of a great
multitude of nations, tribes, peoples, and tongues
standing before the Lamb. The vision evidently
anticipates the eternal blessedness at the end of
time and, perhaps, the great messianic banquet
that will celebrate Christ's marriage with the
church on the eve of the final victory over evil (see

46

Rev 19:9; Luke 13:29). Indeed, the celebrations of All Saints' and All Souls' compose a commensal reunion of all the faithful: the living, the saints and little angels in Heaven, and the souls in Purgatory.

From the year 1826 is a description of a market for the Days of the Dead at the town of Xalapa (Jalapa) in the State of Veracruz. This is by Captain G. F. Lyon, RN, FRS, who despite the 'loss of many papers, and the greater part of my collections, in the wreck of the Panthea, in which I returned to England,' gives an interesting account of eight months spent travelling in Mexico. Lyon had been appointed a Commissioner for the mining companies of *Real del Monte* and *Bolaños*, and was a most observant traveller. His description of the market at Xalapa is too long to quote in full, but he describes every kind of fruit and vegetable, meat and fish on sale in the busy market preceding *Todos Santos*.

November 1. – This was the 'Festividad de todos los Santos,' [All Saints] a grand feast-day; and the town in consequence was crowded with the natives of the neighbouring villages, in addition to its own gaily dressed multitude. In the morning the troops, preceded as usual by discordant trumpets, playing the never-to-be forgotten and eternal 'Bravo's march,' repaired to the church and heard mass; after which a merry bustle and confusion reigned throughout the day, and, contrary to the usual custom on religious festivals, Christianity was not outraged by a procession of the favourite and local idols. The market-place (Plaza del Mercado) was well supplied, and crowded with Indians, who, as in Mexico [City], were the chief traders; displaying their stores spread on mats in the full glare of the sun ... On one side of the market was ranged a temporary double row of booths, for the sale of white and fancy-coloured wax tapers, which were abundantly purchased by all those good Christians who purposed honouring Todos los Santos by an illumination after nightfall. Small tables covered with neat white cloths and tasteful displays of confectionery, were placed at the corners of the streets, and had a pretty effect, with little gay coloured paper banners waving over the dogs, lambs, and nondescripts of painted sugar, which were always surrounded by gazing groups of open-mouthed children. Xalapa indeed is celebrated for its dulces (sweets) ... On this present day of jubilee, all the Xalapenses were in their holiday apparel ... A great proportion of the ladies still adhere to the simply beautiful black Spanish dress, with the graceful veil, or Mantilla; but where they have done other Europeans the honour of imitating them, it is a bungling piece of business, and all sorts of finery and tawdry orna-

50. Stall in the market of La Merced, Mexico City, before the Day of the Dead. Typical paper puppets hang above the stall. Below are rows of paper funeral processions with priests and coffins.

ments are to be seen blended in happy confusion on the same person. In the evening the open windows admitted of my hearing, in almost every house, exceedingly inharmonious airs upon very bad harps, and singing, in a slow, monotonous, nasal tone, by one, two, or more voices, all in the same key.[8]

Again there is mention of sugar figures: one would love to know what the 'nondescripts' might have been.

The sugar skulls so much associated with the Day of the Dead today have not been specifically mentioned so far. Hugo Nutini suggests that their survival as part of the cult of the dead

51. Sugar skulls sold as gifts at *Todos Santos*. The names of the intended recipients are piped in icing-sugar onto the foreheads of the skulls. H 11–15 cms

is an example of convergence between pre-Hispanic Mexican and Spanish Catholic symbolism. He writes:

At first glance, sugar skulls appear to be a survival from pre-Hispanic times, perhaps having to do with the human skulls that were kept as trophies by households or *tepochcallis* (men's houses) and offered to or displayed in honor of a particular god at certain festivals ... But the human skull as a symbol of death has a long history in Christendom, and it could equally well be that the sugar skulls in the ofrenda are of Catholic origin. (Nutini: 1988)

In addition to the skulls of the *tepochcallis*, there were of course the skulls of the *tzompantli*. Some similarity must be allowed between these and the modern sugar skulls. The earliest extant examples are possibly the sugar skulls in the Starr collection preserved in England in the Cambridge University Museum of Archaeology and Anthropology (Starr: 1898).[9] Perhaps the earliest literary mention (given that skulls are not mentioned specifically by Ajofrín) is that of Fanny Calderón de la Barca (see below).

In 1843 John Lloyd Stephens published the second narrative of his travels in the Yucatán with the English artist Frederick Catherwood.[10] His description of human skulls seen in the graveyard of a village near Kabah, and the illustration of one such which accompanies the text, do at least offer an iconographic similarity and a hint of the origins of the practice that the sugar skulls may represent. Recovering from a bout of fever, Stephens records:

The spectacle around was gloomy for sick men ... Death was all around us ... Adjoining the front of the church, and connecting with the convent, was a great charnel house, along the wall of which was a row of skulls. At the top of a pillar forming the abutment of the wall of the staircase was a large vase piled full, and the cross was surmounted with them. Within the enclosure was a promiscuous assemblage of skulls and bones several feet deep. Along the wall, hanging by cords, were the bones and skulls of individuals in

boxes and baskets, or tied up in cloths, with names written upon them, and, as at Ticul, there were the fragments of dresses, while some of the skulls had still adhering to them the long black hair of women.

The floor of the church was interspersed with long patches of cement, which covered graves, and near one of the altars was a box with a glass case, within which were the bones of a woman, the wife of a lively old gentleman whom we were in the habit of seeing every day. They were clean and bright as if polished, with the skull and crossbones in front, the legs and arms laid on the bottom, and the ribs disposed regularly in order, one above the other, as in life, having been so arranged by the husband himself; a strange attention, as it seemed to a deceased wife. At the side of the case was a black board, containing a poetical inscription (in Spanish) written by him.

'Stop mortal!
Look at yourself in this mirror,
And in its pale reflection
Behold your end!
This eclipsed crystal
Had splendour and brilliancy;
But the dreadful blow
Of a fatal destiny
Fell upon Manuela Carillo.

'Born in Nohcacab in the year 1789, married at the same village to Victoriano Machado in 1808, and died on the first of August 1833, after a union of 25 years, and in the forty-fourth of her age.

'He implores your pious prayers.'

The widowed husband wrote several stanzas more, but could not get them on the black board; and made copies for private distribution, one of which is in my hands.

Near this were the bones of a brother of our friend the cura of Ticul and those of a child, and in the choir of the church, in the embrazure of a large window, were rows of skulls, all labelled on the forehead, and containing startling inscriptions. I took up one, and staring me in the face were the words, 'Soy Pedro Moreno: un Ave Maria y un Padre nuestro por Dios, hermano.' 'I am Peter Moreno: an Ave Maria and Paternoster for God's sake, brother.' Another said, 'I am Apolono Balche: A Paternoster and an Ave Maria for God's sake, brother.' This was an old schoolmaster of the padrecito, who had died but two years before.

The padrecito handed me another, which said, 'I am Bartola Arana: a Paternoster,' etc. This was the skull of a Spanish lady whom he had known, young and beautiful, but it could not be distinguished from that of the oldest and ugliest Indian woman. 'I am Anizetta Bib,' was that of a pretty young Indian girl whom he had married, and who died but a year afterward. I took them all up one by one; the padrecito knew them all; one was young, another old; one rich, another poor; one ugly, and another beautiful; but here they were all alike. Every skull bore the name of its owner, and all begged a prayer.

One said, 'I am Richard Joseph de la Merced Truxeque and Arana, who died the twenty-ninth of April of the year 1838, and I am enjoying the kingdom of God forever.' This was the skull of a child, which, dying without sin, had ascended to heaven, and needed not the prayers of man.

In one corner was a mourning box, painted black, with a white border, containing the skull of an uncle of the padrecito. On it was written in Spanish, 'In this box is enclosed the skull of Friar Vicente Ortigon, who died in the village of Cuhul in the year 1820. I beseech thee, pious and charitable reader, to intercede with God for his soul, repeating an Ave Maria and a Paternoster, that he may be released from purgatory, if he should be there, and may go to enjoy the kingdom of heaven. Whoever the reader may be, God will reward his charity. 26th of July, 1837.' The writing bore the name of Juana Hernandez, the mother of the deceased, an old lady then living in the house of the mother of the padrecito.

Accustomed as we were to hold sacred the bones of the dead, the slightest memorial of a departed friend accidentally presented to view bringing with it a shade of sadness, such an exhibition grated harshly upon the feelings. I asked the padrecito why these skulls were not permitted to rest in peace, and he answered, what is perhaps but too true, that in the grave they are forgotten; but when dug up and placed in sight with labels on them, they remind the living of their former existence, of their uncertain state – that their souls may be in purgatory – and appeal to their friends, as with voices from the grave, to pray for them, and have masses said for their souls. It is for this reason, and not from any feeling of wantonness or disrespect, that the skulls of the dead are thus exposed all over the country.

At this point Stephens makes a most interesting observation:

On the second of November, at the celebration of the fete in commemoration *de los fieles difuntos*, all these skulls are brought together and put into the tumulo, a sort of bier hung with black and lighted by blessed candles, and grand mass is said for their souls.

There follows a description of a funerary procession which prompts Stephens to reflect:

With these people death is merely one of the accidents of life. 'Voy a descansar,' 'I am going to rest,' ... 'My labours are ended,' are the words of the Indian as he lies down to die; but to the stranger in that country death is the king of terrors.

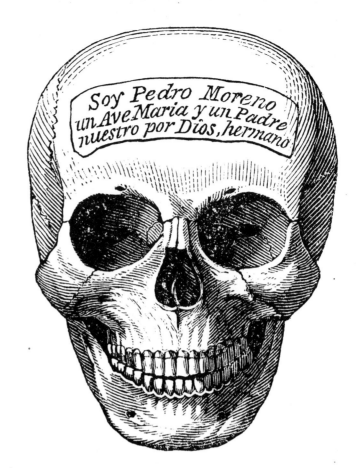

And after the description of the festival of Santo Cristo del Amor which was in progress 'treading lightly on the heels of death,' he concludes the chapter and the volume thus:

and as the padrecito and myself returned to the convent, the chorus reached us ... of women's voices, and seeming to spring from the bottom of every heart,

'Que bonito es el mundo;
Lastima es que yo me muera.'

'How beautiful is the world;
It is a pity that I must die.'

52. Engraving of a skull seen by John Lloyd Stephens in the Yucatán in the mid nineteenth century, when skulls were taken from the ossuaries and exposed to view on the Day of the Dead. The name of the deceased person is shown on the forehead of the skull in the same position as on the sugar skulls of today. In Mexico City *Todos Santos* was also the occasion for displaying the relics of saints housed in the churches (García Cubas: 1945).

53. Cloaked skeleton playing a guitar by José Guadalupe Posada. From a broadsheet entitled 'The Big Cemetery of Lovers' (*El Gran Panteón Amoroso*).

54. Model of skeleton seated on a catafalque or monument, reading a book. The skeleton is made of spring-coiled wire and pottery; the monument is of card. From a collection of Mexican ethnography donated by the North American anthropologist Frederick Starr to the British Folk-Lore Society in 1899. This collection contains some of the oldest surviving objects associated with the Mexican Day of the Dead. Guadalajara, Jalisco. H 23 cms

The label on the brow of the skull Stephens illustrates is in the same position as the cartouche which on sugar skulls is filled with the name of the intended recipient of this Day of the Dead gift. Perhaps this practice, described by Stephens in the Maya area, may once have been more widespread; it could be that as it became obsolete, the less grizzly and more hygienic sugar skulls took on the commemorative function.

In 1934, Robert Redfield and Alfonso Villa R., published their study of Chan Kom, another Maya village of the Yucatán. More than ninety years after Stephens they describe the disinterring of bones during the days of *hanal pixan* (dinner of the souls) or Day of the Dead:

The week between the first two days of hanal pixan and the octave of the festival is the time proper for taking from the graves the bones of any relatives who were interred two or three years before. In the shallow soil of the country, this practice is necessary, to make room for new interments. The occasion is one of ceremony, much resembling in its form the *rosarios* held at the wake.

Two fowls are boiled and *atole* is prepared. In the afternoon two or three men go to the cemetery and take out the bones. When the grave is opened, a little holy water is sprinkled on the bones and they are blessed. The bones are placed on a piece of new cloth and cleaned. Another piece of cloth is put in a small box; the cleansed bones are laid therein and again sanctified with holy water. The box is closed and carried to the little shelter in the cemetery, where a *Pater Noster* is said over them. Then the box is carried back to the village and into the house and placed on a little stand under a table, on which the food [for the dead] is set out. The *maestro cantor* [prayer master] recites the prayers used at the wake. The table of food is then offered to the *maestro cantor*. Another table of food is brought in and served to those present. At night chocolate is served. Holy water is again sprinkled on the box, and that night it is taken to the house in the cemetery and left there.

Another traveller who was in Mexico at the same time as Stephens and Catherwood was Fanny Calderón de la Barca. Born in Scotland in 1804, Frances Erskine Inglis went with her family to the United States of America, where in 1835 she met and married the Spanish Minister, Angel Calderón de la Barca. She travelled with him in Mexico between 1839 and 1842 and while there were official diplomatic duties to pursue, they were also engaged in seeking out information for the author William H. Prescott, then engaged upon his monumental work on the Spanish Conquest of Mexico.[11]

The letters she wrote to her family were so vivid and packed with information about life in Mexico, that Prescott recommended their publication, and they appeared in London in 1843 as *Life in Mexico*, by Madame C—— de la B——.

Among the 'rich stores of instruction and amusement,' as Prescott put it in his introduction to her book, were two descriptions of the celebrations for the Day of the Dead in Mexico. The first is from the twenty-eighth letter, written at Santiago on 3 November 1840:

Yesterday, the second of November, a day which for eight centuries has been set apart in the Catholic Church for Commemorating the dead, the day emphatically known as the 'Día de Muertos,' the churches throughout all the Republic of Mexico present a gloomy spectacle; darkened and hung with black cloth, while in the middle aisle is a coffin, covered also with black, and painted with

skulls and other emblems of mortality. Every one attends church in mourning, and considering the common lot of humanity, there is, perhaps, not one heart over the whole Catholic world, which is not wrung that day, in calling up the memory of the departed.

This description of a church in Mexico City, shows an urban celebration for the Day of the Dead firmly within the recognisable traditions of the Catholic church. A year later, she is more into the swing of things, and more in touch with the prevalent atmosphere of enjoyment that is more usually associated with everyman's experience of the Day of the Dead. From her forty-seventh letter, dated 4 November 1841:

Last Sunday was the festival of All Saints; on the evening of which day, we walked out under the *portales*, with M. and Madame de ——, —— minister and his wife, to look at the illumination, and at the numerous booths filled with *sugar skulls*, &c.; temptingly ranged in grinning rows, to the great edification of the children. In general, there are crowds of well dressed people on the occasion of this fete, but the evening was cold and disagreeable, and though there were a number of ladies, they were enveloped in shawls, and dispersed early. The old women at their booths, with their cracked voices, kept up the constant cry of 'Skulls, *niñas*, skulls!' – but there were also animals done in sugar, of every species, enough to form specimens for a Noah's ark.

Her description could be applied to the sugar market at *La Merced* in present-day Mexico City or that still held each year at Toluca, a town famous for its sweets. Little has changed, except perhaps that the sweets are now sold with the benefit of electric light to highlight their brilliant colours. The skulls are still piled high; there are still enough animals for the Noah's Ark; beautiful *ikat*-dyed *rebozos* or shawls can still be purchased there and are still worn by women from the surrounding villages. The fashionable *monde* to whom Fanny Calderón refers may, however, have worn something grander.

There have indeed been changes – new styles of skull now appear every year. They seem to undergo more rapid transformations than the animals, fruits or figures of hearts and flowers that are sold at this time.

Another example of this descriptive *genre* is from an account given by the Austrian Countess Paula Kolonitz, who journeyed to Mexico in 1864 as a member of the entourage of Carlota, wife of the ill-fated Emperor Max-

imilian.[12] After the sea voyage from Miramar to Veracruz, relieved of official duties, the Countess Paula stayed for three months in Mexico, and subsequently published a memoir of her experiences which appeared in Vienna in 1867. It includes a brief but lively description of the Day of the Dead in Mexico City:

We passed the Day of All Saints in Mexico. In a way it seemed strange to us because it is celebrated with much joy, and with things which shocked and offended the heart with their frivolity, whereas in all the Catholic countries, on this day above all others, honour is given to those we loved in their lifetimes, to those whom we loved very much and whom death has stolen from us.

For many days beforehand, they set up poles and erect shops and stalls in the Main Square (Plaza Mayor) which are then gradually filled with games and sweets. All is symbolic. Everything recalls the Day of the Dead, so that all one sees are small coffins, skulls, skeletons, catafalques and priests with their hats in the style of Don Basilio, as are used in the country; many funeral carriages of all sizes and forms, of wood, sugar or

55. Model procession of pottery, wire and paper representing monks carrying a coffin. Probably Oaxaca City. H 31 cms

cardboard, which are given to children for their solace, delight and amusement. Happy, they run through the narrow alleyways formed by the stalls in the square, looking, delighting, buying. So that this is a day of fiesta. In all the houses at nightfall they put up a table upon which they place the amusing toy catafalques and where they exhibit all kinds of foods and fruits. The children and the maids believe that while the household sleeps, the dead come and sit down and partake of the feast.

At night-time, by the light of torches and lanterns, the elegant world of Mexico flock to the great square. There they pass among the stalls and the street vendors; they laugh, they chatter, they joke, and so ends a day which for them is neither melancholy nor solemn.

Again, the range of toys seems little different from those of today, except perhaps for the priests in their country-style hats. Priests there are, in procession, with coffins on their shoulders, and perhaps these were what the Countess saw, since they were certainly being made in identical form when Frederick Starr (p. 48) put together his collection for the Folk-Lore Society of Britain in the 1890s.

For a view of the Day of the Dead in a rural area, one of the best descriptions is that of Carl Christian Sartorius, who was born in 1796 at Gundernhausen in western Germany. In 1824, after losing his job as a teacher, he travelled to Mexico where he married and settled down, making his home at Mirador, near Huatusco in the State of Veracruz. His own farming venture was successful and he tried to encourage further European and North American settlement in Mexico.

He devoted much time to the study of natural sciences and paid particular attention to the plants and animals of Mexico. His large herbarium was bequeathed to the Smithsonian Institution of Washington, D.C., for which he made meteorological observations right up until the day of his death in January 1872.

His book, *Mexico, Landscapes and Popular Sketches*, was first published in 1858, edited by a Dr Gaspey and illustrated with engravings after original paintings by the artist Moritz Rugendas. The preface to the 1961 reprint of this work tells us that it was 'written about 1850, when Carl Christian Sartorius was in Europe and giving lectures on Mexico to scientific societies.'

His descriptions of the Day of the Dead, are so full and so lively, that they are worth quoting at length. They appear in a chapter entitled 'Three Festivals. Passion-Week, Corpus Christi, All Souls' which, in its first paragraph,

56. Pottery and wire toy in the form of a leaping frog surmounted by a skeleton. Mexico City (Starr Collection). H 12.5 cms

makes a point that could still justly be made today:

In Mexico, the religious festivals have assumed a peculiar character; Indian customs have been in part retained, and are most singularly interwoven with the ceremonies as practised in Europe. These peculiarities, however, must not be sought for in the cities, for on the whole surface of the earth, civilization there levels ancient customs, and fashion scorns that which in distant country towns and villages is still regarded as sacred.

No doubt Sartorius the scientist would be fascinated to find the volume of literature which has been devoted to the 'interweaving' of Indian and European customs and which yet leaves so much unanswered. Although he does not give a precise location for what he describes, and it is no doubt partly a composite view, much of his observation is likely to have been made in the State of Veracruz.

Another festival which is kept by the whole population, but which is of peculiar significance for the Indian, is that of All Saints and All Souls . . . With the Mexicans the festival of *Todos santos* received a national colouring, dating from the aborigines, but gradually adopted by the Mestizoes and even by the Creoles. It is not the festival of the Roman Church, for this is here only a secondary consideration, it is an ancient Indian festival, which the prudence of the Christian priests, who found it too deeply rooted amongst the neophytes, added to the Christian holidays.

All Saints' Day is everywhere preceded by vast purchases. On this day a new dress must be had, new ribands and shoes; the women buy new crockery of all kinds, fine, parti-coloured mats, elegant little baskets of palm-leaves (*tompiatl*), and bright-coloured schikales (the fruit of the *crescentia alata*). But above all the purchase of wax tapers causes much head-breaking in every house. For several weeks beforehand great activity is observed among the retail dealers. Every shop-keeper endeavors to procure wax at a reasonable figure, candle-makers work in his [sic] house preparing tapers of all sizes, and in the evening the whole family is occupied in ornamenting these tapers with strips of coloured paper. There is no house, no cottage without some dollars' worth of tapers; the poorest labourer would rather go without bread, than without wax; and the Indians devote the earnings of weeks to its purchase.

In the larger cities this is less known; the higher classes as they are called, withhold themselves as much as possible from plebeian habits, and we must wander to the villages, if we desire to see this festival in its ancient form.

Whoever is fortunate enough to have a god-father among the Indians – and one can easily attain this good fortune – should visit his *compadres* (god-parents) on the first of November. The street in front of the house is swept very clean, and before the door is a large cross covered with immortelles (*tagetes*). The Indian calls them *sempasochil* and always plants them near his cottage. The house is in festive order, the old saints on the wall are laden with flowers, a wreath of flowers is between them, and two tapers burn in clay candlesticks. No one is at home, but close by, in the kitchen, we distinctly hear the thumping and shaping of the tortillas. Let us look through the doorway into this sanctum of the women. Three stout lasses are preparing the maize on stones, but our *comadre* (godmother) stands there with a knife in her hand, like Judith over Holofernes; happily, though, her victim is only a large turkey. Another, doomed to the same fate, is tied up in a corner; and close by are at least six fat hens, all ready for the pot. 'Who would be so cruel, *comadre*,' we exclaim, after saluting her: 'what are you going to do with this mass of provision? Is one of the girls to be married?' The three look roguishly at each other and laugh. '*Ojala*,' says the old woman chuckling. 'I should then be rid of one of my cares; but the fowls are for the dead, and you will afterwards do us the honour of trying the *tlatonile*.'

Should the reader think of accepting the invitation, we must warn him not to fill his mouth with the proffered dish before trying it; this *tlatonile* looks like a very innocent ragout, but burns like fire, being the genuine extract of unripe Spanish pepper, and none but mouths that are fire proof may venture on it. But we must now explain the meaning of the festival.

The ancient Aztecs held annually a great festival in honour of the dead, and offered the departed death-sacrifices. In walled sepulchres of the

57. Steel engraving from an original sketch by Moritz Rugendas, first published in 1858 to accompany *Mexico, Landscapes and Popular Sketches* by Carl Sartorius. The scene shows a market place of the period.

58. Photograph showing a dead child (*angelito*) and family by Juan de Dios Machain who worked in Ameca, Jalisco, between the end of the nineteenth century and *c*. 1930. Photographs of dead infants were much in demand. The custom of wakes for dead children, during which they were displayed in special costumes and wearing crowns of flowers, had its origin in Spanish tradition. In sixteenth-century Spain, infant funerals were accompanied by dancing and music and the letting-off of rockets, celebrating the infant's immediate ascent to Heaven without passing through Purgatory.

olden time I have found the thigh-bones of turkeys, covered with a dish, and on the pavement surrounding the tombs the bones of little birds, with small pilasters built over them. The sacrifices were probably of various kinds, accordingly as they presume their dead to be in the lustrous house of the sun, in the shady abode of Tlaloc, or in the gloomy Mictlan. Even human sacrifices seem to have taken place, sacrifices of slaves, as in front of a large funeral pyramid, in a round-walled hollow, numerous skulls were found. It is beyond doubt that at these festivals, death-sacrifices, and death-meals took place. The Christian priests suffered these rites to be combined with those of All Souls, and thus the heathen, probably Toltec custom has maintained itself till the present day. The name would lead one to suppose it a gloomy festival, quietly reminding of all the loved ones, whom the earth covers. Neither the Indian nor the Mestizo knows the bitterness of sorrow; he does not fear death; the departure from life is not dreadful in his eyes, he does not crave for the goods he is leaving, and has no care for those who survive him, who have still the fertile earth, and the mild sky. Is it indifference, is it frivolity which a rich tropical nature bestows on her children? I know not; but it is certain, that in the eyes of the people, death does not appear as a black, dismal spectre, that sorrow for the dead does not absorb all the joys of life. The first outbreak of grief is violent, copious showers of tears are shed, but are soon dried. Like the Mussulman, the Mexican says: 'God has willed it, we must all die.' Every Indian thinks thus, and regards it from the practical side. On the occasion of a death the relations and neighbours come and share in the grief, especially throughout the night; when the body remains in the house. The tribute offered is a taper, and something to drink. Prayers are offered up for the repose of the deceased, and

the night is then passed in social games and merriment in the same apartment where the corpse lies on the flo[o]r surrounded with tapers. When death befalls a child under seven years (*parvulos*), it is celebrated as a day of rejoicing, because the soul ascends direct to heaven, without undergoing the transitory state of Purgatory. The little corpse is decked with flowers and ribands, fastened to a board and placed upright in a corner of the cottage, in a sort of niche formed of branches and blossoms, and lighted up with many tapers. On the approach of evening, a few rockets proclaim the *velorio*, music resounds, and the whole night is passed in dancing and merry-making. The god-parents of the children do not altogether approve of it, as they have to pay the reckoning. At these wakes, the company remain assembled until the morning (with children as with adults), and then proceed immediately to the churchyard. The bier is quickly formed of a few sticks, a mat serves for a coffin; if a priest is at hand, preceded by three cross-bearers he hastens to the spot, gives the benediction, and the body is lowered into the earth, to return to earth. Every one present casts in a handful of dust, the grave is filled in, and the mourners depart without any extraordinary impression being produced. If a mother is pitied for having lost her child, she replies: 'I loved the little angel; but I am glad that he is happy, without having to experience the bitterness of life.'

Thus accustomed to make light of that which is inevitable, to dance about the yawning grave, we shall not be surprised to find, that the rites in honour of the departed have rather a joyous than a melancholy character. We repeat that only the Indian and the Mestizo observe the ancient practice, whereas the white Creole rarely imitates the Indian customs.

In the Indian villages the proceedings are as

follows. On the evening of the last day of October, the house is put in the best order, and when it is dark, a new, parti-coloured, woven mat is spread out on the floor of the dwelling. The whole family are assembled in the kitchen, waiting for the meal being prepared, which consists of chocolate, sweet maize porridge, stewed chickens and little tortillas. A portion of each is put if possible into new vessels, and conveyed by the members of the family into the house, where it is placed on the mat; to this is added a peculiar kind of maize-bread, called *elotlascale*, and death-bread, a kind of wheaten-bread without fat, sugar and salt, which is baked for this day only, shaped like a rabbit, a bird etc., and prettily ornamented. On clay candlesticks, corresponding with the number of dishes, thin wax tapers are lighted, not much thicker than a quill; roses, marigolds, and the blossoms of *datura grandiflora* are laid between the plates; and now the head of the family invites the dead children, that is to say those of his own immediate house (his own children, grandchildren, brothers and sisters) to come and regale themselves with the offering. The whole family now return to the kitchen to regale also the living. This is the offering of the children, and every child, according to the age it has attained, has its dish and its taper. Saucers with incense are placed around the mat, and fill the chamber with a dense cloud.

The following day offerings are prepared for

the adults in a similar manner; but all on a larger scale, from the mat to the tapers. Other dishes, too, are added, which would be too hot for the children: turkey in red-pepper broth, tamales, and other highly seasoned dishes; there is moreover a good supply of drink in large mugs, brandy, pulque, castile, and other favourite liquors of the Indians. With the adults less care is exhibited for adorning the room with flowers; but things are added which belonged to the deceased: their sandals, their straw hat, or the hatchet with which they worked. The whole house is filled with incense, which is placed before the pictures of the patron saints, who were undoubtedly introduced, three centuries ago, in the place of the house idols.

The belief, that the souls of the departed visit the places that were dear to them in life, that they sometimes flutter about their dwelling as bright humming-birds, sometimes float above their former homes as clouds, was doubtless handed down by the Toltecs to the subsequent lords of the soil, namely to the Aztecs; and we may assume that it still obtains among the people, although we never succeeded in gaining confirmation of the same from the mouth of an Indian. They are reserved in everything bearing reference to the religion of their fathers; perhaps, owing to their long subjection, their traditions are unconnected, and only here and there to be recognized.

The meal, dedicated to the manes [spirits] of the departed, is not usually consumed by those

59. Two altars in a house in the Totonac village of La Laguna, Veracruz. On the left is the permanent altar for the saints, some housed in wooden *nichos* (display cases). On the right is the altar with the offering of foods and drinks for the souls who return on 1 and 2 November.

who offer it; but is sent to relations and neighbours, from whom similar donation is received. In the villages where there is a mixed population, the young fellows on the look out for fun, go to the dwellings of the Indians, and offer to tell their beads for the repose of the souls. They are welcomed, and the offerings intended for the ghosts, are in part devoured by the living. Let us join a party of them, consisting of young Creoles and a few Mestizoes. They laugh and jest at the silly Indians, who prepare a meal for those who are long since dead. 'Do you recollect, Felipe, how we told our beads in old Mizcoatl's house, and had nearly burst with laughter when long Nicholas filched a glass of sweet liquor from the *ofrenta* (death-meal) and emptied it, and then made the old heathen believe, the shade of his son had drunk it?' – 'To be sure,' returned the other; 'but last year he managed better, and would not admit us until all the liquids had been placed in safety. We made up for it, however, by carrying off a contribution from his fat *huajolote* (turkey), which was not to be despised; and there was drink enough at his neighbour's.'

Talking in this way, the mischievous rogues knocked at the doors, and muttered prayers, feasted at the expence [sic] of the harmless superstition of the poor Indians, and in addition, carried away a tolerable supply of boiled and roast. We quit them, to do honour to the comadre's invitation, and are hospitably entertained. We there learned that only the white ragouts were cooked for the children, which are but moderately spiced, but still burn like a decoction of pepper; further that few families spend less than from six to ten dollars for this feast, and that it is their greatest delight to consume all their favorite dishes on this day. The following day, the church-festival of All Souls, mass is attended, and the women light whole rows of little wax tapers which they stick on the floor before them. This is a harvest day for the priests; for every Indian has a short prayer said for the souls of his departed after divine service, for which he has to dispose two reals (about one shilling) on the altar.

In the evening the women and children proceed to the cemetery, strew the graves with flowers, sprinkle them with holy-water, burn incense, and light innumerable tapers, which are suffered to burn until they go out of themselves. In the clear, beautiful November nights, these grave illuminations afford a magical appearance, when the tapers light up the dark cypresses or orange-trees of the cemetery, and the gloomy walls of the chapel. All is hushed; no sound is heard near the abodes of the dead save the chirp of grasshoppers, like the breath of nature; whilst the expiring flame of the tapers reminds us of the soul quitting its frail earthly tenement.

With one or two small amendments, this could be a description of the Day of the Dead in Veracruz at the present day.

It is still true that to see the most traditional forms of celebration for the Day of the Dead, one must leave urban Mexico. Mexico City, however, because of its ever-growing population of people from rural areas, has become somewhat more a repository for rural customs pertaining to the festival than it was in Sartorius' day. Mexico City has too its own new styles of celebration that have developed in a changing world. It is no longer true to say that there is a lack of interest in indigenous customs.

The buying of new clothes for the Day of the Dead is often spoken of, but in practice is now rarely adhered to. Articles of clothing or household linens are sometimes purchased or made, to place on the *ofrenda* for the dead; they will subsequently be used by living members of the family.

The passing and slightly humorous reference to godparents does not even begin to explain the obligation that this relationship has in Mexico. The terms *comadre* and *compadre* can be used in an informal way as a sign of friendship; the system of *compadrazgo* is, however, of enormous social importance and carries with it formal obligations upon the godparents which there is a requirement to fulfil in the correct manner and at the correct time.

Still recognisable today is the 'head-breaking' nature of the purchases: expenditure for *Todos Santos* can be a heavy burden for a family, perhaps especially so in rural Mestizo communities where the *ofrendas* for those who have died within the last year can be especially costly and elaborate. The building of an expensive *ofrenda* confers prestige within a community as does the ability to offer bread and chocolate to all comers when they visit the house to pay homage.

Children are sometimes still laid out in special costumes and there is still differentiation between the foods offered to children and adults. That so much that Sartorius wrote could still be applicable to events 140 years later speaks to the persistence of traditions in some parts of rural Mexico; the process of change is now proceeding at a much accelerated rate.

60. An ossuary, central Mexico. Formerly ossuaries were used to house bones
and skulls dug up some months after burial. Such relics sometimes became
cult objects (Galinier: 1987).

The Here and Now

61. Engraving from a *calavera* (broadsheet) of a skeleton as 'Father Time' with hour-glass and scythe. By José Guadalupe Posada, 1905.

Cyclic time is another way toward absorption, transformation, and sublimation. The date that recurs is a return of previous time, an immersion in a past which is at once that of each individual and that of the group. As the wheel of time revolves, it allows the society to recover buried, or repressed, psychic structures so as to reincorporate them in a present that is also a past. It is not only the return of the ancients and antiquity; it is the possibility that each individual possesses of recovering his living portion of the past. (Paz: 1974)

In the years following the end of the wars for Independence in 1821 and the beginnings of the Revolutionary period *c.* 1910, many dramatic movements unfolded in Mexican history as the new state made erratic progress towards nationhood.[1] Mexico City remained the hub of political and social life; the state capitals and other provincial cities grew in size and offered some of the diversions of urban life. The smaller rural townships changed little and the life in the Indian villages scarcely at all.

Two forms of popular art provide an insight into the life of the times. Events of moment in personal life had their popular expression in ex votos, most commonly in the form of scenes painted on sheets of tin or other cheap metal. These representations of miraculous happenings or disastrous events averted by supernatural intervention were usually accompanied by a brief explanatory text. Gratitude was expressed for escape from death or disaster.

Even before Independence, public events were documented and sometimes satirised in the newspapers and broadsheets, often accompanied by illustrative woodcuts, etchings and engravings and, after 1826, lithographs. The 'penny press', the *prensa de un centavo*, became, by the middle of the nineteenth century, one of the most important vehicles for social and political satire. The satirical element owed much to the caricatures and cartoons of nineteenth-century European tradition. The spirit was that of the Spanish lampoons or *pasquins*, satiric verses posted in public places (Childs and Altman: 1982). There was also access to the contemporary works of the French, German and British caricaturists and cartoonists (Bailey: 1970).

For the Day of the Dead, there were special broadsheets known as *calaveras* (literally, 'skulls') with verses supposedly written by the dead as mocking 'obituaries' for the living (Monsiváis: 1987). They were illustrated with skeleton figures in all manner of styles and postures deriving in part from the imagery of the eighteenth century (as for example the skeletons painted on the funerary catafalques) which in turn hark back to the traditions of medieval art. There was also the influence of illustrations from books such as the celebrated *La Portentosa Vida de la Muerte*[2] (The Portentous Life of Death) in which skeleton figures were animated as in life.

Many of the artists remained anonymous, which afforded them some protection in times of censorship of the press. Two in particular, however, have become well-known, partly because of the attention given to them by the post-Revolutionary artists of Mexico. Both worked for the printer and publisher Antonio Vanegas Arroyo who produced many popular religious images and *oraciones* as well as the songs and broadsheets publicising important events and giving news of accidents and disasters. Manuel Manilla worked for Vanegas Arroyo from 1882 until *c.* 1890, as one of several artists employed to produce the striking graphic images that accompanied the popular texts. The tradition of the skull and skeleton in modern dress was already well-established. In journals such as *El Calavera* (The Skull), which commenced publication in 1847, the skeleton image played its part in the commentary upon events such as the war against the United States over Texas (Stellweg: 1988). Manilla worked within this tradition; his successor in the house of Arroyo, José Guadalupe Posada (1852–1913), took up that tradition and developed it. Posada's cavorting skeletons in modern dress took to the life of the day with gusto, mocking the antics of the living.

The life and works of Posada are well-documented elsewhere (Rothenstein: 1989, Posada: 1963, 1972). It is sufficient to note that many of the images he created in his *calaveras* are still present today in the popular imagery of

62. Engraving showing Death addressing skulls and skeletons in a grave-yard. In the background is a tram with skeleton passengers. By José Guadalupe Posada, 1910.

the urban celebration of the Day of the Dead. Perhaps the most universally recognised is the figure of *La Catrina*, the servant girl in the fashionable dress favoured by her mistresses, the grand ladies of the *Porfiriato*.[3] The broad-brimmed and befeathered hat atop the skull head of *La Catrina* is enough to evoke this whole tradition of satire and the wry vision of the world and its follies so brilliantly expressed by Posada.

These were the days when, in Mexico City, death took to the tramways:

Except in the cases of the wealthy, the street-cars are always used for funerals, a special car painted black being employed. Every day, and almost every hour of the day, you can see funeral cars running out to the suburban cemeteries. The hearse-car, elaborately draped with black cloth, and surmounted by plumes and a cross, with raised dais for coffin, goes first; and then come two ordinary cars of solemn black for the mourners. This funeral train is only for the well-to-do. For the poor there is a car completely closed, with doors at the back, and fitted with shelves upon which the coffins are stacked. attached to this is a second-class car, painted black, and inscribed 'Funebre,' in which relatives and friends ride to the cemetery. (Carson: 1909)

A popular verse illustrated by Posada makes a wry reference to the final journey to the cemetery:

> This happy skull
>   today invites all mortals
>   to come on a visit to the infernal regions.
> There'll be special trains
>   for your enjoyment on this trip
>   and there's no need to dress up for it.[4]

Posada died in 1913, three years after the start of the Revolution that began Mexico's next

great period of struggle and strife. Between 1910 and 1917, the images of death took on new meaning as the Revolution took an enormous toll of the population. It is estimated that as many as one million Mexicans died in this period when 'familiarity with death was universal, stronger in the rural areas where indeed the differences between the period of the Porfirian dictatorship and the bellicose period were minimal. (In 1910, the average life span in the

63. Papier mâché model of a bus with skeleton passengers *en route* to the 'Atomic Cemetery'. Made by Pablo Morales, this piece forms part of a larger work, 'The Apocalypse', assembled by the Linares family. Mexico City. H 85 cms

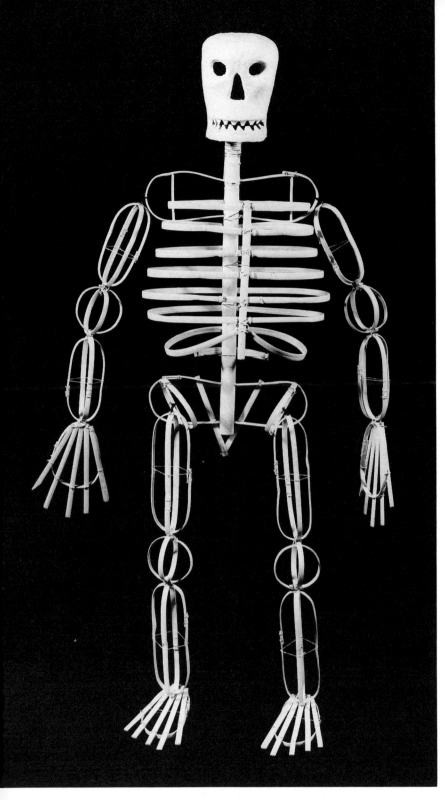

The 1920s saw a greatly increased interest in these and indeed all of Mexico's popular arts, especially those produced by the Indian population. The self-styled Dr Atl[6] (the painter Gerardo Murillo) wrote his book *Las Artes Populares de México* (Popular Arts in Mexico) in 1921 and founded the *Comité Nacional de las Artes Populares*. He was one of a number of younger artists and intellectuals who, reacting against the fashions and tastes of the *Porfiriato* when the preference was for foreign culture, took a renewed interest in Indian life and customs. There was a heightened interest in everything Mexican. The artistic, literary and scholarly communities of Mexico all turned to the exploration of Mexico's ancient history and the indigenous populations of the country. For the first time since the early Colonial period, the culture and lifestyle of the Indian peoples took centre stage.

In the fields of archaeological and anthropological investigation too, Mexican scholars entered a new highly productive period. There was at the same time an upsurge of interest from scholars of other countries. The resulting body of literature in many languages is immense.

Included in anthropological studies from the early decades of this century up until the present day are many accounts and some interpretations of the Day of the Dead; a selection of these works will be found in the bibliography at the end of this book. One of the most recent works is a comprehensive regional study of the Tlaxcala region based upon the author's enviable thirty or more years of experience in the field (Nutini: 1988).

A general account of the Day of the Dead in Mexico was given in the first chapter of this book, with some suggestion as to how the festival varies between rural and urban settings. There are also distinctive regional variations, and some places where the *ofrendas* are unusual or unique in form. The fieldwork and collecting which formed the basis of this account and the collections displayed in the exhibition at the Museum of Mankind in London were for the most part carried out in the States of Veracruz and Puebla.

In the towns of Xalapa and Papantla in Veracruz, we were fortunate to meet and receive much assistance from Totonac anthropologists who have carried out research into the Day of the Dead among the Totonac-speaking communities of the region. They were generous in

64. Cane and papier mâché skeleton figure from Tepoztlán, Morelos. Such figures were carried by people going from house to house on the Day of the Dead, collecting alms and food offerings. H 96 cms

countryside was thirty-four years)' (Monsiváis: 1987). The songs of the Revolutionary period are filled with references to death; they reflect the anguish of the times and defiance in the face of the ever-present threat of death.

Look here death – don't be inhuman,
Don't come back tomorrow, – let me live,
Remembering that tomorrow
Campaign trumpets will call us to fight.[5]

making arrangements for us to meet and work with several Totonac informants and also in providing us with the published results of their own work. It seems fitting to provide a translation of their own description of the Totonac Day of the Dead, *Ninín*, which summarises the accounts they collected in Totonac and then translated into Spanish.

The following is an extract from an article by Domingo García García and Crescencio García Ramos, anthropologists and founding members of CODELIT, the *Colegio del Idioma Totonaca* (College of Totonac Language).

Ninín: the Dead among the Totonac

The Totonac live in the north of the State of Veracruz. They are a coastal people living in thirteen municipalities in the region of the town of Papantla, a town divided between peoples who speak highland and coastal dialects. Those who speak highland dialects are found between

Espinal and Zozocolco de Hidalgo, Veracruz, on the eastern borders of the State of Puebla. The other group is found towards the northeast of Puebla ... There is a further group of Totonac who live in the highlands between Misantla and Xalapa who, however, retain few Totonac characteristics.

To this day, the Totonac carefully guard and maintain some of the mythical and magico-religious beliefs which are fundamental to the coherence and continuity of their community life. Something of this historic cultural tradition imbues the rites performed at particular times of the year. Philosophical beliefs are latent in the [collective] memory of the people who continue to speak a language that is the embodiment of their unique and splendid culture.

Despite the commonly held belief that the religious practices of the Totonac were swept away by the Spanish evangelists, these in fact still survive. In a way, the imposed Spanish-European influences have resulted in the re-affirmation of some of the practices dedicated to the veneration of the Totonac deities. The

65. Small offering table for the *ánima sola* attached to the outside wall of a Totonac house at El Cedro, Veracruz. Offerings are placed here for the souls of those who have no living relatives or are otherwise excluded from the main household altar for the dead.

famines and sickness. The belief was that such evils and sufferings were part of the earthly world. When the souls of the dead passed to the other world they no longer suffered, but still relied upon the indispensable assistance of the living. The destiny of the soul was determined by the manner of a person's death rather than by good or bad behaviour during life. Death was not the occasion of sorrow nor a subject of terror and fear. The living relatives helped the dead during their transition to the afterlife by carrying out everything necessary to ensure that the soul would arrive as easily as possible at Kalinin, the realm of the dead, or Kapoqlhwan, the place of the shades. This was consistent with the belief in the *listakni*, the spirit-soul – that which gives us life. This immortal part goes to its place of destiny, guided by the gods, the divine Lords.

In Kalinin dwells Linín, he who brings about our death – and is the motive and cause of death. He is the Lord of the Dead and lives beneath the earth where we will all go to be with him. It is also believed that some of the spirit-souls will be taken by Aktsín or Aksini, the god or Lord who metes out punishment to such of the *listakni* or souls as die tragically – for example, those who die by drowning and those who are murdered. These souls wander for four years at the command of Aktsín; when it rains and there is lightning and thunder, and the level of the streams and rivers rise, people hear noises and strange voices. They say that these are made by the dead whom Aktsín has set to the digging out of new streams and rivers in order to entrap more victims. After four years, the souls of these dead are set free, and go to accompany Chichiní, the Sun in the east. This is also the fate of those who die in battle and in childbirth, or who were midwives, priests, dancers, musicians or seers. They will help the sun to rise and ensure that he is not conquered by Linín in his trajectory. Once the souls are free, purified and perfect, they finally attain immortality and are transformed into birds, insects, butterflies, clouds, stars and planets. As such, they help Chichiní in his daily progress from the place where he is born, Kalakapulhni, in the east, to his home in the west, where he dies, entering the underworld, Katampín.

[An invocation is recited:] Invocation to the Dead and to the Lords [gods]

Humbly we make this offering to you; we stand here in the waiting place, still and at rest throughout the day and night; here we have our songs and

66. Totonac altar for the household saints, decorated for the Day of the Dead with papers ornamented with cut-out designs. El Tajín, Veracruz.

process of evangelisation also changed some aspects of the Totonac world view. The gods – the Lords, creators and protectors of the Totonac were replaced by the Catholic Saints. The calendar of festivals was altered as were the music and songs, invocations, and the nature of cosmological belief. For example, the worship of one supreme deity [was introduced], as was the personification of evil: Tlajaná, the triumphant devil who rules in hell. In Totonac belief, there is no [concept of] hell; all the supreme deities, the gods and goddesses, creators and progenitors, had good attributes. Only when they were neglected by mankind and not given the sustenance due to them, did they send punishments such as droughts, our words. Hear the noise of the rockets[7] and the ringing of the bells. When you come to this place we sing, we play and dance to your traditional music. Everyone is gathered here with great joy; you have absolved us with the Lords, who suffer no displeasure, nor disputes; we have no wish to cause any nuisance, animosity or envy. Behold the honour bestowed in your memory, with this humble little offering from our harvest, as a sign of gratitude for your benevolence and your visit to this transient place. You, Lords, Creators and Progenitors, the givers of all vital knowledge, of memory, we offer you the perfume of flowers and the music of our songs. You will not be troubled; all our transient hopes are vested in you at this humble spot: *kantiyán*, your sacred house. Eat and partake some of our harvest: the *wati* (*tamal* of meat and bone) which is your sustenance. Today, you must forgive us for troubling you and tomorrow you will go from here to your kingdom.

After setting up the offering and making the invocation, the people wait at the entrances to their houses and say that they are humbly complying with the customs taught to them by their forbears. They speak of an event of long ago which befell a man from these parts. He did not believe in the dead, and made no preparations for the Day of the Dead; he didn't await [the return of] his dead parents. He went off with his friends as usual, and set out for home when the ceremony was almost at an end. He noticed that there were many people following him, but that all were the dead who were returning to the other world. Among them were his Mother and Father who were returning empty-handed with no offering, whereas all the other dead were laden down with their offerings. His own dead carried only a piece of broken pottery as an incense burner, so that they were burning their hands and by way of food, had only some *pisis* (vegetable broth, *guisado de malanga*); they were crying and very sad. Then the man no longer doubted [that the dead returned]; he rushed home to set out his offering, because what he had seen had caused him great sadness. But shortly after arriving home, he started to feel sick and nauseous and later fell ill. A little while later he suddenly died. The food which he had at the last ordered for the offering to his dead parents, served as the food for his funeral. This is the story of that poor man. Today when recalling this story people say: 'So, it really is necessary to make an offering to the little dead ones.' They maintain the belief that the souls return in the form of insects to partake of the essence which emanates from the food of the offering. The constant repetition of this and

similar stories of death, year after year, helps keeps the celebration alive.

Today, this important tradition is transformed into a convivial feast for the living, shared with their dead and their gods. It also establishes unity: the reaffirmation of personal relationships, and those within the family, with *compadres* and the entire community in the temporal space of the universe.

Litakaxtawilan: The preparations

In the community of Escolín, the preparations [for the Day of the Dead] begin almost two months ahead of the event. Some sell part of their harvest, others go to work as labourers to

67. Offering for the returning souls in the same Totonac house as Fig. 66, set up in a separate room. New kerchiefs and cloths for the use of the dead are seen among the fruits and flowers.

get together the necessities required for the offering. So, on the day of San Lucas they cut the bananas (*plátano de castilla*), *kanáseqna* for the offering for *Ninín* (the Day of the Dead). They cut the canes and poles for the assembling of the altar; enough wood for the baking of the bread and cooking of the *tamales*; the sugar cane is crushed, to extract the sweet juice and to make the loaf sugar. They go into the country-side to collect wild honey, *kiwitaxkat*, and the beeswax, *lilhtam* for the candles. They make the pots – pottery griddles, incense burners, dishes and toys; they make and embroider the napkins; they dig up the sweet potatoes (*camotes*), the cassava (*yucas*) and *jícamas* (tuberous plant); the cocoa beans (*cacao*) are milled; suffi-cient maize is prepared. Eight days before [the festival] they clean the paths that lead to the houses and clear the undergrowth in the cemeteries: usually the farm-workers do this. Each family cleans and weeds the patio of their house, and makes everything scrupulously clean including the inside of the house. Five days before *Ninín* they start to heat up the bread ovens; they gather together the banana leaves and the corn husks (*totomoxtle*) for the [cooking

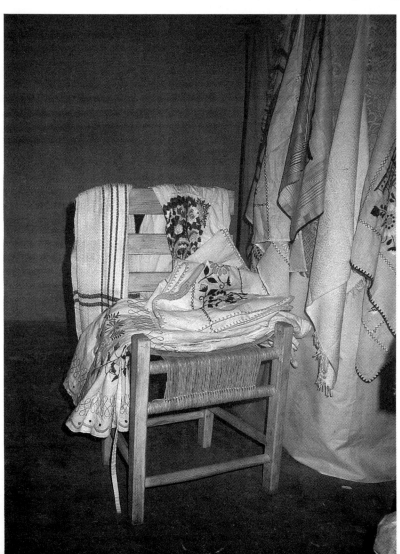

68. Chair set beside an offering for the dead; on it is placed a new hand-embroidered woman's costume in Totonac style, as well as commercially manufactured cloths. El Tajín, Veracruz.

of] the *tamales* and *bollitos* (small sweet *tamales*); also the calabashes, oranges and the palm stems for making [the plaited] 'stars' (*stakunin*) and 'suns' (*chichinin*) [for decoration]; the *tepejilote* or little palm, the *qalhpuxam* or 'flower of the dead' [*cempasúchil*], the *sempiterna* flowers (*pas-maxanat*), the cockscomb flowers (*la mano de león*) and the *limonaria* (scented flower). Fin-ally, on the days of 30 and 31 October, the pigs and poultry are slaughtered. Then the *tamales* of chili and meat for the adult dead are pre-pared and those with salt for the dead children.

Ninín is celebrated in four phases:
1. San Lucas on 18 October.
2. *Ninín*, the Day of the Dead, (*Todos Santos* or All Saints') from 31 October to 2 November.
3. *Xa aktumajat*, the *octava* on 8 and 9 November.
4. San Andrés (*Sanandres*) on 30 November.

1. San Lucas is the day when the celebrations begin in memory of those who have died tragi-cally, which means, those who have died by drowning or assassination.

A small offering of food is placed on the [household] altar for the saints, consisting of *mole* (meat in spicy sauce), bread, coffee or chocolate and *tamales*; it is decorated with [pla-ited] palm 'star' ornaments and palm leaves. If they are remembering a particular dead person, the *padrinos de la cruz* (godfathers of the cross) will take part with the family and prayer-makers, who will recite rosaries. The event comes to an end when the cross is taken to the cemetery where part of the food offering will be placed [upon the grave].

2. *Ninín*, the cult of the dead
This celebration is dedicated to the young and the adult dead. When the decoration of the altar (*puchaw*) is complete, on 31 October at the middle of the day (*tastunut*) they wait for the souls of the children. This day is known as the day of the little ones (children) or *laqsqatanín*. The food offering [for the children] consists of *tamales* without meat or chili seasoning, bread, chocolate, *tachula* (*tortillas* filled with *pipián*), anise-flavoured *bollitos*, maize (*elote*), *totopos* (maize-flour biscuits), sweet preserves, fruits, clothing, toys and water. Incense is burned when the candles are lit, accompanied by a short prayer. Rockets are let off. Once the food has been placed upon the altar, they leave the doors of the house open so that [the souls] can enter and consume the pure essence of the

64

Cleaning and decorating the graves in the cemetery outside the Otomí village of San Pablito, Puebla. The villagers walk in procession carrying *cempasúchil* and other flowers to decorate the graves.

PLATE 9

a. Truck taking *cempa-súchil* ('flowers of the dead') to market before the Festival of the Dead in the town of Atlixco, Puebla.
b. Women selling beeswax candles for *Todos Santos* in the market place of Tantoyuca, Veracruz.

opposite
a. Stall with paraphernalia for the Day of the Dead in the market of La Merced, Mexico City. Offered for sale are painted and blackware pottery incense burners, pottery dishes and mugs, small gourds and baskets from many regions of Mexico.
b. The sugar market at Toluca (*feria del alfeñique*). A display of sugar skulls for the Day of the Dead made by Wenceslao Rívas Contreras, one of the most celebrated sugar-workers in the State of Mexico.

PLATE II

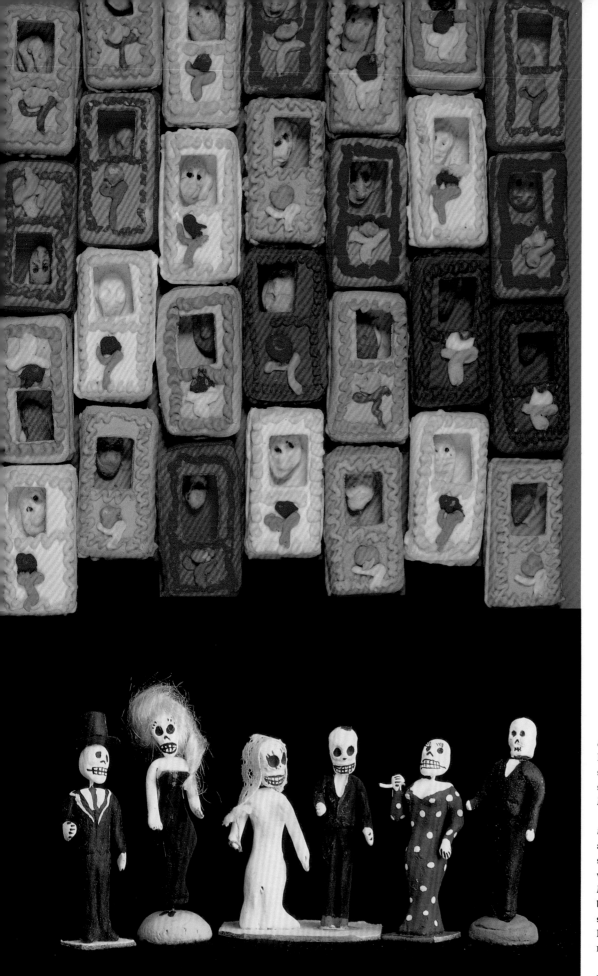

opposite PLATE 12
**Painted papier mâché
skull decorated with
spangles of glitter.
Mexico City.** H 27 cms

this page
**a. Multi-coloured miniature
sugar coffins showing skulls
within. Toluca, State of
Mexico.** L (approx.) 6-7 cms
**b. Miniature pottery
skeleton figures. States of
Puebla and Morelos.**
H (approx) 6 cms

PLATE 13

a. Offering in a public building, Mexico City. Included are skulls and skeletons of papier mâché and pottery. Also, reproductions of *La Catrina* by José Guadalupe Posada. The floor is decorated with metallic paper cuts, *cempasúchil* petals and dried chili peppers. Made by Maurilio Rojas of San Salvador Huixcolotla, Puebla.
b & c. Lifesize sugar skulls representing a bride and groom. Made by Wenceslao Rívas Contreras. Toluca, State of Mexico. H (approx.) 34 cms

Mestizo family *ofrenda* (offering) in the town of Chicontepec, Veracruz. The arch framing the offering is decorated with yellow *cempasúchil* flowers and the magenta and (less common) greenish *mano de león* (cockscomb) flowers. The wall behind the photographs, candles, crucifixes and other ornaments is decorated with red metallic paper overlaid with a white hand-made cloth.

PLATE 14

PLATE 15

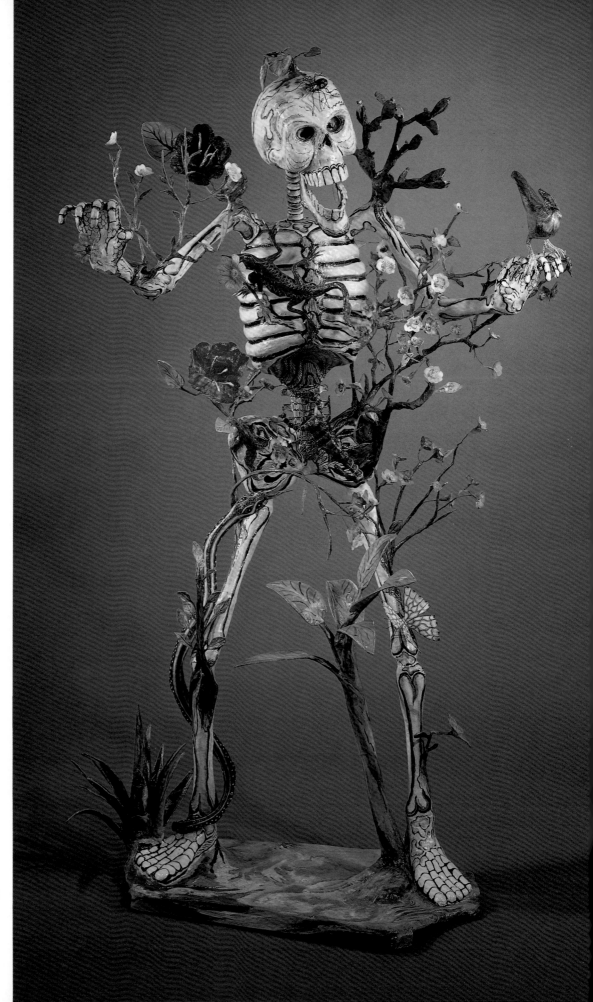

Lifesize painted papier
mâché skeleton decorated
with flowering branches,
a bird, a snake, animals and
insects. Made by Felipe
Linares. Mexico City.
H **170 cms**

PLATE 16

foods. The afternoon passes and night falls; they receive the hymn-singers who intone the '*Ayudemos Almas*', the '*Pues Padecistes*', the '*Señor de Tampico*', the '*Divina Pastora*', '*Buenos Días Paloma Blanca*' (Good Morning White Dove) among other hymns. At midday on 1 November, the souls of the children withdraw and the souls of the adults arrive. The food offering is changed: *tamales* with chili in all varieties, *bollitos*, *totopos*, chocolate, holy (blessed) water, alcohol, tobacco, clothing and musical instruments. Incense is burned three times during the day, and the adult souls withdraw on 2 November at midday.

Subsequently, the families take part of the food offering to the cemetery to place upon the tombs. During the course of 2 November the exchange of food offerings between godparents and families takes place. During this time, miniature 'altars' are set up on the outside walls of the houses for orphans who have no family, whether children or adults. The belief is that these spirits do not enter the house to take food from the altar. Their offering is small: a nightlight, water, two little *tamales*, bread and chocolate. Everyone, all the living and the dead of the Totonac nation, is included in the sequence of ritual events.

The cross on the tomb is set up facing the west, where the head of the deceased is placed, and from where it is believed that the dead will depart for the other world. The living go to rest facing towards the east so that the following day they will accompany the rising sun. Throughout the night hours voices can be heard everywhere, as the singers chant their hymns:

So you were conceived
without stain
ave María
Full of grace

And at first light:

Good day white dove
Today I come to greet you
Acknowledging your beauty
In your celestial kingdom

At the close of the ceremonies:

Depart, depart, depart
souls in agony;
may the sacred rosary
break your chains.

The noise of the rockets is unceasing as are the barking of dogs and cries of little children; the cooking pots give off the [savoury aroma] of *tamales*, [which mingles] with the wood-smoke from the fires; there is the smell of the incense and flowers and aromatic steaming chocolate, as well as of the 'bread for the dead'. In the light of the candles, all this brings a harmony to the night, uniting the living and the dead in a world chilled by winds from the north and watched over by the moon and the stars; everything remains in perfect harmony until the rising of the sun (Chichiní).

At some time during this night when no-one sleeps, a visit is made to the cemetery. The mourners take with them a small food offering, candles and incense. The tomb is adorned with a cross, the image of a saint, and an arch decorated with 'stars'. As on the [household] altar the tomb is hung with 12 or 13 [plaited palm] 'stars' which represent the 'heavens' [levels] of the afterworld – the 'Milky Way' through which the souls have to pass. Twelve stars are placed for a woman and thirteen represent a man and the principal divinity: Chichiní.

3. *Xa Aktumajat*, '*La Octava*', (the Octave): 8–9 November

The dead are received again – for nine days they have been visiting the homes [of the living]. On the eighth day, [people] bid farewell to the children and on the ninth day, to the adults. The altar is decorated once more with an offering of flowers and food, which is smaller than that made before.

4. San Andrés (*Sanandres*): 30 November

The celebrations for the dead come to an end. Although for some people they end with the *octava*, for others there is this further occasion for final farewells until the time when the dead will return the following year. Those who believe this put up their own special altar or use the [household] altar of the Catholic saints to venerate the dead; they bid them farewell with an offering of flowers and food. Usually people take advantage of the opportunity to have a vigil for the cross of one of the dead, inviting the godparents or 'sponsors' of the cross, relatives and friends. Once the offering is set up, a rosary is recited (*taqalhtawaga*), hymns are sung, part of the food is consumed at midday and, in the afternoon, they partake of chocolate and bread and go to the cemetery, taking the cross and part of the offering. By way of farewell they recite a rosary and some hymns are sung so that the dead person will not return to trouble the family. For this reason, they offer sufficient *tamales*, *tortillas*, turkey in *mole* sauce, wine, bread, chocolate, songs and flowers. The people return to their everyday lives; they go back to work, to the tending and cultivation of their fields in preparation for the new season of maize-sowing which is fast approaching.

The whole ritual cycle, as has been said, is concerned with agricultural success; it is the consecration by means of the image. An offering is made to the dead – to death – of the things that have been sown, tended and harvested: oranges, mandarins, calabash, maize, the family pig, etc. *Todos Santos* exercises and perpetrates the non-medianised bond between life and death (by the transference of the living to the dead: the latter eat what they always ate with their family, just as before); between human activity and the agricultural cycle (by means of the essential coincidence between the time of harvest – the resurgence of the seed as fruit – and that of honouring the dead – who also return and issue out of the afterworld), and at the same time it is the immediate bond between all people – men, women, the old and the young – of the Totonac community, it is evidently a collective force of an economic and social nature, which demands a family and group event as an obligation (actually more important than ever because of the danger that it will disappear) to honour our beloved dead ones.

Mention has been made of *mestizo* styles of offering that are either unique or very unusual. Two such are the special offerings for those who have died in the previous year at Huaquechula, Puebla, and the 'living offerings' of Iguala in the State of Guerrero.

Offerings at Huaquechula

In a tract of land between the volcanos of Ixtaccihuatl, Popocatepetl and Malintzin, lies the small town of Huaquechula; this is the Tlaxcalteca Valley region in the southern part of the State of Puebla. The region is an agricultural one, producing maize, alfalfa, avocados and flowers. Sugar cane was formerly important, but has recently declined. The land was rich in pre-Hispanic times and in the early Colonial period fruit trees, wheat, barley and other new crops were introduced which, alongside the traditional crops, found their way into the markets of Atlixco and the city of Puebla. Cattle ranching was also successful. A wide variety of fruits, flowers and herbs are still produced.

The Franciscan convent of San Martín was founded in Huaquechula and such of the buildings as remain dominate the centre of the town. The two *barrios* of the town come together in the celebration of important festivals, including

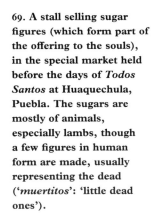

69. A stall selling sugar figures (which form part of the offering to the souls), in the special market held before the days of *Todos Santos* at Huaquechula, Puebla. The sugars are mostly of animals, especially lambs, though a few figures in human form are made, usually representing the dead ('*muertitos*': 'little dead ones').

Todos Santos. The *ofrendas* made here on the Day of the Dead for those who have died in the previous year are spectacular and unlike anything known from elsewhere.

The market held at Huaquechula before the Day of the Dead has the bright polychrome pottery made especially for the *ofrendas*. There are incense burners, candlesticks and figurines, painted either in mat or gloss commercial paints, often over a white slip. Fragments of glitter are sometimes added to brighten the effect. The simplest forms rely entirely upon painted patterns, usually floral designs, for their decoration. Other candlesticks and incense burners have mould-made figures projecting from the rims or applied to the body of the object. These include figures of children or adults, carrying musical instruments or fruits as if for offerings, and small winged cherubs; there are also full-figure saints (Saint Michael is the most common) and Virgins.

More spectacular items with much applied decoration can be had, but are usually made on commission. These combine the usual figures with spear-shaped 'leaves' and flower heads in baroque profusion. Both incense burners and candlesticks can be decorated in this fashion and are used alongside factory-made pottery acquired in the nearby town of Atlixco. These

are usually of angels or sometimes weeping children (*llorones*). In wealthy households, an array of metal candlesticks, some obviously family heirlooms and some perhaps borrowed, are used in front of and on the *ofrendas*.

Also in the crowded market are a few people selling pottery from other towns. A whole row of stalls under the shelter of some trees has the vendors of the sugar figures that are made locally: most common are lambs, predominantly white with pink decoration and sometimes including a tassel or some paper decoration on the head. There is the occasional figure of a *muertecito* (dead person) in a coffin. A little further on, the bread sellers offer a wide variety of breads, small cakes and biscuits. As always there are the flower sellers, setting out their bundles of brilliant *cempasúchil*, cockscombs and other flowers.

The overall effect of a Huaquechula *ofrenda* is quite staggering. Many houses in Huaquechula have rooms with high ceilings, perhaps as much as 12 to 15 feet high, and the *ofrenda* reaches close to the ceiling beams. In wealthier houses they are brilliantly lit with electric light; in humbler homes, the effect is still magnificent by candlelight.

They are built in tiers and, as Froylan

70. Locally made polychrome painted pottery incense burners in the market at Huaquechula, Puebla. These *incensarios* have hand-modelled or moulded ornaments of figures carrying offerings, sacred-hearts, saints and angels. They are used alongside factory-produced pottery figures of angels and weeping children on the *ofrendas* of Huaquechula, Puebla.

71. Detail of one of the large white *ofrendas* in the unique style of Huaquechula, Puebla.

edging papers with punched-out geometric designs, are made locally (see figs. 100–1), and the style of the designs suggests that they are an older feature of the decorative repertoire.

Families who cannot afford the fabric for making an *ofrenda* now sometimes use thin sheets of white plastic, which look remarkably effective. *Ofrendas* made for children are miniature versions of the adult ones. It is a matter of heartfelt obligation to prepare the *ofrendas*, costly as they are.

It is obvious that the building of a fine *ofrenda* confers prestige upon a family, as does the ability to offer bread and chocolate or more substantial meals to many visitors. Yet the overriding atmosphere is one of the fulfilment of obligation to the dead. A new road making access from Puebla City easy and increased national awareness of the value of older traditions as part of the national identity will bring change to Huaquechula as more outsiders flock to see the spectacular *ofrendas*.

Living offerings at Iguala

In the town of Iguala in the State of Guerrero, there is also a custom of building very special offerings for adults who have died within the preceding year. In addition to the more usual offerings and altars for the dead which are the custom of the town, there are the '*tumbas*' and '*tumbas vivientes*' (tombs and living tombs). In her account of the Day of the Dead in Iguala, María Teresa Sepúlveda gives a very full description of these *tableaux* for the recent dead (Sepúlveda: 1973).

She writes that the origin of the custom is not known. As in Huaquechula, people say: 'this is what we do: this is the custom of our ancestors.' The 'tombs' are scenic arrangements made by the family of the dead person, or by specialists hired to make them. The main room of the house is cleared of furniture and a scene constructed with cardboard, corrugated paper and tissue, showing rocks and mountains against a starry sky; it is decorated with plants or green-painted sawdust. In the centre will be placed a carved wooden figure of a saint, or a cross – perhaps borrowed from a nearby church or chapel. Sometimes there might be a cardboard image representing Christ, a Dolorosa or a Guardian Angel. Beneath this is a coffin; either a real one hired for the occasion, or one made-up in wood. On or above the coffin will be a portrait of the dead person, a glass of wine, a

Martínez told us (p. 92), can be free-standing, though most we saw were set against a wall. The origin of this peculiar form of *ofrenda* is not known; the only free-standing example that we saw was, in plan, like a fortification with projecting buttresses at each corner of the lowest tier. A possible origin that suggests itself is the form of the funerary catafalques described on page 43. Nor could we gain any explanation for the use of white materials for making the *ofrendas*. The yards upon yards of white satin and net, the gold braid, the gold paper stars and printed 'scraps' of angels and cherubs, are all available in the shops selling religious paraphernalia in Atlixco. Only the *barandales*, the white dish of salt, one of rice flour with a host, and a bottle of water which has been blessed at the church.

The wine and the rice flour are the symbols of spiritual sustenance; the blessed water allows the souls to quench their thirst. The symbolic significance of the salt is not known: it is placed there because it is 'customary'; perhaps, as in other places, it is seen as a purifying element. (Sepúlveda: 1973)

Beside the coffin is an inscription with the dates of birth and death of the person concerned and some verses in their memory. Some families place the food offering around the coffin whilst others set this out in an adjoining room. Sepúl-

veda gives an example of the type of memorial tribute that may appear on the inscription:

Dear Father:

Since your pure, white soul flew to heaven to remember you in this world is our only consolation. In all places and at all times we feel your loving presence at our side. Death has taken from us whom we loved, but your memory is always alive in our hearts. Lord, the soul which you took to the heavens was the greatest treasure of our hearts. He has fulfilled your blessed will. With a soul full of deep grief we will continue to follow the path to which your precious life has led us.

   Rest in peace
      your wife, sons, daughters
                  and grandchildren.

72. The 'Living Dead' (*muertos vivientes*). Detail of a 'living' offering in the town of Iguala, Guerrero. Such tableaux are arranged and enacted on 1 November by the relatives of persons who have died within the last year. In the background is a cloth with a lifesize figure of Christ painted upon it. Around the model coffin in the foreground are grouped children dressed as angels, 'death' holding a scythe, and a bandaged body. These 'actors' are usually relatives of the deceased.

Some families follow the custom of arranging the bed of the deceased: they cover it with the best quilt and place on it embroidered cloths and floral decorations. During this day no one will use this room, so that the soul of the dead can rest in his bed without disturbance.[8]

For the 'living tombs' they also make a scenic arrangement with a coffin, candles, flowers and plants; but, in addition, the families hire mourners and other people who will represent a scene from the life of Christ: the Oration of the Garden, the Solitude, the Last Supper, the Baptism of Christ, The Holy Trinity . . . The simplest form is the tomb with 'little angels', or perhaps the representation of the way the person died (if he died violently and not through illness). Some 'living tombs' have background music; a recording of an oratorio or a mass.

The relatives and friends exchange offerings when they visit the 'tombs' or 'living tombs'. They take away bread, fruit, candles or flowers in plates or baskets covered with embroidered cloths specially made for the occasion. They receive in turn, home-made bread. The 'tombs' are open to the public. People go around the town on trucks and buses or on foot in groups of from 10–15 persons, between 11 at night and 1 in the morning, they let off rockets at the house entrances where there is a tomb. Visitors are received with a cup of sweet wine, biscuits and bread.

The family keep vigil throughout the night and the next day go to the cemetery to leave flowers and candles. If the dead one belonged to a cofradía or brotherhood, the members accompany the family during the vigil and at the burial, giving something to the costs and they have the obligation of preparing the 'living tomb' at Todos Santos. (Sepúlveda: 1973)

There is one final manifestation of the Day of the Dead that should be mentioned to round out the picture of the festival. Today, many of the Mexican communities living in the United States of America also celebrate the Day of the Dead. For those who are are able to return to Mexico they will often choose this time of year

73. Part of a 'living offering' for the Day of the Dead at Iguala, Guerrero. A photograph of the deceased is set above the model coffin in the foreground. Some verses written in her honour are framed in a painted scroll beneath the photograph. Two young female relatives dressed as angels sit on either side of the coffin against a background of plants.

for their visit. Those who remain in Chicago or Washington, Los Angeles or New York or any of the cities where a substantial Mexican community flourishes, will celebrate *Todos Santos*. In part the celebrations are traditional in that an offering will be made in the home. Visits to the cemeteries are of lesser importance unless the family have relatives who have died and been buried in the United States.

In some cities such as Los Angeles, the Day of the Dead has in the last decade developed into an occasion for a parade and a fiesta involving several thousand people (Childs and Altman: 1982). There is music and dancing in the streets; elaborate costumes and masks are worn and figures are carried in the processions. Many of the most traditional Mexican foods associated with the Day of the Dead in Mexico are sold (*atole* and *pan de muertos*), and *ofrendas* are made everywhere, decorated with objects either manufactured locally or imported from Mexico. So infectious is the spirit of the event that non-Latin areas of Los Angeles have been caught up in its exuberance. The day ends with the celebration of a mass.

Elsewhere, in New York for example, there are exhibitions and celebrations. The Alternative Museum in New York has staged several special exhibitions taking the theme of the Day of the Dead as a point of departure for displays which perhaps focus on problems facing the local community or provide an opportunity for the display of the work of Mexican artists resident in the United States. The accompanying catalogues provide texts in Spanish and in English explaining the customs of the Mexican Day of the Dead. In several cities there are special programmes and publications for school children.

The Day of the Dead as the most distinctively Mexican of celebrations has become, for those far from home, a focus for the preservation of national identity. The Day of the Dead is alive and well both in its native land and abroad wherever Mexican culture is celebrated.

74. A man wearing a skull mask and 'skeleton' costume during the celebrations for the Day of the Dead, Hollywood Boulevard, Los Angeles, California. The Day of the Dead is now widely celebrated by Mexican communities throughout the United States of America. The photographer comments that in this instance the celebrations are a combination of the Mexican Day of the Dead and Halloween.

Part II

_____

Interviews

75. 'Weeping children' (*llorones*)**. These commercially produced pottery figures are bought each year before the Day of the Dead by the inhabitants of Huaquechula, Puebla. They are used to adorn the altars for the souls of people who have died within the preceding year.**

Introduction

The ten interviews which follow were all recorded in Spanish in 1988 and 1989. Although they have been translated and edited, an attempt has been made to retain the spirit and the phrasing of the spoken text. These first person accounts describe the beliefs, rituals, religious commitment and artistic endeavour embodied today in the ancient festival of the Days of the Dead, or *Todos Santos*.

Celebrations are evoked within the cultural context of each community. Some of the people interviewed live in cities and towns – namely Mexico City, Puebla City and Toluca; others live in rural settings in the States of Puebla and Veracruz. Two interviews offer an insight into Totonac traditions near the archaeological site of El Tajín: while Fredy Méndez offers a factual account of festivities in the region, Juan Simbrón links *Todos Santos* with early Totonac history and mythology. Although the other speakers are Mestizo, traits from Náhuatl[1] culture are clearly discernible in San Salvador Huixcolotla and Huaquechula. The age of informants also varies: Fredy Méndez is in his twenties, while Consuelo García Urrutia was seventy-eight at the time of her interview. All stress the serious nature of this festival, yet agree that the arrival of their dead brings great pleasure and tranquility.

76. **Fredy Méndez and his sister wearing traditional Totonac dress in La Congregación del Tajín, Veracruz.**

Fredy Méndez

(La Congregación del Tajín, State of Veracruz)

Before the Conquest the lands of the Totonac were known as Totonacapan; today their descendants live in south-eastern Veracruz and northern Puebla. According to the National Census of 1980, the Totonac language is spoken by more than 185,836 people. Differences between highland and lowland culture are marked. The archaeological site of El Tajín is located in northern Veracruz; built in the mouth of a thickly vegetated valley, it lies 50 km from the Gulf of Mexico and 15 km west of Papantla. This area currently supports a large Totonac population, yet the formal establishment of the present community is relatively recent. In the late nineteenth century the Mexican government opened up a great stretch of the Papantla area to settlement; many of those who purchased plots of land were Totonac.

Fredy Méndez lives with his family beside the road which passes El Tajín.[1] They own a strip of land, and make a living selling beer and soft drinks to motorists and tourists. Fredy, now in his twenties, is respected in the region for his embroidery skills. There is, as he explains, a shortage of jobs. 'In Papantla or Poza Rica there is little work to be had. Many people here embroider – men, women and children. I started when I was ten or twelve. No one taught me; I learned by myself. I embroider skirts, blouses, servilletas [cloths] and tablecloths.' During Todos Santos Fredy regularly receives awards and compliments for the splendour of his ofrendas. Judges from the town of Papantla visit ofrendas in local homes; they also assess exhibition ofrendas mounted in the town centre.[2]

In nearly every Totonac house, the religious shrine or altar is a focus for artistic expression. Catholic saints and holy images are venerated, and frequently displayed in wooden, glass-fronted nichos.[3] During the festival of Ninín (the Totonac term for the Days of the Dead) returning souls are received with lavish and costly offerings. These may be arranged with those of the saints; alternatively they may occupy a second, temporary altar.[4] The visual appearance of these ofrendas can vary widely from house to house. Balloons and colourful cut-outs of tissue-paper are a recent innovation; suspended palm-leaf suns and stars, flowers, foliage

77. Household saints' altar in the Totonac village of El Cedro, Veracruz. A temporary altar for returning souls is set up beside it during *Todos Santos*. Saints and souls both receive offerings of incense, candles, food and drink. The carved wooden saints wear miniature garments; behind them are a number of Holy pictures.

and clusters of fruit have a much longer history. Fredy gave the cost of his materials as 300,000 pesos, which works out at about £75.00 (US$125.00). No sum was suggested for the food. Because people buy things slowly over several weeks, they rarely calculate the total outlay.

Although the State of Veracruz is rich in pottery, its produce is rarely seen beyond the locality where it is made. Before Todos Santos *cooking utensils and incense burners, some shaped like birds, are made for family use in many houses by women who rely on nearby clay deposits. Sometimes objects are fired indoors in the embers of the cooking stove; sometimes they are fired outside without a kiln. A rapidly diminishing supply of firewood – the result of widespread deforestation – now threatens this ancient tradition.*

The spiritual conquest of Totonacapan dates from the very arrival of the Spaniards. Today traits of the old religion are fewer in the lowlands than in the highlands. Catholicism is a powerful unifying force, and evangelical sects have made little headway. Prayers and rituals are often led by rezan-

deros (prayer-makers). According to Fredy, 'Such a man would take an interest in this subject from an early age. He learns the prayers from an older man – perhaps his father; when the older man dies, or when he's too old to carry on, the younger man inherits his hand-written books. Rezanderos in El Tajín are farmers; they sing alabanzas *(Catholic hymns of praise) when the dead return.' In the* Handbook of Middle American Indians, *H. R. Harvey and Isabel Kelly (1969) write: 'The most common ritual numbers are four and seven, but eight and twelve also occur. Reference to twenty- and eighty-day periods strengthens the assumption that the Totonac shared the Mesoamerican calendar.'[5] Some of these numbers occur in the following pages.*

Fredy Méndez was interviewed in 1988 in the company of his father and his mother. Both contributed information, and confirmed his statements. Although Fredy was not taught Totonac as a child, he has since learned to speak it fluently. He takes great pride in his cultural heritage, and hopes Totonac customs can survive.

Fredy Méndez

We have lived in this region for a long, long time. My great-grandparents moved from a place nearby, and settled in El Tajín. They knew many stories about the pyramids, but these have mostly been forgotten. Who the builders were, no one is sure. I don't think they were our ancestors. If the original inhabitants had survived, their ruins would not have been forgotten and buried underground. Perhaps the Spaniards killed them all. Some people say there are spirits in the ruins of El Tajín, but they lived long ago and they do us no harm.[6]

We are Totonac, and we are Catholics. We go to mass, as we have always done, and observe the ceremonies of the Catholic Church. The Protestants want us to abandon our beliefs.[7] They say we waste our money on foolishness. People whose faith is weak are easily persuaded. In these parts, however, there are few converts. When Protestants talk, we listen politely and buy their books, but we don't read them. We are faithful to our festivals and saints.

Each year during *Todos Santos* the dead return. This is the most important festival of the year. It is not a time for making merry. It is a sad and solemn time, as when someone close to us dies, yet it gives us pleasure to receive our dead. We do the things our ancestors did: my father follows his parents' teachings, and I will continue to do the same. The dead come to eat: they come to consume our offerings of food and drink. These must be set out with pleasure and affection. If I decide to make you a present, I do it whole-heartedly, because I want to. It must be like this during *Todos Santos*. The souls do not force us to give them anything. If we give, it must be because we truly want to.

As the festival approaches, we accumulate the things we need. When we want something costly, like new clothing, we put money aside over many weeks. So it is with *Todos Santos*. Last year we spent 300,000 pesos on materials alone, without including the cost of food. During October, and maybe September, our purchases include plates, paper, candles and other goods; we buy chili peppers, sugar, salt, *cacao*, coffee, cinnamon, and twelve kilos of wheat flour. In this way we make our preparations.

Not everyone takes the same amount of trouble. Not everyone has the same amount of skill. To do something good takes time, enthusiasm and a love of tradition. I like things to be ornate, not simple and uncomplicated. From the ceiling we hang tissue-paper cut-outs in many colours. These are laborious to make: if the blade slips even slightly, the sheet is wasted. Some

people barely pattern their paper, but I create birds, animals, flowers and people; I even show the main pyramid of El Tajín.[8] This technique was uncommon in my father's youth. Instead, he uses tissue paper to cover rope or strips of wood: by tying the paper at intervals with string, he shapes the paper into bubbles.

On 29 October my mother grinds *cacao* on her *metate* (grinding stone). She adds sugar, cinnamon, hard-boiled egg yolks, and powdered cloves. She prefers not to add biscuit crumbs, as some people do. This mixture is kneaded and rolled flat, like a *tortilla*. Then she fashions it by hand into different shapes. Some are inspired by nature, while others refer to things that no longer exist. Not everyone does this: some women make unadorned circles,

78. Making paper decorations for the Day of the Dead in Cerro del Carbón, Veracruz. Designs are cut with a sharp blade. The patterned sheet of paper is then stuck down on to a second sheet of a contrasting colour. Such decorations are pinned round altars during celebrations (see figs 15 and 66). The pottery vessels on shelves in front of the house serve as hives for native stingless bees.

79. Totonac food offering for the Day of the Dead. In the centre are figures made from chocolate. Papantla region, Veracruz.

without even a pattern. My mother, by contrast, scores the surface, and makes them pretty, as her mother and her grandmother taught her. After about two hours, the figures harden. Some will lie flat upon the altar; others will be hung up on threads. Long ago my family found some seals of stone; they were very ancient, and came out of the ground. My grandmother used these seals to imprint her chocolate with designs; then, sad to say, the seals were lost.

29 October is also the time when bread dough is mixed; my mother does this at the end of the day. On the 30th we bake bread in the oven outside. People who have no oven buy bread from us, but we keep ten or fifteen kilos to feed our visitors. On the 30th, too, we hang our paper banners, and suspend our wooden board for the *ofrenda*. This board should be flat, so first we lay it under bricks. The *altar colgante* (hanging altar) is usual still in countless homes, where it hangs on ropes from the ceiling during the month of November. A white cloth covers it and hangs down around it. Many families, however, prefer a table; in modern houses, they may have no choice – a hanging altar requires a beam, or some other method of support.

31 October is La Vigilia,[9] and we work hard to finish our *ofrenda*. Some people barely dress their altar: they spread out a white cloth, and offer only water, bread and a few *tamales*. Other people, by contrast, lavishly decorate two quite separate altars. One is for all saints, while the second is for all souls; both altars carry flowers, candles and food. Families in Plan de Hidalgo and Plan de Palmar have many holy images, and many saints of wood or plaster. In houses such as these, the saints' altar is permanent: it remains in full view all the year round. We too have saints, although not so many, but we keep

ours in a private place; we shield them from visitors, who might swear or become drunk. When *Todos Santos* comes, these other families mount a second altar beside or opposite the first, according to the space available. This is what my grandparents did. If we, in our house, had lots of images and lots of saints, then we might follow their example and have two altars. As it is, we have just one.

We love our surroundings, and the fruits of nature; we hang clusters of bananas, *jícamas*, limes, oranges and *mandarinas*. We put out flowers – yellow flowers, and others if we want. We deck the altar with green *tepejilote* leaves,[10] and we fashion suns, stars and pineapples from the *palma de coyol*.[11] We cut the fronds ourselves nearby. These are the adornments that we make. At the centre goes an image of the Virgin of Guadalupe or the Sacred Heart. In front we lay a *petate* on the ground.

If we have photographs of the deceased we put them out, but many families have none. There should be a chair, so that the dead can sit and eat. There should be towels and a dish of water, so that the dead can wash their hands. We need ribbons, incense burners, shoulderbags, embroidered *servilletas*, and cloths. The dead use these cloths to carry away their food. Of course this is a belief – they can't physically take it away. Sometimes we put out clothing. The dead go to the grave in the clothes they have used. When they return each year, we give them what we can afford: a newly embroidered kerchief, a blouse, or a skirt. If you like, you can put out other things as well – a *machete* or a comb.

Candles for the dead are supported by split logs and split sticks. There are yellow candles and white candles. Once we preferred the yellow ones of beeswax, but now they are poorly made and oily; as soon as they get hot, they start to bend. Today we find the white ones better; they are made from paraffin wax, and they are harder. We also offer candles in glasses.

There are many classes of *copal* (incense).[12] High-quality *copal* costs 24,000 pesos a kilo, but some varieties are more expensive. Cheaper ones are bad value: they won't burn and the smell is poor. Good *copal* is white in tone; bad *copal* is usually dark. The kind we buy is from the State of Puebla. During *Todos Santos* wealthy families use half a kilo over three days; we make do with less. The cost is high, so we use a quarter of a kilo, and chiefly burn it when food is placed on the altar. Incense drives evil spirits away. They are attracted by the

80. Suspended household altar in the home of Fredy Méndez (see also plate 20b; fig. 14). Adornments include papercuts and hanging figures made from the *coyol* palm. Candles are set into a section cut from the stem of a banana plant. Laid out on low chairs are newly made women's garments, handtowels and a man's hat; these are for the use of the returning souls. Although the central cloth is from Tenango de Doria, Hidalgo, all other embroidery is the work of Fredy Méndez.

aroma of food, and by the candles. The devil would also like to share the food of all souls, but the smell of incense keeps him away.

The day of La Vigilia, from the hour of noon, is for the souls of dead children. 1 November is for adult souls, who also arrive at noon. Although the dead can find their way home from the cemetery, we lay a path of flowers near the door to lead them inside. When they leave us on the 2nd, they need no path.

Between 31 October and 2 November, past generations were careful always to leave the front door open, so that the souls of the deceased could enter. My grandmother was constantly worried, and was forever checking that the door had not been accidentally shut. Younger people are less concerned, but there is one rule which we must obey: while the festival lasts, we treat all living beings with kindness. This includes dogs, cats, even flies or mosquitoes. If you should see a fly on the rim of a cup, don't frighten it away – it is a dead relative who has returned. If a moth sits on a *servilleta*, leave it be; welcome every living creature.

The dead come to eat *tamales* and to drink hot chocolate. What they take is vapour, or steam, from the food. They don't digest it physically: they extract the goodness from what we provide. This is an ancient belief; it comes to us from our grandparents, or maybe it's older still. Each year we receive our relatives with joy. We sit near the altar to keep them company, just as we would if they were alive. We are not able to talk with the dead, though there are those who can. Some people possess this knowledge. Because they study books on Satan, they know

how to converse with the dead. Individuals can visit these people, if they want to contact their dead. A murder victim could say who had killed him, and why. Several women near Papantla have these powers.[13] We, during *Todos Santos*, do not; we merely sense the presence of those we love.

We burn incense, and we feel glad. We offer food, and we say: 'Eat'. Always, we do this with good grace. If people are irritable and resentful, the dead know it. They become ill, and they vomit. Our duty is to make them happy. The poor must do the best they can. Hard-up families offer bread and water, if that is all they can afford: what matters is the feeling in their hearts. Some people, however, make no *ofrenda*. They have lost faith in the return of all souls. 'Why should I spend my savings on the dead?' they ask. 'I can use my money in better ways.' These people, after *Todos Santos*, frequently fall ill. The dead say: 'In this house, nothing has been done for us' and misfortune may follow. People who neglect their dead have been known to fall, to sicken with fever, maybe even to die. I myself have seen such cases. When such a person starts to vomit, he or she must see a doctor, take medicine, garlic and other remedies, pray and say the rosary. We, in this house, have never been ill, because we respect and welcome our dead.

We feed dead children with *comida blanca* ('white' food); this means that it contains no chili. Red meat is never given. Instead we provide broth, and *tamales* with egg and sesame seeds, chicken, fish, and squash with shrimps. For these *tamales* we use maize dough and salt. We put out *refrescos* (soft fizzy drinks) and hot chocolate prepared at home. We cook sweet dishes from pumpkin, banana, boiled *camote* (sweet potato) and yucca. We serve toasted sesame seeds, and toasted pumpkin seeds with *panela* (brown cane sugar). We make *totopos*, which look like square *tortillas*. For these we use maize dough, eggs, lard, aniseed and *panela*. Fried until they are crispy, they last about two weeks. To decorate the altar, we hang up *bollitos de anís*: wrapped in maize husks and steamed, they contain maize dough, *panela*, carbonate, lard and aniseed.

Dead adults eat many of the things I've listed; they too like *totopos* and *bollitos de anís*, sweets dishes, fruit, chocolate, *refrescos*, and home-baked bread in a *batea* (wooden dish). In addition they like meat and chili, so we make them *tamales* with pork, and serve hot *mole* sauce with turkey and *tortillas*. We offer them

81. **Locally fired cooking pot. Food is being prepared in the open air for the Ceremony of the Cross (see page 82). El Tajín, Veracruz.**

coffee, cigarettes, beer, and sometimes *refino* (*aguardiente*, or cane alcohol). Some things, like *mole*, are best served in earthenware dishes, but for other foods we prefer fine china. A single plate, which might have cost 200 pesos a few years back, is now priced at 20,000 pesos or more. The best make is called Ánfora. It costs a lot, but it's still the one we like the most. Those who can afford it buy new dishes for *Todos Santos*; those who can't offer the best of what they have. Many families also need new cooking pots for this time of the year. These are made or bought with care. A good earthenware pot, if you treat it well, can last ten or fifteen years.

In other places, so I've been told, people wear masks, dance and play music when the dead return. This is not the custom here. Instead, we have *alabanzas*. These are sung by four men, who go in groups from house to house. On 1 November they sing in the evening and late into the night; then, on 2 November, they sing again. They sing *Los ángeles en el cielo* (The Angels in Heaven), *El Señor de Tampico* (Our Lord of Tampico) and other songs besides. Householders give them food to eat and alcohol to drink. There is little music other than this. In our region we have brass bands: if a dead man had been a musician, his family might pay a group of musicians to play for him; or his fellow musicians might come and play for free.[14] But this is rare.

I have a holy picture which shows two roads: the road of virtue and the road of evil. When someone dies, the soul rises up and the body goes below. The good ascend to Heaven, but those who have robbed or killed must go to Hell. Our altars, our offerings and our *alabanzas* are for *los fieles difuntos* (the faithful departed); we are welcoming pure souls from Heaven. We cannot be sure that the wicked return from Hell, but, in case they do, we offer them their own *ofrenda*. Outside the house, on a narrow shelf or table, we put bread, chocolate and flowers. Those who have sinned may neither enter the house, nor approach the blessed altar; they must remain outside. This altar is for errant souls, for souls in torment, and for orphans.[15]

At midday on 2 November the dead depart. Those who have been well received go laden with bananas, *tamales*, *mole* and good things. Those who have been poorly received return empty-handed and grieving to the grave. Some people here have even seen them, and heard their lamentations. When the visiting spirits have withdrawn, we visit each other in our homes, and exchange gifts of food. On this day, we welcome relatives and friends; as the hours pass, they come and go, talking and eating. We like to offer hospitality. There is *mole* with turkey or chicken, rice, and *tamales*; there is hot chocolate and bread.

On the 2nd or 3rd we go to the cemetery: this is our duty. We sprinkle lime over the grave, as if clothing the dead person in white, and we offer bread, chocolate, *tamales*, *bollitos de anís*, *totopos*, fruit, candles and flowers from the altar at home. We lay a leaf on the grave, then we spread out the food; we perfume the air with incense, and we light our candles. When we go home, we leave the food behind.

This is not the end of our celebrations. On the eighth day of November we set a small quantity of food upon the altar.[16] Then, at the end of November, comes the day of San Andrés. We offer him *tamales*, chocolate, bread and many things, just as we did the other saints on All Saints' Day. Dead adults and dead children both return: together, on this day, they make their last farewell. *Todos Santos*, you see, lasts all month long.

Even though we know the dead will visit us on earth, we feel grief and sorrow if our loved ones die. When this sad moment comes at last, a crucifix is placed on the dead person's breast, to offer protection against the devil. Then the body is washed, and dressed in its finest clothes. A man who is *de calzón* is arrayed in the newest *calzón* he owns.[17] People may go to the grave with all their clothing, although some families like to keep a few garments in memory. Forty years and more ago, when a woman died, she was buried like a bride in her white skirt, her blouse and her *quexquén* (*quechquemitl*, or shoulder cape). She wore her gold earrings, her gold necklace and her gold rings. Now these things go to her daughter, or her daughter-in-law.

When a man dies, his wife prepares him for burial; when a woman dies, her husband prepares her for burial. This task may also be done by the *compadre* or *comadre*. In adult life, at the time of our marriage, we form a life-long bond with a man and woman: they become our *compadre* and our *comadre*, just as we become theirs.[18] When death occurs, they must immediately be told. We also run to tell the chief *rezandero* who arrives as fast as he can, bringing with him one, or three companions. He asks for a *petate* and a blanket, so that they can kneel and pray during the night-long vigil.

82. Professional prayer-makers (*rezanderos*) during the Ceremony of the Cross (see text). They kneel on a rolled up palm mat (*petate*) before the dead woman's altar, blessing both it and the cross (visible here above their shoulders). Later the cross will be placed on her grave in the cemetery. El Tajín, Veracruz.

flowers, and light twelve candles – six along one side, and six along the other. These don't need to be tall; if necessary, we cut big candles into smaller pieces. Then we erect a provisional cross.

When a death has occurred, someone goes asking for donations. He or she goes from house to house, asking for eggs and *nixtamal* (maize boiled in water with slaked lime). Four days after death, this is used to make egg *tamales*. For these four days, the dead person's house has remained unswept, inside and outside. Then, on the fourth day, the chief *rezandero* sweeps: he asks for a bucket of holy water and *aguacatillo* leaves. With these, he drives away the evil spirits. He sprinkles water, and he sweeps. This is his task, and he must do it alone. He gathers the refuse in a bag, a sack or a blanket. He takes it away, prays, and burns it; to do this, he needs *aguardiente*. Then he returns to the house, asks again for the *petate* and the blanket, and says three prayers. On the ninth day after death, he comes again to the house, and again says three prayers.

Eighty days after death, we erect a permanent cross. Next week my father will be *el padrino de la cruz* (godfather of the cross) for a woman who died aged ninety.[21] In the house where she lived there will be an altar for *la difunta* (dead woman). This altar will be decorated as if for *Todos Santos*; so too will the permanent altar of the saints. There will be flowers, food, incense and candles. New clothes will be set out for the dead woman; later, these will be worn by the living. The *rezanderos* will kneel on a *petate*. They will pray for the soul of the dead woman; they will bless the cross, and the *ofrenda*. There will be food in abundance for relatives and friends. Afterwards the flowers and the cross will be taken to the cemetery.

All regions and all peoples have their own traditions. I take our traditions seriously and am forever asking questions. I want to know how things were done and why. It saddens me that some young people now reject our culture, and take no interest in our past. Many customs are already lost. As the years pass, and as old people die, memories are blurred. We live next to the pyramids, yet we know next to nothing of their creators. They too had their traditions and beliefs. One day our descendants will also forget how we dressed, how we behaved, and what we believed.

The coffin is placed on a table; beneath it we put the dead person's belongings – his *machete*, his *coa* (digging stick), his shoes and his blankets. Forty years ago, the *rezanderos* would ask for all these things, and take them away for their own use. Now we are becoming modern: today these things go to the next of kin, and not to the *rezanderos*.

When someone dies, we cut a short length of *carrizo* (stiff and hollow reed). Into this little cup we pour water and two or three fresh-water *acamayitas* (small crustaceans).[19] This goes in the coffin, so that the spirit will have something to eat and drink. Some people also put in miniature *gorditas* (puffed maize cakes), and throw pieces of *tortilla* on top of the coffin. The dead person is thus assured of water and maize on his journey.

On the day following death, the body is borne away for burial.[20] The chief *rezandero* will say three prayers; often, he chants in Latin. In the cemetery, he blesses the grave, which has been dug for a fee by the community's own policemen. Then, when the coffin is in the ground, each relative drops a handful of earth on it, making the form of the cross. After the coffin has been properly interred, we offer

Juan Simbrón

(La Congregación del Tajín, State of Veracruz)

Juan Simbrón lives with his extended family near the archaeological site of El Tajín. This is his account of its construction, and of early Totonac history, agriculture and religion. Ninín *is described within the cycle of the seasons.*

El Tajín is set among low hills, and surrounded by thick vegetation. Although its nucleus covers some sixty hectares, subsidiary ruins are scattered over several thousand hectares. First occupied around AD 150, *its period of peak activity was approximately* AD 600 *to* 900. *At the heart of El Tajín stands the four-sided Pyramid of the Niches. Faced with carved stone blocks, it rises in six tiers to an upper sanctuary. Around the sides are 365 square niches – the number of days in the solar year.*[1]

83. **Juan Simbrón with his violin in his home near La Congregación del Tajín, Veracruz.**

84. **The Pyramid of the Niches at El Tajín, Veracruz. Visible archaeological remains at the site are of late Classic and early post-Classic date (*c.* AD 600–1300).**

Respected locally as an orator and natural leader, Juan Simbrón received little formal education. Totonac is his first language, and he feels sure that his ancestors built El Tajín. Not all his neighbours share this certainty, and archaeologists have yet to prove conclusively that today's Totonac are directly descended from the creators of El Tajín.[2]

The following narrative chronicles the achievements of the ancient Totonac, when they were the masters of their lands. Now their ecology is threatened: in recent decades oil exploration by Petroleos Mexicanos, cattle ranching by Mestizos and extensive deforestation have disrupted traditional agriculture in low-lying regions. Vanilla production has plummeted, while crafts which rely on natural resources are in decline.

Each week Juan Simbrón discusses these and other pressing problems in Mexico City, where he goes to work for the CNC (Confederación Nacional Campesina). He meets regularly with representatives of Indian organisations from within Mexico and beyond, and is a fervent supporter of bilingual, bicultural education for Totonac children.

'What shall we do, comrade?' the Indian scientist said. 'We will build a monument, but we will build it with stages, stairs and niches. We will build our own *calendario Galván viejo*,[3] and we will take measurements. How many days are there in a month? Some months have thirty-one, some have twenty-eight and some have thirty.' This is how the Indian scientists made their calculations – those who excelled in honour, wisdom and learning. There was no formal schooling in those days, but the Totonac drew on their own intelligence. 'This is how it will be', they said. 'We will become mechanised. We will build something resembling the tower of David.' It became known as the pyramids, as El Tajín.

They built it from wood, from great wooden planks of a size we no longer see, from pure wood. They joined these planks together, until they had constructed 365 niches, because a wise man told them that this was the number of days in a year. 'What account shall we take of January?' 'It will be a time of drizzling rain, cold, and driving wind.' 'What account shall we take of February?' 'It will be a time of near madness, half wet and half cold.' 'How many confrontations will there be in the year, when the sun fights with the earth? When will there be eclipses of the sun and the moon? What names shall we give to the four directions, the stars,

and the chief planet ... ? How shall we call these things? How many days will there be in each year? For how many days each year must the chief planet travel?' A seminar was held: these matters were discussed. The Totonac scientists conversed, and they agreed: the ruin[4] would contain niches; it would be wonderful to behold. When it was inaugurated, all the scientists of the world would see it, and recognise its worth.

They took the measurements of the sun and time; they took the measurements of the water in the sea, the rivers, the wells and the springs. They measured the coast, they measured the north and the south-west ... They took the measurements of everything. And when they had completed their work, the monument turned to stone. It turned to stone as a result of offerings they made, for they sacrificed a Christian on that spot. The Father of Faith said: 'You will sacrifice your child.' 'Yes, it shall be a sacrifice. My son[5] will become the Host, will become the celebration of the Holy Mass. We will celebrate the Host, with the blood of the dead one, of the Lord.' So they seized him, they killed him, they cut his throat, they sacrificed him on a stone, on a platform of stone. They laid the boy down, they killed him, and with his blood they consecrated the Host. They celebrated mass, they performed the dances of the *Guaguas* and the *Voladores*,[6] and the King said: 'We need music for this celebration.' In that year, in that moment, the ruin was formed, the great Totonac house of the Totonac people, and it turned to stone. This was marvellous! This was incredible! They made it with wood, but it became stone.

After this everything grew steadily, and each year for forty years the King said: 'The end of the world is coming.' When forty years had passed, each person went off to found a village. Some travelled east, some travelled north, some travelled south, and some travelled west. Each person settled and founded a village, while Totonac culture continued on its course. There was cold, there were eclipses of the sun, of the sea and the moon: people measured these things, and obtained something called maize. It took root like any fruit-bearing plant and it was food. 'What shall we do with it?' they asked. 'We will cook it, and we will taste it.' They began to cook it; they began to boil the grains of maize, and they chewed them without salt, because for 140 years the Totonac nation had not eaten salt. They did not know salt. There was another group who did use salt, but this

Juan Simbrón

Totonac group did not. In punishment, they had not been given salt.

Meanwhile the King maintained his course and continued with his dances and traditions. Each year he celebrated Corpus Christi; each year he celebrated each and every festival. As March approached, they asked: 'What does it mean?' 'It means that Lent is coming. It is time to go courting: young men know what spring means. The birds sing: they gladden the woods, the earth, the people, the village and the community.' In this time the indigenous people who lived here owned the sea, the rivers, the earth, the vanilla plants, the fruit trees and the fish . . . They owned every kind of mine, whether of sand, of stone, of gold or of bronze. They owned every kind of mine that lay beneath the surface of the earth. For the indigenous inhabitants were scientists. When there was sickness, people asked: 'What shall we do?' 'We will celebrate the Holy Mass.' And each year, every twelve months, they sacrificed a Christian. But they also made an offering of cheese, they made an offering of squash.[7] They made many offerings of the things that they produced. Each year, Holy Week, the period of sacrifice, came and went; each year the months of March and April came and went.

In May, people asked: 'What thing should we do now, in time of drought?' 'We will clear the vegetation, and plant maize without fertilizer, because the earth is ready fertilised.' They planted maize, and an old grandmother appeared with a great grinding stone: she began to grind the maize. They began to grind the maize, to make *pulque*,[8] to make *mezcal*. She said: 'Let us add water, let us boil water, let us try something out, let us see how it tastes.' Because the water contained natural limestone, what emerged was *nixtamal*. Then they began to grind and grind and grind, until maize dough covered the great grinding stone. Together, working together, all the Indian women made a vast *tortilla*, and the only thing lacking was salt. There was water, there were bananas, fruits, avocadoes, mangoes . . . There were enormous chili peppers which they ground without salt, and ate with this same *tortilla*. To cook it, they made a great *comal* (griddle) and heated it over charcoal, over flames, because they had no proper stove. In this way they made *tortillas*, in this way they became organised, in this way indigenous people came to understand one another.

'How many times each month is the moon full?' 'Only once; first comes the new moon,

85. Totonac *ofrenda* (offering) for saints and souls in the home of Simón Gómez Atzín near Papantla, Veracruz. Grouped around the base of the altar are locally fired incense burners and candle holders. An arch with palm 'stars' and *tepejilote* leaves surrounds the table. Foods include special breads and chocolate figures.

mother crying. I am to blame: I asked you to offer *malango*. It has poisoned her, and she is dying. My mother beat me with a stone.' His wife began to kill the pig, but before she could finish, he fell down dead. A shadow had claimed him, and he died. At his funeral they ate the pig.[13]

We believe this story, and we celebrate this festival with our faith. Always, always, because it is written. Like Christmas, Candlemas, Holy Week and Corpus Christi, we celebrate this *fiesta* every year. We meet our obligations with open doors, and welcome those who come and those who sing. Sometimes we hear voices outside, talking, chatting cheerfully, and making noise. We look outside, and see no one. But we

hear the voices of a multitude of people: these are the visiting *ánimas* (souls); these are *los fieles difuntos*. They don't really eat. They enjoy the smell of blessed food and coffee; they enjoy the aroma of everything. We put out cigarettes, tobacco, incense, and they arrive happy. It's the same with us: we smell *mezcal* and we say: 'Oh, I'd like a sip of that'; or we feel tempted by a cigarette. So it is with *los fieles difuntos*. We make our offerings with a good heart. If we do this with joy, then there will be no sickness: everything will be tranquil during *Todos Santos*. This is our custom. Seeing is believing. Now you yourselves have seen our festival; you will tell the world how it is with us.

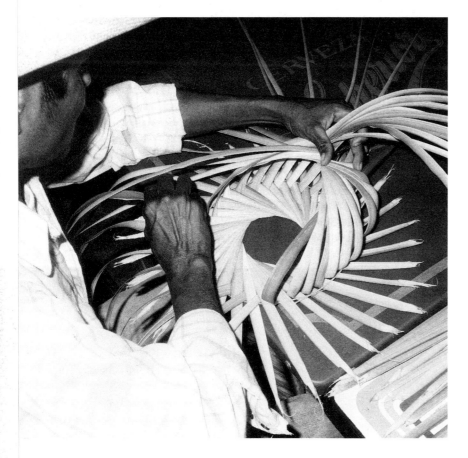

89 and 90. Making a '*piña*' ('pineapple') using the fronds of the *Coyol* palm. Such figures are suspended above household altars to honour the saints and the returning souls during *Todos Santos*. El Tajín, Veracruz.

Froylan Martínez Cuenca

(Huaquechula, State of Puebla)

91. **Froylan Martínez Cuenca of Huaquechula, Puebla.**

Huaquechula, in Puebla State, is a small Mestizo town with a partially disused Colonial monastery and unpaved streets. Many of its inhabitants have gone in search of work to Mexico City or, often illegally, to Los Angeles and New York. Those who can, return during Todos Santos *to honour the memory of the dead; as in most other places, this is done with an* ofrenda. *Unusually, however, Huaquechula has evolved a monumental and spectacular* ofrenda, *described by locals as an 'altar', for those who have died within the year. These elaborate constructions are built over several days by specialists, who are paid by the bereaved for their time, inventiveness and skill.*[1]

Froylan Martínez Cuenca has been building altars for the newly dead for over twenty-five years. Highly praised by fellow townspeople for his talents, he also makes sprays of white artificial flowers for the souls of dead children. Froylan used to work as a primary schoolteacher, but in 1989, when this interview was done, he held a job in local government. The fixed nature of this employment barred him from building altars during the current season, but he hopes to return to this task in future years.

When asked, Froylan put the cost of a fine adult altar at around five million pesos. This sum, if converted at average exchange rates for 1989, works out at £1,250.00 ($2000.00). In 1990 the minimum daily wage in Mexico City was less than 10,000 pesos (approximately £2.50 or $4.00). Froylan's estimate is probably excessive, but it gives an idea of money spent to receive the newly dead. The cost of hospitality is also high. As he explains, the bereaved must offer food and drink to all who visit a new ofrenda. *In the main room of wealthy homes, in full view of the altar, trestle tables are set up to welcome a steady stream of relatives and friends. In 1989 their numbers were enlarged by eager sightseers from Puebla City and beyond. As the fame of Huaquechula's altars spreads, the intimacy of the celebrations may be threatened.*

Ours is an ancient tradition and an ancient faith: each year we are visited by the souls of the dead. Because my knowledge and my experience are limited, I cannot tell you how or when this tradition began, but I know that we – the people of Huaquechula – have inherited it from our ancestors; it has been passed down from generation to generation, and I don't think it will ever end. I learned about it more than forty years ago from my parents, and children today learn about it in the same way. In later life they will say: 'Our fathers and our mothers did things this way; we must follow their example.'

Because we are Catholics, we believe that the souls of the dead are purified in purgatory. They go before God the Father, and to Heaven – if this is what they deserve. Each year, during *Todos Santos*, they return to earth. There are sceptics, it is true, who don't believe in the return of the dead. They say: 'If the dead are comfortable in Heaven, why would they want to return to earth? And if they're in the other place, they wouldn't be allowed to leave!' I have no answer. Each person knows what he believes. Each person must keep his own faith. But here in Huaquechula you will find few houses without an *ofrenda*. No sacrifice is too great.

ánimas – these are the souls of the adult dead. Their arrival is marked at two o'clock by the solemn tolling of a knell.

We wait for our visitors at home. We receive them with incense and with flower petals, when we hear the church bells sound. Children are welcomed with the coloured petals of gladioli and with white chrysanthemum petals. For adults we use petals from the flower of death: it belongs to ancient tradition and comes to us from our ancestors – even the poorest among us will buy *cempasúchil*[2] for the dead. We sprinkle the petals to make a path: it guides the souls from the street, through the house to the waiting *ofrenda*. A trail of incense also invites the souls to enter. Incense is an aroma which rises up to Heaven; it is carried on the air to our Lord.

When the dead arrive, you feel their presence. You can't talk with them; you don't call their names. You go out and meet them when you hear the bell. As soon as they arrive, you light the candles of the *ofrenda*. Everything must be ready. When we hear the tolling of the bell we feel happy and peaceful; we go out to meet them, and feel glad that they have come. If flesh-and-blood human beings visit us, we see them before our eyes and we feel happy. We cannot see the souls, but we rejoice that they are with us.

Because I live alone, I don't prepare cooked dishes for the dead. I offer them candles, incense, flowers, fruit, sweet breads and whatever else I can. On 1 November without fail I visit my brother's house. He has a wife and daughters and they prepare food for the *ánimas*. As soon as I have welcomed the *ánimas* to my house, I go to his to eat. It gives our dead parents pleasure to see us happy and united. Imagine how sad they would feel were I to turn down my brother's invitation. We should always try to give our parents pleasure, so I go gladly to my brother's house.

When my father was alive, he said to my mother: 'Put out an *ayate* (carrying cloth) for me when I am gone; I shall want to carry away the things you offer me during *Todos Santos*.' After his death, each year, my mother used religiously to give him an *ayate*. She was a careful woman, God rest her soul; after *Todos Santos*, she would always say: 'The day has passed; I shall put away this *ayate* until next year.' My brother used to remonstrate: 'No, mother, let us make use of this *ayate*. Next year, with God's help, we will buy my father a new one.' She always replied: 'No, we should keep this one. Who knows if next year we'll be able to

92. *Todos Santos* altar for saints and souls in the house of Froylan Martínez Cuenca of Huaquechula, Puebla. Pinned to the wall is a chenille picture of Christ. On the offering table are apples, breads, candles and imported joss sticks from India. A rich display of flowers and foliage includes *cempasúchil*, asters, gladioli and potted ferns. On the floor, scattered *cempasúchil* petals form the path which leads the returning souls to the *ofrenda*.

Even the humblest family will have flowers, fruit, bread, incense and candles to receive the dead.

According to my parents and my grandparents, the dead come out of the sky in formation. They go to the church, then return to their homes. Those who die in accidents arrive on 28 October. This is the day of San Simón, and they come on this day because he was a martyr. 31 October belongs to children – baptised and unbaptised. When they die, their souls go to Heaven and they become angels of the Virgin Mary; we call them *angelitos* (little angels). At two o'clock the church bells ring to tell us they've arrived. 1 November belongs to the

Froylan Martínez Cuenca

afford another.' But my brother would insist: 'The day has passed: now we should use this one. Don't lose faith. Next year, with God's permission, we will buy our father a new *ayate*.' And so, each year, my father had a new *ayate*. Now my mother is dead, but my brother and my sister maintain this custom. Each year, too, they offer my mother a new basket. Like my father, she is able to carry away her share of the *ofrenda*.

In our family we receive the adult dead together – the *ofrenda* is for close relatives and for those who died in distant times. There is something for everyone – maybe just a piece of fruit or a morsel of bread, but something. This is as our mother taught us. She also taught us to welcome the *ánima sola*, or errant soul without a family or home to go to. During *Todos Santos* many people light a candle by the roadside for the *ánima sola*, and protect the flame from the wind with bricks. But our mother, may she rest in peace, would say: 'Why should the *ánima sola* remain by the roadside? How disrespectful! We should make these unfortunate souls as welcome as the souls of our loved ones. All should get the same treatment.' Each year, therefore, when my mother offered bread, chocolate, fruit and *mole* to the dead, the *ánima sola* was welcomed at the same table as our own souls. Today we follow her example. My *ofrenda* is for everyone and for the *ánima sola* too.[3]

Every village, every municipality, has its own customs. Here in Huaquechula we reserve a special welcome for new souls – for those who have died during the preceding year. If, however, someone should die in late October, then

93. Women seated on a palm mat (*petate*) before the large white altar of a relative who has died within the preceding year. His photograph is centrally placed on the lowest level. Huaquechula, Puebla.

he or she will not visit before next year; he or she must act as caretaker, and stay behind in that other place. When new souls first come back to earth, they are termed *de ofrenda nueva*. I don't know how this tradition came about. For as long as I can remember, new *angelitos* and new *ánimas* have been honoured with elaborately constructed monuments or altars. No expense is spared, and the *ofrenda nueva* has pride of place. If it is for a child's soul, then adult souls are received at a side table or even in another room. If it is for an adult soul, then the reverse is true. In our family we follow our mother's teachings: when she died, we welcomed all other souls to her *ofrenda*, but this is rare.

It takes special knowledge to build an altar, or *ofrenda nueva*. Several people here can do it – I am not the only one. We go to immense trouble, and feel proud of our achievements. Now the tradition has begun to spread.[4] There are people in neighbouring villages who admire the splendour of our work. They would like to welcome their new dead as we do, but lack the necessary skill. Increasingly, we are invited to build altars for the bereaved in other places.

I first started building altars twenty, maybe even twenty-five years ago. No one taught me how – I just worked things out as I went along. There are few rules; it's really a matter of personal taste. This year, because of my job in local government, I wasn't able to make a single altar. Five or six people asked me, but I had regretfully to turn them down. I'm used to building two, three, even four altars a year. It takes three days for three people to make an altar. I operate with two helpers; they are friends who work with no one else. I never make sketches before I start. Inspiration comes in the moment. My helpers sometimes say: 'You're clever, why don't you make sketches?' But I reply: 'No, you'll find out later what we're going to do. It'll be something good, never fear.'

Because most altars stand against the wall, you see them from the front. Once, however, I made an altar with two views: one side was shaped like a gigantic chalice with the Host, emanating rays of light; the other took the form of the tabernacle, where the consecrated host is kept. Sometimes I include green plants in my design. I like to see green leaves against an all-white background. Before Huaquechula had electric light, we would illuminate our altars with small candles in wired containers. They hung from the ceiling in wavelets, and looked lovely at night when they were lit. Just imagine

all those lights shimmering in the darkness! Now we use electric light bulbs. I integrate these into each altar, and often I use fairy or Christmas lights as well.

In truth, everything depends upon the space I'm given. It's no use planning altars in advance. Ideas flow when I see the room: only then can I visualise an altar's shape. I want each one to be unique. If I build three altars, they will all be special. Sometimes you hear people grumbling about the altars others build: 'Who made this one?' 'So-and-so.' 'Doesn't he know how to do anything different? He's done the same thing here that he did there.' Or: 'This altar isn't at all impressive – if only we'd asked someone else.' I take pains to avoid this sort of criticism. We work fast and carefully, and do the best we can. When people praise our altars, we feel very pleased and proud.

We use a lot of tables, large and small, to create the structure. We use wooden crates, and planks of wood that we cut to size. Everything is made ready before we start. When I know the shape an altar will take, I make a list of the things I'll need – so many wooden crates, so many metres of white material, so many sheets of card, so many paper angels, so many stars, so many *llorones* (plaster figures of weeping

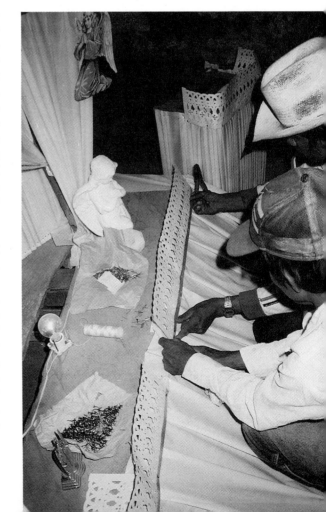

94. **Altar-builders at work. They are pinning a *barandal* (decorative border of thin card) to the edge of the altar. In this instance white plastic sheeting replaces the costlier satin of more wealthy households. Huaquechula, Puebla.**

children), so many *barandales* (decorative borders of hand-punched card). Then there are the tin-tacks and the nails, the lightbulbs, the electric wall-sockets, the fairy lights and so on. The final list can be alarming – everything these days is costly. I can't give you an exact figure for this year, but I would guess that an average adult altar, with thirty metres of material, could cost five million pesos. Children's altars are smaller and less expensive.

There is something we always do for *angelitos*. To welcome a boy's soul, we put a baby Jesus, a male angel or a *lloroncito* (weeping boy) at the top of the altar. To welcome a girl's soul, we put the Virgin Mary there. It's different for adult souls. To welcome male and female souls we put a figure of Christ at the top. If, in the case of a woman, we have no figure of Christ, then we use a white cross, and tie a white or a purple ribbon across it.

Barandales are made in Huaquechula, but we buy most other things from shops in Atlixco. There are several types of white material that we can use, but satin is best and looks the smartest. For the two-sided altar I've described, I used a total of eighty metres – forty in front and forty behind. Sometimes hard-up families make do with white polythene sheeting. Not everyone buys everything new; if the bereaved dismantle an altar with care, they can keep many things for future use. Five years ago we gave my mother her *ofrenda nueva*: my brother still has the material, and I have most of the adornments. Last year several people wanted me to lend them things, and this year a man sought to borrow the *barandales*. 'But of course', I tell them. It costs a terrible lot to buy everything from scratch; most people have friends and relatives who will lend them things if necessary.

There have been altars like these in Huaquechula for as long as I can remember, and for many years before that. How they evolved, I do not know. They haven't always been white. When I was a child they were covered with tissue-paper cut into different patterns. If the altar was for adults, these sheets were laid over purple ones; if the altar was for children, they were laid over blue or some other colour. The effect was lovely. After that altars were dressed in crêpe paper. Then, a few years later, things changed again: people began to use material. I think our forebears grew abler as time passed. We are still using material today – or plastic

95. Corner of an *ofrenda nueva* (offering for the recently deceased) in Huaquechula, Puebla. The edges are bordered with variously patterned *barandales* (paper strips with punched out designs). Tall wax candles are decorated with sprays of artificial silk flowers, some still protected by cellophane. The flower sprays and *barandales* are of local manufacture, but commercially produced pottery figures (shown here) are purchased in nearby towns.

93

sheeting if money is short – and I think that altars will stay as they are. Whatever the cost, whatever the hardship, each new soul must have its new *ofrenda*.

When the altar is built, relatives add the finishing touches. It was customary, in the past, to put out a wine-filled glass goblet, shaped like the chalice, and the Host – unconsecrated, of course. Without these, no adult altar was complete. This is no longer done, because it goes against the wishes of the Church: priests grew unwilling to give out the Host. Today, as before, relatives offer flowers in vases, candle holders and incense burners. There are many potters in Huaquechula, yet not all are equally good. As with altars, so with other skills: there is always someone who works better than the rest. If the dead person is a woman, we select an incense burner with a female figure, and vice versa. We also offer figures of *alfeñique* (sugar paste): we choose lambs in memory of the Lamb of God, and birds, because they sing to God.

For children everything is done in miniature. On 31 October the *padrinos* (godparents) go to the house of the *angelito*: with them they carry the *ofrenda*. Minuscule rounds of chocolate and diminutive bread figures are covered with a tiny *servilleta*. If the *ofrenda* is for a girl, it is packed in a little basket; if it is for a boy, it is carried on a small tray. Godparents must also take a decorated candle and a candle holder. For a girl the candle holder will display a Virgin; for a boy it will display a male angel. In the house of the *angelito* cooked dishes are prepared and served in tiny vessels. If a child ate normal food before its death, it may be offered *pipiancito* (pumpkin seed sauce) with miniature *tortillas*, or *molito de olores* – the *mole* sauce that goes with turkey. But if it died before it was weaned, or was too small to lift a mug, then we give it milk in a feeding bottle.

One year, so I've been told, there was a sick child here in Huaquechula. When 31 October came, his mother set up the *ofrenda* for his brother who had died; then she went shopping in the market-place, and was delayed past the hour of two. When at last she returned, the sick boy scolded her: 'Make haste, mother. As you can see, my brother is already here.' 'Where?' the mother asked, for she could see nothing. 'Over there, by the table. He came with a crowd of friends. They were singing merrily; they left my brother here, then went to visit other houses.' That boy was fortunate indeed: he saw the blessed *angelitos* returning to their homes.

On 1 November, our welcome is for dead adults. The duty of the living is to provide the things they liked in life. If a man enjoyed drinking, we give him a bottle of spirits; if he liked beer, we lay on a few beers; if he liked *pulque*, then we see he gets *pulque*. Or, if a man liked smoking, we give him his favourite cigarettes. This is our obligation. On this day, too, we serve food in abundance. There will be *tamales*, *pipián* and *mole de olores*; there will be ripe apples, oranges, bananas and *tejocotes* (choke-cherries). We offer hot chocolate, and several kinds of bread: *hojaldras*, *rosquetes* and human figures called *muertos* (dead people) with their hands just so. And we have white *pan de agua* (water bread), because it is said that our Lord gave out this bread during the Last Supper.

I think the dead extract the aroma and flavour of the food. When the souls have partaken of their *ofrenda*, the difference is plain. If we put out a glass of water, the level drops. When we offer fruit, bread and other foodstuffs, they have a strong and distinctive aroma; afterwards we can feel the change. The living eat the food of the dead, but the aroma and the taste have fled.

It is customary, when we enter the house of an *ofrenda nueva*, to offer a candle as an act of devotion. Each visitor must donate a candle, though some will be put by for later. Eventually, however, all must be lit in the soul's honour, and allowed to burn right down. If a whole family visits, a single candle will do. Of course there are limits. You know how young people like to stay out after dark? Sometimes a group of ten or fifteen lads will get together, and go visiting altars with one candle between them! Don't think that most of us go visiting for fun, however. Householders must offer food and drink to all who come, but we do not visit with this in mind. We don't go because we want *mole* or hot chocolate; we go because it is our duty.

At two o'clock, when the church bells sound, we suffer grief for the death of our loved ones; then we feel at peace because they are with us until the 2nd. They leave, adults and children together, on *el día de las bendiciones* (the day of blessings). We go to mass at 6 am for this moment of parting: the blessed souls are returning to heaven, from whence they came. During Holy Mass we bid farewell to our loved ones, who are leaving us again. On this morning my mother, may she rest in peace, used to get up at 4 or 5: she lit candles, perfumed the house with incense, kindled the fire and served hot chocolate in mugs. She knew the dead would soon be leaving, so she gave them their breakfast first. I don't know if other families do this. Today my brother's wife gets up at 5 to make hot chocolate; we carry on as our mother taught us.

After mass the faithful go home, then on to the cemetery. There are two cemeteries here: in Santa María we stay all morning until maybe noon; in La Trinidad people go in the afternoon. We put flowers on graves, pray, burn incense and light candles. For the newly dead we take *ceras compuestas* (decorated candles). We adorn our graves, and sprinkle them with holy water. I've been told of people in other places who take food to the cemetery; I think they have breakfast among the graves. Here an individual might take a piece of fruit to eat, but in neither cemetery is this a regular thing. Customs vary from town to town. Here, for example, the dead are not received with music, yet in nearby Tezonteopan de Bonilla there's a band. During *Todos Santos* it goes from house to house, playing music at all the *ofrendas*. When someone dies, there is music all night long in the dead person's house, and music at the burial too.

Death in Huaquechula confers many obligations on the living. A sick adult who is near death is accompanied by relatives and friends; they gather at the bedside and pray. When the sick person relinquishes his soul at last, news is taken to the church, and the *agonías* (death knells) sound. If a man dies, the bell tolls five *agonías*: each *agonía* comprises five clangs, making a total of twenty-five clangs. If a woman dies, the bell tolls six *agonías*: each *agonía* comprises six clangs, making a total of thirty-six clangs. Next day, before the funeral, the bells toll a *doble* – just as they do when the adult dead return. Each cemetery has a chapel with a bell: it too tolls a *doble* when the coffin-bearers bring the corpse. Those who live in the high part of Huaquechula are buried in Santa María. Those who live in the lower part, below the monastery, are buried in La Trinidad. We light three candles on the day of burial, because the soul is struggling with the earth: the light will intercede with God the Father.

When a child lies dying, no prayers are said. Church bells sound to announce the death: if they ring up here, we know it's on our side of the town; if they ring in the monastery, we know it's over there. As people talk, the identity of the child is known: 'Just imagine, that was so-and-so's son who died.' Next day the bells announce the funeral; whoever wants to come is welcome.

When someone dies at home in bed, we place a small altar on the spot. In front of it we make a cross of sand, then we sprinkle lime on the sand to whiten it. We lay the corpse on the ground, over the cross, and rest the head on bricks; then we cover the corpse with a white sheet. The feet should always be shod with *ixcatles*: these are sandals made of *ixtle* (agave fibre).[5] Sometimes we put them on just before death, sometimes we wait until after death. I don't know why we do this – I only know it's a devotion that we must perform. *Ixcatles* are made by people from a distant village; occasionally they come to Huaquechula to sell firewood. At all times we see them interweaving strands of *ixtle*, their fingers working ceaselessly as they journey to and fro. They deliver the *ixcatles* to someone in Huaquechula. When death approaches, we go to this person, and buy *ixcatles* for our loved one.

The corpse remains on the cross while the coffin is made. If the deceased was a woman, we gather up her dresses and her other garments, and put them in the coffin. If it was a man, we put in his shirts and trousers. We lay these in the coffin, and place the corpse on top. We don't include any other possessions – just clothing. We lay a small crucifix on the breast of the dead

96. Pottery produced in Huaquechula, Puebla. The candle holder (left) and the incense burner (right) are embellished with mould-made flowers, cherubs and the Archangel Michael. Pottery is given a white slip, then decorated with commercial paints. H (approx.) 20 and 15 cms

man or woman; just before the coffin is taken away for burial, we remove the crucifix and lay it down on the altar. When finally we 'raise the shadow', this crucifix is passed from hand to hand, so that everyone can hold and adore it. Exactly one week after death, at precisely the same hour of day or night, we 'raise the shadow'. Friends and relatives together say the blessed rosary, and recite prayers for the welfare of the soul. When the shadow is rising, we trail clouds of incense, sprinkle holy water and throw flowers over the area which the shadow occupied. Then we leave the house and show it how to reach the graveyard. The soul is departing: during these moments the blessed spirit leaves the home.[6]

Sadly, not everyone can die at home. Some men go away to work, and many die in the USA.[7] When a corpse reaches Huaquechula, the bells toll for its arrival, and later for its burial. If someone dies in the fields, or in New York, we can't raise their shadow because this is not the place of death, so in front of the house altar we lay out a wooden cross, or we form a cross with flowers. One week after death we raise the cross, and pray as I've described.

The *novenario* (novena, devotion lasting nine days) is always performed, whether someone dies at home or not. We say the blessed rosary at 8pm, for nine consecutive evenings, starting during the onset of death. Here in Huaquechula we have *rezanderos* (prayer-makers), specialists who commend our souls to God.[8] Such a person is summoned to lead us in our prayers. One week after burial, the *novenario* ends. If someone dies on Tuesday and is buried on Wednesday, we raise the shadow the following Tuesday and say the last rosary on Wednesday. After that everything is over. We take away the flowers, and that's the end. But we know, come *Todos Santos*, that the dead will return. We will remember the dead in sorrow, yet rejoice that they have come.

These, then, are our beliefs. Sadly, this year in Huaquechula, three new souls were left without *ofrendas*. Their families have broken with tradition. They receive neither the old dead nor the new dead, and treat the day of *Todos Santos* like any other; they have been converted by evangelists. Meanwhile, the rest of us keep faith. Next year, if God is willing, I shall build *ofrendas* once again.

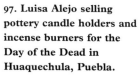

97. Luisa Alejo selling pottery candle holders and incense burners for the Day of the Dead in Huaquechula, Puebla.

PLATE 17 **Model *ofrenda* of wood, paper and pottery, showing a crucifix, candles, skulls and traditional foods and fruits. Oaxaca State. H 37 cms**

Model catafalque made of card and tissue paper with painted decoration of
skulls and crosses. Tiered catafalques, often decorated with painted scenes,
were used in funerary processions and ceremonies during the Colonial period.
Toy catafalques are mentioned in early descriptions of festivities for the Day
of the Dead. Oaxaca City. H 29.5 cms

PLATE 18

PLATE 19

Mestizo household altar for the Day of the Dead in the town of Huaquechula, Puebla. Elaborate 'altars', their form perhaps derived from the tiered catafalques of the Colonial period, are built by specialist makers in houses where there has been a death in the preceding year. In this instance two dead relatives are commemorated.

Over a structure of boxes and wood, up to eighty metres of white satin are draped and pinned into pleats and ruches and ornaments of various kinds are added before the food-offering is set out.

a. Totonac Indian suspended *ofrenda* in the Méndez family house near El Tajín, Veracruz. The traditional Totonac altar is decorated with palm leaf ornaments said to represent the sun, stars and pineapples. As well as all the most traditional local items, the
Méndez offering includes an embroidered cloth (centre) from Tenango de Doria, Hidalgo.
b. Interior of a Totonac house in Plan de Palmar, Veracruz, showing two altars side by
side. The larger (right) is the permanent household altar for the Saints; the smaller altar
is for the offerings to the dead souls at *Todos Santos*.

Pottery candelabrum in the
form of a 'Tree of Life'
showing devils and figures
wearing regional costumes
of Mexico with offerings of
food, fruit and breads at
their feet. Made by Alfonso
Castillo. Izúcar de Mata-
moros, Puebla. H 105 cms

PLATE 20

PLATE 21

a. Otomí villagers walking in procession to the cemetery outside San Pablito, Puebla. They carry baskets with crosses, decorated candles and *cempasúchil* flowers. One woman holds a pottery incense burner.
b. The cemetery at Hueyapan, Morelos. A Nahua woman wearing an *ikat*-dyed *rebozo* (shawl) kneels beside a tomb. The graves are adorned with *cempasúchil* flowers and petals.

PLATE 22

a. Pairs of *Xantolo* dancers performing in the Nahua village of Zapotitla, Hidalgo. On 1 and 2 November, the dancers go from house to house. Male dancers traditionally take the role of women, borrowing dresses from female relatives. Masks are carved from wood, but commercially produced masks of rubber and plastic are increasingly used.

b. Decorative banner of tissue paper (*papel picado*) with a design punched out with chisels of various sizes. It shows musicians playing trumpet and guitar and a skull and bones. San Salvador Huixcolotla, Puebla. L 75 cms

PLATE 23

Carving of painted wood showing Death (as a woman) dancing with the Devil. Death and the Devil appear together in a number of regional dances, and are often represented in Mexican popular art. Arrasola, Oaxaca. H 32 cms

PLATE 24

Candido Reyes Castillo

(Huaquechula, State of Puebla)

Candido Reyes Castillo has been building altars for the newly dead of Huaquechula, in the State of Puebla, for more than forty years. These visually splendid altars, commissioned by the bereaved for Todos Santos, honour those who have died during the preceding year. During the rest of the year Candido devotes himself to agriculture. With pride, he recalls a visit in the mid 1980s to Puebla City: 'I was invited by local government to build an altar in a public building. There it was seen by many people, and photographed for the regional newspaper.'

In 1988, when this interview was recorded, Candido had built an altar in his own home for a dead relative; a shortage of money had curtailed its size and splendour. The exchange rate then stood at approximately four thousand pesos to the pound, so an average adult altar, according to Candido, was costing around £575 ($925). Candido's interview reaffirmed several points discussed earlier by Froylan Martínez Cuenca; these have been omitted, to avoid repetition.

98. Candido Reyes Castillo (born in 1923) in the Colonial monastery of San Martín where he works as guardian. Huaquechula, Puebla.

99. Highly embellished polychrome painted candle holder with mould-made decorations showing foliage, flowers and putti; the figure of God is flanked by two archangels. Made by Ignacio Peralta. Huaquechula, Puebla. H (approx.) 32 cms

Our altars for the new dead are unique to Hua-quechula. A few people in outlying hamlets make them too, but that is all. I have taught my son everything I know. I, in my turn, learnt the skill from my father when I was ten years old. I used to follow him around, sticking papers and helping out. Altars were as imposing then as they are today, rising up in storeys towards the ceiling.

We used tissue-paper in those far-off days. White sheets were cut out to show angels, flowers and other designs; they looked lovely, like crochet. We laid these white sheets over coloured tissue-paper, allowing the black, purple or yellow of the background to show through. The effect was beautiful to see. Today there is almost no one left who patterns tissue-paper in this way; if people want this work, they buy it from outside. Our *barandales*, too, have changed. When I was a child, they were cut to show pots of flowers and other things; we used to shade them in with coloured crayons. Now they come in narrow strips, and they are never coloured.

Since my boyhood, altars have developed in several phases. Tissue-paper was replaced by wallpaper – the kind people use in towns and cities to make their houses elegant. After that we tried another sort of paper, then switched to crêpe paper, which was delicate to work with. Each year prices were rising, and the cost of paper was escalating. Back in 1938 or 1940, as I remember, a single sheet cost fifteen *centavos*. So my father talked like this to the bereaved: 'Look how expensive paper has become. We buy it, we take it down and we burn it. What a waste! If you want an altar, why not buy material instead of paper? When *Todos Santos* has passed, you could take the material down with care; you could re-use it for another altar, or even dress your children in it.'

That's how we came to work with material. There were some lovely materials in 1940. Today satin is our favourite kind. We buy only white; we pleat it and mould it to the base with small nails and tacks. For maximum splendour I might use seventy or eighty metres, but less ambitious altars can be achieved with thirty-five

or even twenty metres. The base is wood. It has to be strong, because we climb all over it as we work; it has to support our weight, and the weight of all the fixtures and fittings. These are secured with nails, tacks, screws and wire.

Electric lighting is very important. If it's well done, it transforms the altar into something wonderful. Sometimes we illuminate it from below; sometimes we illuminate each storey individually. It depends on the skill of each creator. There's more to lighting than merely connecting up the wires. If the bulbs are hung too high, the whole effect is spoilt. Bad lighting makes everything look flat and dead, but good lighting shines through the white, and throws the altar into relief.

Some rules must be observed. A child's altar should feature a *niño Dios* (baby Jesus). You might have two, if money allows, but if you can afford only one, then it must go at the very top. An adult altar will usually include a photograph of the deceased; this goes low down, where it can be seen by each and every visitor. At the top we put a crucifix.

It can take four people eight days to make a good altar. People pay us for our time and skill. This year I made eight altars. I had seven helpers, including my son, so we became a team of eight. On each altar we spent three days, making a total of twenty-four. Before we start I need to design the different parts, so each altar takes roughly a month from start to finish. The shape is determined by the space we're given, and by the finances of the owner. Poor people can't provide much wood or satin, yet they ask us to make them something nice, with the cheapest of ingredients. We do our best, and people are grateful. By eking out the materials and by scaling down the size, we try to give them something good. We can't provide them with the most beautiful altar, yet we try not to provide them with the worst! Other people, by contrast, say: 'Give us the finest altar possible. Ask for anything you need.' Then we adjust our designs accordingly, and spare no expense.

It costs a lot to make a new altar. It shows our love for the dead person; it is the last thing he or she will receive from us on earth. In later years

100 and 101. Two *barandales*, shown here in silhouette. According to Candido Reyes Castillo, *barandales* were formerly coloured with floral and other motifs; today they are white and display repeat designs punched out with chisels. Huaquechula, Puebla.

98

Candido Reyes Castillo

our *ofrendas* resemble those in other places, but the first one should be something special. This year an average adult altar might cost approximately 2,300,000 pesos – and that's without the extras or the food. For a full week, starting on 31 October, we offer hospitality to all who come. To each visitor we must give something, even if it's only a cup of chocolate and a piece of bread. This is the tradition of Huaquechula.

30 November, the day of San Andrés, was important once, when our shops gave credit. In the old days people used to come to Huaquechula from outlying hamlets, and stock up for their *ofrendas*. You could get your *cacao*, your sugar, your flour and so on for *Todos Santos*, and pay only at the end of the month. San Andrés acted as treasurer, obliging debtors to pay when his day arrived. He was in charge of finances, but he didn't manage things too well. Now shops have stopped using San Andrés as guarantor! It's cash up front, and no credit.

When we visit the *ofrendas* of the dead, we take a candle as a gift. Some are partially coloured and decorated in high relief. You won't find these just anywhere – they are a speciality here. So, too, are painted pottery incense burners and candle holders, *barandales*, and the sprays of white artificial flowers that godparents bestow on dead godchildren. Other things we buy in shops in Puebla City, Atlixco, Izúcar de Matamoros or Cuautla.

I can't say what form the dead take on their return, but I like to think they come as doves. When the spirit leaves the body, it flies away. Some people here have seen white doves on altars, and the Holy Ghost is like a dove, so I think our souls return as doves to earth. Of course, there are those who say the dead do not return, but I know they do. I feel sure of this, because when we offer food to the deceased, it loses its aroma and its taste.

Some people here have even seen the dead. Once there was a widow who left her house during *Todos Santos* to visit another *ofrenda* and offer a candle. During her absence, a group of visitors came with candles to see her, hoping to pay their respects to her dead husband. Surprised to find her out, they peeped through the keyhole, and saw candles burning brightly and the dead man kneeling in front of his own altar. Quickly they went to find the widow in the house of her relatives. 'Hurry home', they told her. 'Your husband is there. We have seen and heard him praying in front of the altar.' When the widow arrived home with her visitors, the

102. **Caritina Díaz making figures of sugar sheep with curly coats. Huaquechula, Puebla.**

house was empty. Some people have the ability to see strange things, don't you agree?

Dead children come on 31 October, dead adults on 1 November. Dead children are offered lambs, ducks or baskets of *alfeñique*, diminutive breads and round tablets of chocolate, fruit and a cup of milk. If we can, we give our children coloured flowers: chrysanthemum, gladioli and *cempasúchil*. A tiny candle and a little incense complete the *ofrenda*. Often we are short of money: what we can't afford, we must do without. For dead adults we prepare turkey with chili, *mole*, beans, *pipián* and several types of *tamal*. We offer holy water in a glass, and buy cigarettes, brandy or beer according to taste.

Although we don't lay clothing on the altar, we do put dead people's garments with them in the coffin. We used to bury them with their belongings – a man, for example, might go to the grave with his *machete* – but this custom has nearly vanished. Today we bury the dead with just their clothing, a jug of water, and a bouquet of roses. In the old days the dead took their valuables with them; women were buried with their finest jewellery. It made the living uneasy to wear something belonging to the dead – we imagined they might come behind us, and frighten us. But that was superstition; we feel differently today. Why send a rich man to the grave with all his wealth, when it could help us who are alive?

New altars can stay up for three, four and five months – or longer if necessary. But if things have been lent, and if they are required by their owners, then an altar might come down after just fifteen or twenty days. Wooden crates are often used to provide the structure, and they may be needed for the harvest. Ideally, however, a new altar should remain *para el cabo de año* – until the day when death occurred. When *Todos Santos* has passed, we cover the altar over. A year after death, we tidy it up. We go to mass; then we return home, light candles and eat breakfast with our relatives and friends.

103. **Candles decorated with bands of metallic paper and printed paper putti in the market for *Todos Santos*. Atlixco, Puebla.**

Luis Vivanco

(San Salvador Huixcolotla,
State of Puebla)

104. Luis Vivanco.
San Salvador Huixcolotla,
Puebla.

105. Tissue paper banner
for *Todos Santos* showing
angels kneeling beside a
cross. The design has been
punched out with sharp
chisels. This is the
preferred style in San
Salvador Huixcolotla and
surrounding villages.
Made by Miguel Reynoso
Zabaleta. W 70 cms

old men, who were about the age that I am now. They made decorations for the church: they cut tissue-paper with scissors. A few of us then started using *fierritos*,[1] or tiny chisels with sharp points. These were made by a man called Crisanto Lovato, who came originally from Guanajuato. I worked with three *fierritos* when I began, but gradually I commissioned more and more. I still have a set from those early days. When other people saw what we were doing, they too took up this work. But we were the originators, we were the ones who started it. Designs were simpler by far than they are today – our ideas came out of our own heads. Now I'm the only one who's still alive. My descendants have really developed their skills; they do better work than I ever did. I sold my papers throughout the region. I sold my papers in Mexico City: people there examined them with care, and asked how I had done them. I'm old now, and my sight is failing; I can't work properly any more. Our craft has come a long way since its beginnings. Ours is the only village which works with *fierritos*. There is only one Huixcolotla.

Luis Vivanco was interviewed in the same year. Aged sixty-three, he did not recollect the use of scissors. His father, from whom he learnt his craft, worked only with fierritos. *Vivanco describes the growing complexity of designs, and the demands of his clients in Mexico City. Initially his repertoire included medium-sized banners which could be pinned to the wall or linked by strings, tiny paper flags on sticks, paper chains and lanterns. Now it includes tablecloths and large, round* murales, *which serve as decorative wall hangings.*

Víctor Fosado Vázquez, on page 132, describes the spirit of rivalry which exists in many villages. It is, he suggests, a relatively recent development, with ever increasing numbers of artisans competing for the attention of buyers from outside their own community. Professional jealousies are strong in San Salvador Huixcolotla, where two families – the Vivancos and the Rojas – devote themselves full-time to paper cutting. Rojas is the surname shared by five of Pedro Mauricio's grandsons. Maurilio Rojas, aged twenty-two in 1989, said:

You can't imagine the envy there is in this village. Someone from here – I don't know who – went around Mexico City saying that my grandfather had stopped working and that no one else in his family could cut paper. Lies! We are his grandsons, and we are fully committed to the craft, but things aren't easy. To be honest, we have a problem with the Vivancos. They live near the entrance to this village, while we live over on the far side. If ever strangers come looking for artisans, they see them arrive and then take them over. I wish there were a greater sense of fair play.

106. **Pedro Mauricio (left), his wife (right) and his daughter, Irene Mauricio Reynoso (centre). San Salvador Huixcolotla, Puebla.**

The Mestizo village of San Salvador Huixcolotla lies approximately 50 km from Puebla City. Although agriculture is the chief pursuit, it is combined in many homes with the art of cutting paper banners for local festivals and, increasingly, for 'sophisticated' purchasers in Mexico City and abroad. Death is now a frequent theme.

Pedro Mauricio is one of the oldest inhabitants of the village, and one of the first to practise the craft of paper-cutting in its present form. In 1989, when he was eighty-eight years old, he explained how the skill evolved:

Paper has been cut in this village for ninety years and more. When I began to do this work some fifty-five years ago, I followed the example of two

Luis Vivanco

Maurilio Rojas has a message for us:

When I show this work to people who aren't familiar with it, someone will invariably say: 'My auntie, my grandfather, or my cousins's uncle can do this – it's done with scissors.' With scissors this work would take an age! Then again there are people who think we use a press. If we did, we would have no flexibility – we would be unable to change our designs from day to day. Someone who used a press would continually have to make new plates, but we need only our *fierritos*. Please tell whoever asks, that our papercuts are made by hand.

107. **Maurilio Rojas at work. Using sharp chisels, he cuts through up to fifty sheets of tissue paper. San Salvador Huixcolotla, Puebla.**

Creating images of death does not disturb me. I've cut so many, and never felt afraid. Recently I had a visit from a priest. He saw skeletons dancing and drinking *pulque*. 'This is very wrong', he said. 'Death is sacred, yet you are joking with it.' 'But Father', I told him, 'this is what I do to earn a living.'

I don't know how the craft of cutting paper came about. When I was eight years old I learned it from my father. Images were simple in those far-off days: flowers, leaves, doves . . . . Our craft wasn't famous like it is today. Proper pictures, of the sort I make, began only forty or fifty years ago. Fifty years ago we sold our wares in local village squares. When *Todos Santos* came, we went from house to house, and people bought our work for their *ofrendas*. Then we started over again, peddling portraits of the Virgin of Guadalupe for 12 December,[2] and nativity scenes for Christmas celebrations.

I did not plan to cut paper all my life. I worked as a musician in my youth, and travelled the region with different bands. I was hoping, when my mother died, to join the Mexico City naval band, but my married brothers urged me to come home. They said our father must not live alone. Because I was his youngest son, I returned to keep him company and help him with his land. For years we sold cut papers during all the big fairs – in Atlixco, San Martín Texmelucan, Tlaxcala and Chalco. People from Mexico City took an interest in our work, and young Víctor Fosado gave me my first important chance: he made me draw and cut out different things.[3] For three months I was on trial. My first big sale was for forty pesos, which seemed a lot of money at the time.

Now I have customers in Mexico City and the USA. God has helped me, and given me inspiration. Tequila companies and restaurants ask me to pattern banners with their names. Surprisingly, my best orders from shops are always *calaveras*. I make them for *Todos Santos*, but they sell all year round. Simple skeletons of bones were how I started, but people wanted more variety. I do skeletons on horseback, skeleton balloon sellers, skeleton cockfights and skeleton weddings; I do *la catrina*[4] full figure, in period clothes. Often my customers suggest new themes. 'What shall we try next, Don Luis?' they ask. 'Could you do a skeleton funeral with skeleton drunks?'

I don't know why people in Mexico City like death to be shown so cheerfully – custom, I suppose, for *Todos Santos*. No one in San Salvador Huixcolotla or surrounding villages would buy the skeletons that I sell to my customers there. Here people want living things: angels, birds, the chalice, crosses – maybe even coffins, but never skeletons.

Local commissions form a large part of my work, just as they did in earlier days. For village festivals, here and elsewhere, I show patron saints, the blessed Virgin and heroes from history for *las fiestas patrias*.[5] On the Day of San Salvador, there is always a profusion of paper banners outside our church. We used to put them inside as well, but since its redecoration at great expense, paper banners are forbidden. Even the burning of candles is carefully controlled. I also make banners for local families. I do christenings – babies with feeding bottles and doves – first communions, fifteenth birthdays[6] and weddings. People tell me what they want. They give me names and phrases: *fulano y fulana, felicidades* (so-and-so and so-and-so, congratulations). Houses look lovely during celebrations, their yards festooned with paper banners. I also make paper-chains and *farolitos* (paper lanterns).

108. Sheets of tissue paper with a punched design showing a skeletonised singer holding a microphone. The top sheet is the *patrón* (pattern): the chisels follow the outline which is still clearly visible. From a long banner made by Maurilio Rojas. San Salvador Huixcolotla, Puebla. w. 49 cms

To perforate paper we use *fierritos*, a hammer and a sheet of lead. We make a *patrón* (paper pattern) to guide us in our work, and lay it over some fifty tissue-paper sheets; the lead plate goes underneath. Because the *fierritos* wear out quite fast, we need to replace them constantly. I have fifty-eight at the present time, but often commission new ones to increase my range. With less than fifty, we cannot work. Some *fierritos* will fill in for others, but some we cannot do without. They are made by a man in Acatzingo, and sometimes by a man in Tepeaca. Other blacksmiths don't want to know! We beg them to help us, and offer good payment, but they refuse to take on this work.

Although tissue-paper is traditional here, foreigners and people in Mexico City like papers with a metallic sheen. These are for show and special luxury. Because of their thickness, twenty sheets only may be patterned at one time. Plastic is another recent innovation, for open-air display within the region. Many villages now adorn their streets with weatherproof banners of coloured polythene. If wind blows and rain falls, tissue-paper is quickly destroyed. When patterning plastic, I cut twenty-five or thirty sheets together. Paper can be glued to take the strings; plastic needs to be laboriously sewn. But if villagers prefer to honour San Martín or San Pedro in plastic, then I'll fulfil the commission and do my best.

Paper cutting is a family tradition. Already my small grandchildren are learning fast – they grab my *fierritos* and pattern scraps of paper. There are six of us who work full time: myself, my brothers and our sons. Sometimes I think we undercharge for our labour and skill. But rather than sitting idly at home, we make a living, and earn enough to get by. Some people work just now and then, and devote their energies to agriculture. I have two and a half hectares of my own. This year I grew tomatoes, but I left the harvest to rot in the fields: the selling price was just too low. The cost of the wooden packing cases would have outweighed any profit. For my wife and myself I grow maize and beans, but this year we had no rain.

Sometimes, when I tend my fields at night, people ask me if I see the dead. I don't of course; in any case the dead are dead, and cannot harm us here on earth. According to our religion, there is an afterlife. Everything depends on a person's deeds, and whether he died in a state of grace. Did he confess and take communion? If the answer is yes, then the soul goes straight to Heaven. Otherwise it goes to purgatory, but will escape eventually with the mercy of God. We worry when someone meets an accidental or a violent end: only God knows whether his soul is damned eternally.

Old people say we cross a river when we die. We can only cross it with the help of a dog.[7] If we don't look after dogs in life, they won't help us after death. If people here see you hitting a dog, someone will be sure to say: 'Don't do that, or it will never help you cross that river.' We have a woman neighbour whose mother died – she was laid out, then she came back to life. Her daughter asked her what she had seen. 'I saw a great, wide road; then I came to a river. Lots of dogs were trying to bite me. On the other side of the river were children, and they tried to pull me across.' That's all the old lady could remember. She had been dead a whole day, and they were about to bury her. I believe this story must be true: she died, and she came back. This happened ten years ago; soon afterwards she died for good.

If we dream of the dead, we are not frightened. If my wife dreams of her mother, we give her a mass. When we make our *ofrenda* for *Todos Santos*, we can't see or feel that someone is there. But when we think the souls are with us, we say the rosary, and we feel contented because our loved ones have come. On 31 October the *angelitos* arrive in the afternoon at three. We await their arrival with flowers, incense and candles, and we decorate the *ofrenda* with brightly coloured papercuts of

Luis Vivanco

doves and angels. There are tiny breads and sweets, small baskets and miniature toys.

On 1 November at three o'clock the *angelitos* depart and the *ánimas* come. Papercuts now should be black or white: a patterned black sheet is laid on a background of white, while a patterned white sheet is laid on a background of black. We offer *cempasúchil* flowers, holy water, *pan colorado* and *pezuñas*,[8] beer, *pulque* and fruit in abundance. On the 2nd we serve baked pumpkin, *mole*, fresh maize, *tortillas*, mutton broth, *memelas*,[9] boiled *chayotes* and *tamales* – *tamales* with *rajitas* (green chiles), *tamales* with meat and sweet *tamales*. These are rushed piping hot from the stove to the *ofrenda*. When three o'clock comes and the dead depart, we burn incense. We scatter *cempasúchil* flowers to make a pathway; in the past, we even used to let off rockets. Afterwards it is our duty to repair to the cemetery, and beautify the graves of our loved ones with flowers.

One family only does not welcome the dead: they have rejected Catholicism, and belong to an evangelical sect. The rest of us are sustained by our own true faith. There was once a man, it is said, who had no money to receive his dead. Instead of food, he offered a stone. On 2 November he actually saw the dead leave, and he saw his own mother struggling under the weight of that stone. Afterwards he scraped and saved: when *Todos Santos* came again, he gave his mother a good *ofrenda*.[10] Because of this, we trust in the return of all souls. We hold masses; we offer food and drink in our homes; we fill the graveyard to overflowing with flowers. We believe our dead remember us, just as we remember them.

The following additional information is provided by Irene Mauricio Reynoso:

When a baby dies, we feel less pain than we do for the death of an adult. We say: 'It was only tiny'. We feel sad, of course, but a wife grieves more for the loss of a husband; a mother grieves more for the loss of a son or daughter. If you lose a baby, you can give birth to another. But you can never replace an adult: we suffer most when an adult dies.

When the souls of dead children return, we say the rosary, and we give them tiny playthings of palm and clay. We also buy them red and black candlesticks from the nearby village of Amozoc. When the dead arrive, we say the rosary, we burn incense, and we sprinkle water

on the ground – ordinary water. We do these things again next day, when they leave. We also sprinkle flower petals from a basket.

At three o'clock on 1 November, we make a path with white petals, because the *angelitos* are going. And immediately afterwards we make a path with *cempasúchil* because the adult souls are arriving. We change the flowers, and we also change the candles. We put out black candlesticks from Amozoc. Sometimes, too, we sprinkle fragments of paper on the ground; these are left over from making papercuts. People here stick papercuts on walls, hang them up on strings, and put them round the table of the *ofrenda*. Sometimes they build them into pyramids with five levels or less. All this varies from house to house.

We offer all kinds of food – we are not like the inhabitants of Mexico City, who prepare a tiny table, a few flowers, and nothing more. We offer everything the dead enjoyed. I cook things with special flavour, because it is the flavour, or the aroma, that the dead extract. The dead don't physically eat the food: we believe that they come and kiss it. Later, we eat it ourselves. Some people eat extremely slowly, making everything last, because the *ofrenda* has been blessed by the dead. The dead suffer if we make no preparations for their return. We do the best we can, because we never know when our turn will come. Death could strike at any time. When we arrive at our own *ofrenda*, we would grieve if nothing had been done.

109. **Tissue paper banner showing two skeletons drinking. San Salvador Huixcolotla, Puebla.**
W **70 cms**

110. Tissue paper banners for *Todos Santos* by different artists.
San Salvador Huixcolotla, Puebla. Maximum W 70 cms

Consuelo García Urrutia

(Toluca, State of Mexico)

Toluca, in the State of Mexico, is famed for its figures of alfeñique *(sugar paste); these are sold each year during* la feria del alfeñique – *the sugar fair which precedes the Festival of the Dead.[1] Consuelo García Urrutia lives in a modern house in the centre of town. Interviewed in 1988, she was seventy-eight years old. Few outsiders, seeing her stall overflowing with sugar animals and birds, imagine the months of work required. During the interview she used the word* borreguitos *to describe sugar lambs, but she also applied it in a collective sense to sugar figures in general, and sometimes, by extension, to the moulds employed in their creation. In the translation which follows, her intended meaning is always given.*

III. Consuelo García Urrutia with a bull made from *alfeñique* (sugar paste) for *Todos Santos*. Toluca, State of Mexico.

My sugar figures are destined solely for *Todos Santos*. I learnt the skill from my mother; she learnt it from her mother, and so on for generations. Now I'm the only one left. After my mother's death, my sister and I went on working together. We made quantities of sugar figures and never missed a year. Then, two years and three months ago, my sister died. I find it hard to manage without her. My range still includes pigs, chickens, cats, deer, bulls, lambs and giraffes, but I no longer make dogs or elephants as my mother did. Large figures, which require heavy moulds, are especially difficult for someone working alone. Although I can manage large lambs, I stopped making large bulls when my sister died. I still have two that we made together. I sold the rest, but I kept two bulls and a pig, because I knew I'd never make any more.

I work very hard. Often I start in March or April. I never know how many figures I've made, but this year I used three fifty-kilo sacks of icing sugar – that's a hundred and fifty kilos! I'm glad to say I sold almost everything, and made a profit. My sugar figures are wholly edible, except where I've used glitter. If you take care of them they'll last as long as you want them to, because they're properly made in the old-fashioned way.

I use icing sugar, egg whites and a special powder which binds them together. I also add a few drops of lemon juice, to whiten the mixture. We make the powder ourselves from a root which we call *chautl*. It looks a bit like a potato, and belongs to the *pápalo* plant which grows wild in the mountains outside Toluca.[2] Because this powder keeps, I prepare it every second year, when the weather is hot. In May, or even earlier, plants and roots are transported in baskets and sacks to the market in Toluca. First you wash *chautl* roots carefully to get rid of the earth, then you peel and slice them. After that you leave them in hot sun for a week, turning them regularly. They should end up nice and crisp, like *chicharrón* (pork crackling). Without sun, however, they spoil and give you mottled sweets.

My ancestors used to grind *chautl* roots on a

metate (grinding stone), but I do it electrically. I sieve the powder, then add the other ingredients. The mixture at this stage is runny and should be beaten. Next I leave it for a day to firm up, and work it like dough. It can be stored in a dish – earthenware is best because it retains moisture. In the past we used to cover the dish with leaves, but now we use a plastic bag. That's progress! Finally I wrap the whole thing in a damp cloth, to stop the mixture from going hard.

I go to a lot of trouble to find good egg whites. If water gets in, the sweets will suffer. I used to buy egg whites here in Toluca from a woman who makes *Ronpope* (eggnog). One year, however, she must have been short because she topped up the egg whites with water. I made all my sugar figures and put them away. Later, when I unpacked them, they had turned translucent and flaky! Now I travel by bus all the way to Tulancingo, where they make a lot of *Ronpope*.

I bring back about six litres – if I keep them in my refrigerator, they last for two weeks. It is worth the trouble: with pure egg whites, your sugar figures will be firm and able to withstand damp. Younger sweetmakers tell me I'm foolish to spend money on egg whites. They use water, gum and who knows what else – maybe even cereal! They've offered to teach me their methods, but I prefer the old ones.

Each year, before starting work, I wash my moulds thoroughly and dry them in the sun. No matter how carefully one puts moulds away, they always collect dust. I still use my mother's moulds. I can't be sure, but I think they came from Metepec. They were solidly made in those days, with a lovely smooth finish. Today's moulds are rough, perhaps because the clay isn't well worked. Each year, just before the sweet-making season, a man from Mepetec sets up a stall in Toluca's Friday market. He has moulds for different animals. One year I bought

112. **Stall during the sugar fair (*la feria del alfeñique*) before *Todos Santos*. On display are paper puppets in the form of skeletons, skulls of sugar and chocolate, and all kinds of sweets. Toluca, State of Mexico.**

three or four dozen small ones: when I washed them, however, they began to break up, they just came apart! It's the same with many of today's *cazuelas* (earthenware cooking pots). They're not well made like they used to be.

I do everything stage by stage, starting with my mould-work. At each stage the order is the same: I graduate from small sizes to medium sizes, and finish on large. This year the moulding took from March until June. It's a laborious process. Step one is like making pastry because

113. Consuelo García Urrutia with pottery moulds for making sugar figures. Toluca, State of Mexico.

I flatten the sugar-dough with a smooth rolling pin; then I use a second rolling pin with a rough surface. For the body of each animal I cut away two sections of the right size, and fit them into two identical moulds; these are brought together to ensure a perfect fit. After a day or so I lift the moulds off, and put both sections together in a box, so that they can't get separated. When I've accumulated as many pairs as I'm going to make in each given size, I stick them together. For this I use a second mixture which is more liquid than the first, although it has the same ingredients. It, too, is kept covered with a damp cloth.

Next I mould the heads, starting as usual with the smallest. I try to vary the position, so that some animals look sideways or upwards, and not simply straight ahead. Only when I reach the largest size do I fashion the heads by hand. Next I paint in the eyes and other facial features. I buy little bottles of colour, which say 'Made in Mexico', from the market of La Merced. Each is accompanied by its own brush.

The front legs come next, starting again with the smallest. For this I need a *pateador*[3] – this is a length of wood which has been hollowed out to support the animals. If you balanced them on the floor at this stage, they would fall over and break. Trying to balance a procession of two-legged animals on the *pateador* is a bit of a circus as it is! I don't know how other people manage. I imagine some just prop them up against strips of wood, but mine are properly hollowed out. I have a *pateador* to suit every size of animal. If they are very small, I can fit up to one hundred on one *pateador*; if the animals are very large, then the *pateador* will only support six. When all the front legs have been done, I turn the animals round and do the back ones.

Now the animals have four legs, so I start on their ears. If they are deer or bulls, I do their antlers or horns as well, and then their tails. At this stage I may add a little water to my original mixture. I sit at the table and model by hand. As before, I do one batch at a time, moving up in sizes. The largest animals are the most detailed, because I try to make them as different from one another as possible. Sometimes the ears take two days to dry; when they are firm I attach a temporary paper cape to them. This supports the horns while they harden. This part of the process is very time-consuming.

By September I have begun to give the animals their raised coats. This is virtually the last stage. I use icing sugar, egg white and a few drops of lemon juice. The mixture has to be fairly liquid, so that I can apply it in globules. When October arrives I do very little. I add finishing touches: I give each animal its little tuft or tassel, I tie on the odd satin bow, and I wrap large animals in cellophane.

La feria del alfeñique is the high point of our year. It draws visitors from miles around. This year, by 13 October, the *portales* (arcades) were packed along two whole sides with stalls. Don't be deceived, however. There are many stall-holders who don't make their own figures, and many who are not even from here. Some bring crystallised fruits from Mexico City. I think this is wrong. This is an *alfeñique* fair, not a chocolate or an anything else fair! So I tell my companions: 'We must make more of an effort! It's all right to include a few dried fruits among our wares – I do it myself – but the bulk of what we sell must be *alfeñique*.' This year there were stalls selling no *alfeñique* at all – just skulls of sugar or chocolate. Sadly, fewer and fewer people are willing to make the effort.

I discuss these and other problems with fellow members of the sugar-workers' association. We form quite a united group, and have a woman representative who liaises with the town council. She's very active on our behalf, so we held a lunch in her honour after this year's fair. We also took the opportunity to thank the councillors for allowing us to use the *portales*. 'On the contrary', they replied, 'you are the ones who should be thanked. You are perpetuating the traditions of Toluca with your beautiful creations.'

Relations haven't always been this amicable – in the past we've had some bad experiences! When Toluca had a woman as municipal president, she made us suffer dreadfully. One year she organised a fair which coincided with *Todos Santos*, so she sent us to the outskirts of the town. We made such losses that year! Our strip of land became a sea of mud: the more it rained, the yellower our sweets became! After that my companions begged to be allowed back into *La Plaza de Castro*, but she gave each of us a minuscule space measuring no more than a metre across. I felt so angry. 'A lemon-seller might be happy with a metre', I told her, 'but I'm a professional woman, and I expect better treatment!' That year again we made terrible losses.

That was over six years ago. The municipal president who followed her allowed us to use the *portales*, but with one condition: we had to smarten up. He wanted us to have identical stalls. This threw us into quite a panic, because it costs money to buy new stalls! It wasn't such a problem for me – although I may not have a lot of money, I had enough to buy my stall outright. But many people, who have to live the whole year on what they make during the sugar fair, had to buy theirs in instalments.

Now these problems are behind us: we're allowed to remain in one place, with room to display our wares. I just wish the authorities would promise never to treat us so badly again. Because, as they themselves admit, our presence enhances Toluca's image. Our *feria* attracts more visitors than any other event, and visitors spend money in the town. Then there are the licence fees we pay the council – these amount to quite a tidy sum! There have been moments in the past when we almost lost our will to continue. Now I hope those times are gone.

Making *alfeñique* is slow work, especially at my age. When each day finishes, you feel disappointed at the little you've achieved. Yet I long to pass on what I know. When I die, no one in my family will follow the tradition. My daughter helps me when she can, but she has a career as a chemist. My grandson is studying English. Only my nephew is keen: occasionally he helps me do the animals' coats. 'Bring your wife', I tell him. 'Let me teach you what I know.' Now I'm asking the council to organise classes in the town. I'd teach anyone who wanted to learn, and expect no payment. I want to leave something behind me, when I die. Last year, when building was going on in the garden, I buried some of my mother's moulds. 'These have no further use', I thought. 'Better that I should break and bury them.' So I buried a small elephant, a bull and a large pig in memory of my mother and sister. 'Better to do away with these now', I thought. 'Someone in the future will need to dispose of them, so I'll save them the trouble.'

114. Wenceslao Rívas Contreras beside his market stall during *la feria del alfeñique* (the sugar fair). Toluca, State of Mexico.

Wenceslao Rívas Contreras

(Toluca, State of Mexico)

A professional sweetmaker by trade, Wenceslao Rívas Contreras has devoted himself almost exclusively in recent years to the creation of chocolate and, more particularly, sugar skulls. These are sold each year during la feria del alfeñique *in Toluca, in the State of Mexico. When he was interviewed in 1988, Wenceslao was seventy-one years old and the recipient of numerous prizes, yet his desire to create skulls with* más vista *(more visual appeal) remains undiminished. In 1989 his sugar skulls were bedizened for the first time with long eyelashes of metallic paper; many also had gaping jaws, as described below.*

During the fair, names are inscribed in icing sugar as required on the foreheads of skulls. People who decide to eat these fragile reminders of human mortality are rewarded with the taste of chile *and other flavours. Brilliant colours could prove less appetising, however. In common with many craftworkers, Wenceslao refers to his dyes as 'vegetable colourants', yet the label on each small bottle states: 'Artificial colourant. Colouring concentrate. Excipient of sodium chloride. The use of this colouring in foods or drinks requires special authorisation.'*

With regret, Wenceslao says he can find no one who will work with him on a regular basis. His sons sometimes help with production and sales, but show no desire to follow the family calling; one now works full-time in the local Sabritas factory, manufacturing potato crisps. By contrast Wenceslao's daughter, Miriam Rívas Malagón, has designed a range of sugar skulls inspired by Hollywood starlets of the 1930s. Called las gringas rubias *(North American blondes) they show* la muerte sexy *(sexy death).*

115. Sugar skulls with yellow hair, pink cheeks and eyes of green metallic paper. Made by Miriam Rívas Malagón, they were inspired by *las gringas rubias* (North American blondes). Toluca, State of Mexico.

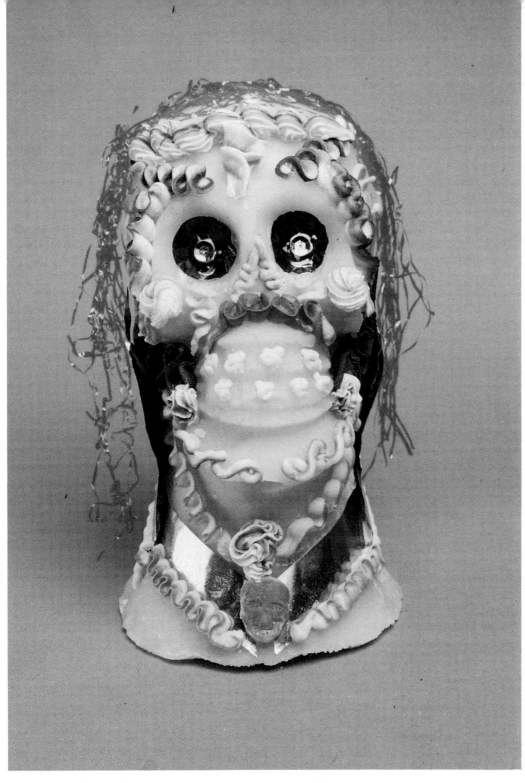

116. Profusely decorated
sugar skull, made by
Wenceslao Rívas
Contreras for sale
during *la feria del
alfeñique*. Toluca, State
of Mexico.

Sugar skulls come in all shapes and sizes: some
have flattened features, others have prominent
cheekbones – the variations are infinite. Most
sugar-workers arc not innovators, however.
Their chief concern is profit. Either they repeat
what has gone before, or they copy the designs
of others. My aim, by contrast, is to keep ahead.
Each year I like to surprise the public with
different models based on new ideas. When the
bustle of the fair is over and the clearing up is
done, I take time to review my designs and to

try out future forms in plaster or plasticine. At
the moment I'm studying the lower jaw. It's
never clearly shown by sugar-workers, but I'm
hoping to create a full skull, with gaping jaws. It
will look more naturalistic, more imposing.

I have pottery moulds going back over
twenty-five years, mostly of my own design.
These were made locally in Metepec. Moulds
for small and medium-sized skulls come in two
or three sections; but if the skulls are large, or if
you want a lot of detail such as facial features,

117. Work table in the home of Wenceslao Rívas Contreras. Shown here are sugar skulls, a pumpkin, and other small sugar ornaments. In the centre is a pottery mould, made in sections in the nearby town of Metepec. Toluca, State of Mexico.

then four sections are best. When making moulds, potters in Metepec attach a nylon thread to the prototype and pack the raw clay around it. Then they use the nylon thread to cut through the clay. The future mould, still in one piece, is fired. Afterwards, when the potter taps the mould, it separates into sections along the lines that were cut.

In practice moulds never turn out as well as you hope. There are always rough bits and bits that stick out. To clean these up I use a file, a bit of sandpaper or a broken-off saw blade. Before embarking on production, I always try out new moulds. It's such a problem getting them right. In Metepec I know only three or four potters who make moulds – most are busy with cooking-vessels or 'trees of life.'[1] Some moulds look fine, but break up later when they're washed. In Metepec clay is not refined as carefully as it should be.

Skull-making often starts in April. The basic recipe is simple: mix five kilos of sugar with one and a half litres of water, then add the juice from half a large lemon, or a whole one if it's small. A level soupspoon of cream of tartar helps whiten the sugar and improves the consistency. Fruit juice, colouring or flavouring may also be added. The mixture goes in a pan on the stove until it bubbles. I used one and a half metric tons of sugar this year – enough for a mountain of skulls!

During moulding, I often start with smaller sizes and work my way up; or I may reverse the process and start with the heaviest. When all the skulls are cast, decoration begins. Icing sugar and egg whites, with added colouring, provide the sugar paste for piping. Using a cone of waxed paper, I apply each colour separately, and finish with white. It's like decorating a cake, but it takes a lot longer – some skulls are embellished with four and five colours. Before I start moulding, in the spring, I make sugar flowers, hats and diadems: these are now added for extra splendour. Not even in Mexico City are skulls so ornate!

Small sizes sell best. Large skulls are costly and beyond the means of many people. My best customers are courting couples: boyfriends want to impress their girlfriends and vice versa. If asked, I'll add names and humorous inscriptions. A skull destined for a mother-in-law may say: 'This is how I want to see you ... sweet as sugar' or 'made of chocolate'! Of course, she'll choose the kindest meaning! I've a bad head for

114

rhymes. Some people improvise verses in the tradition of the *calavera*,[2] but I don't have this skill. It's something for the young. When customers ask for verses, I refer them to my son Miguel.

I've often been told to stick to what's Mexican, yet I enjoy trying my hand at different things. Ten years ago I added skulls in pumpkins to my range. Pumpkins are a feature of Halloween in North America, but I'll make them if I can sell them, and witches as well! I want my displays to have variety, and my customers to have choice. In truth, although these various styles all sell, skulls sell best – they belong to us, to Mexico! Sugar lambs are popular too, but I see these as a Spanish tradition. It would be hard to say how sugar skulls first started. People tell you this and that, but I don't think anyone knows for certain. Probably the custom evolved gradually, long ago.[3]

Sweetmaking is in my blood; it's a family craft dating back generations. My father, who came originally from Jalisco, joined my mother in Uruapan, Michoacán. There he made regional sweets of all types for all seasons, and sugar skulls for *Todos Santos*. These were rough and unsophisticated, however, more like dog skulls than human ones. The fault lay with local potters: they made pots and simple figures shaped like corn-cobs or animals, but could manage little else. Although my father bought his moulds in many places, such as Patamban and Quiroga, they were always thick and lumpen. In those days the demand for sugar skulls was slight, for he made just a few each year and rarely added names. Also for *Todos Santos* he fashioned human figures from a sticky mixture known as *pasta de limón* (lemon paste); using his hands and a knife, he shaped his *muertitos* (dead people), and painted them prettily.

When I left home, the family skills served me well. In my prime, I could make 110 different sweets and puddings! In 1933 I settled in Toluca, but left in 1948 for North America. You see and learn so much when you're on the move! In 1952 I won first prize in a Mexican sweetmaking contest, and earned a good living making sweets in Texas. I had no ties, I worked hard and I enjoyed my youth. Then, in 1962, I settled once again in Toluca, and devoted myself seriously to sweets and sugar skulls. At first I relied on ready-made moulds. Someone, I remember, brought me a skull-mould from Oaxaca, but it was so lop-sided that I cast it aside. Then I decided to design my own moulds. Now I can make cheerful skulls, fero-

cious skulls, and skulls with sad eyes. I want to give them maximum expression, I want to make them come alive.

I haven't always been as solitary as you see me now. Once I had forty-three employees – or forty-three problems daily! We produced every type of sweet and pudding, but the anguish was terrible. What seizures of rage. In the end my gall-bladder was removed in hospital. Those employees did everything but work. At the outset I went regularly to Mexico City: I made deliveries, then bought fruit and other raw materials. As soon as my back was turned, the party began. My employees spent their time eating. How they enjoyed my absences. They would walk off with everything – sacks of sugar, pans . . .

In the end I said to myself: 'Enough is enough. This business belongs to me – not them.' I was paying for the raw materials, but watching them vanish and getting left with the crumbs. I tried half-measures: I set up three retail outlets of my own in Toluca, and stopped delivering goods to the city. But things got no better. 'There's just one solution', I said. 'I'll cut right back, and devote myself to what I do best. That way lies peace, and maybe even a peso I can call my own!' So I sent my staff packing! Never again! Outsiders just bring you grief and rage.

Now I devote myself to *Todos Santos*. Most of the work I do myself. My brother and my daughter sometimes help with the moulding, while Enrique, my son, takes part in the decoration. Between the three or four of us we cover everything. My advice is to keep operations small, with no employees. In the old days, when I had a workforce, we started skull-making in August. Now I start much earlier, and next year I plan to start earlier still. If the sugar skulls are finished by August, I devote myself to working with chocolate. This year I used one metric ton. My entire stock is destined for the fair.

In all my Mexican travels, I've seen nothing to equal the fair of Toluca. Many places produce sweets and sugar figures for *Todos Santos*, but few can rival the State of Mexico. The fair is exhausting and sales are high. With my children's help I run my own stalls and keep my own accounts. I've lost all trust in outsiders – I like to know whether I'm selling my goods or giving them away. Although sixty or seventy stall-holders take part in the fair, few families actually make what they sell. Most have neither the time nor the skill. They buy their merchandise wholesale from Mexico City and sometimes from me. Theoretically, for the purpose of this fair, Toluca's sugar-workers have formed a 'union'. But without rules or discipline, we're in a bad way.

In my time in Toluca I've seen many changes. In 1933 it was a small town, with narrow streets. Now it's ten times the size. There are factories and heavy industry, and the people are more alert. As a lad I never thought I'd be here so long. Now, at seventy-one, my travels are behind me; I've my daughter and a grandchild to support. In Europe or North America,

this work might be better paid. I've won several prizes here, but there's no money involved – only official recognition, which is welcome of course. We're a poor country. My best reward – the one that really matters – comes when passers-by pause in surprise and pleasure to stare at my stall. I can't stop planning new designs. As I talk, I'm visualising a pair of Aztec skulls, with plumes and ear-ornaments, all done in sugar. If you come back, and if God gives me life, we'll see whether I've achieved my aim. We'll see if I've created something new.

118. Skull face emerging from a pumpkin. Nothing more graphically expresses the merging of the traditions of Halloween with those of the Day of the Dead. Made in sugar. Mexico City. H 20.5 cms

María Antonieta Sánchez
de Escamilla

(Puebla City)

119. Dinner table set with food and other offerings for the returning souls. This installation, by María Antonieta Sánchez de Escamilla, was awarded first prize during a *concurso* (contest) for Day of the Dead *ofrendas* in La Casa de la Cultura, Puebla City.

María Antonieta Sánchez de Escamilla lives in the City of Puebla, and has worked for nearly twenty years as a nursery school teacher. She now runs her own nursery school, the Kinder Fantasilandia. Her views on the Festival of the Dead are, she thinks, representative of the urban middle class in Puebla State. With the support of her pupils and their families, she takes part each year in an exhibiting competition of ofrendas *organised by La Casa de la Cultura (The House of Culture). Here official encouragement is given to the popular arts and traditions of Puebla.*

In 1989, when this interview was recorded, María Antonieta Sánchez de Escamilla had just been awarded first prize: she had chosen to show an old-style, Puebla City ofrenda. In her own home the dead are received at the dinner table, just as they were when her parents were alive. The table is set as for a meal; the invisible guests are offered food and drink, and many of their favourite belongings. The title of this ofrenda *was La última cena (The Last Supper). In past years she has presented a minia-*
turised ofrenda, *and an imaginary* ofrenda *for a fifteen-year-old. 'I saw her as thoroughly modern, so I didn't offer her* tamales *or* mole*. I put out jeans and a T-shirt, her school books, an old doll, flowers and perfume. I used roses and hands to symbolise her life; she passed from the bloom of youth to death.' As this description suggests, the* ofrendas *displayed in La Casa de la Cultura vacillate between authenticity and extreme theatricality. When traditions are promoted in a 'sophisticated' setting for a large audience, this is perhaps inevitable.*

The dates given by María Antonieta Sánchez de Escamilla do not coincide in every respect with those provided by other informants from Puebla City. The following description of events is offered by Martha Reyes C.:

At midday, on 28 October, we receive the souls of those who have been killed or murdered. They leave at midday on the 29th, and their place is taken by *los accidentados* (those who die in accidents). At midday, on the 30th, children arrive from limbo. At midday, on the 31st, we greet all baptised children. Then on 1 November at midday the souls of the adult dead arrive, and they stay with us until midday on the 2nd.

Such discrepancies are not unusual. The days which precede Todos Santos *are differently assigned by different people.*

Like other people in other lands, we are unwilling to let go of our dead. We cling to their memory, and hope one day to be reunited. This is human nature. In Mexico, however, we are fortunate: our pre-Hispanic past and our Catholic beliefs allow us to retain our links with the dead. We know they will return to us each year, and our sense of separation is lessened. *Ofrendas* give our memories a tangible form; we express our affections in an intimate way. We

120. Candle holder of polychrome painted pottery in the form of a female skeleton from Izúcar de Matamoros. A wide range of pottery for the Day of the Dead is produced here and in other centres in the State of Puebla. H 14 cms

say: 'If he or she were alive, this is what he or she would like.' Perhaps this is more of a consolation for us, the living.

In Puebla City crafts and special foods abound. Each year, as the festival approaches, potters in the Barrio de la Luz stockpile their wares. These include black-glazed candlesticks and incense burners, punch bowls and miniature pottery vessels for miniature *ofrendas*. In the Barrio de Santa Clara toymakers devise ingenious funeral processions where priests have chick-pea heads and paper robes. Delicious sweets and sugar figures are also produced ahead of time. Some merchandise arrives from other places. Although families in Puebla City use scissors to pattern tissue-paper banners for home consumption, most prefer elaborately cut scenes with angels and doves from San Salvador Huixcolotla. During the month of October these seasonal items are displayed in shops and markets. The Victoria, which used to be our principal market, no longer exists. By searching, however, we find what we need to receive our dead.

Today the Festival of the Dead has official support. Forty years ago it was strongly discouraged. In the 1950s, when I was a child in school, we were ridiculed for believing in *ofrendas*. If we admitted having one at home, we were laughed at for our credulity. Those who honoured the Days of the Dead, so it was said, were the victims of superstition and hallucination. My teacher asked me to explain this to my parents: 'Tell them this is nonsense; tell them they are making a foolish mistake', she said. 'The dead can never visit us here on earth.'

By 1972, when I started teaching, the position had changed. I think the Government became nervous during the 1960s, when hippies were news. As many youngsters lost respect for festivals and traditions, they rejected the values of home and family; rebellion, drink and drugs were often the result. So the authorities revised their views and decided to support our vanishing traditions. It suits the Government for us to stay as we are; if we awake from our slumbers and our passivity, good and bad things might happen! Now the Government wants to shore up our sense of pride and national identity. Mexico's future lies with its children: when official policy was reversed, La Secretaría de Educación Pública (The Ministry of Education) asked schools and nursery schools to promote Mexican culture; teachers, who had mocked our traditions, were told to endorse them.

María Antonieta Sánchez de Escamilla

These aims are my aims. After the Spanish Conquest we lost our identity – today we hardly know if we're Aztec, Spanish or North American! I teach my pupils to honour our pre-Hispanic past, and to love our customs. Can you imagine, before 1972 many lovely songs for children were banned in schools. The authorities wanted them to hear modern music. There's nothing wrong with modern music, but shouldn't we try to keep a balance? The authorities insisted that Cri-Cri and similar songs encouraged children to fantasise, and failed to equip them for the modern world. Lies! We all need to keep a sense of wonder. Fortunately the authorities realised their mistake: children's songs were reinstated. Now our traditions are respected, and we're encouraged to believe in the Days of the Dead.

Children in Mexico learn about death at an early age. I think this is healthy. I tell my pupils to live each day as if it were their last; if we followed this rule, we would all behave better than we do. I don't want children to fear death; I want them to respect life. I explain that our loved ones never really die while we remember them. During the Days of the Dead we show our affection for the deceased. This festival belongs to them, just as our birthdays belong to us. Most of my pupils have lost a loved one: they all have someone to remember. I stress the importance of *ofrendas* and ask them what they'll offer the dead. I think it's good for children to confront the idea of death, and also the idea of their own mortality. Sometimes a child feels squeamish about death, and admits to fearing skulls and skeletons. When this happens, I tell my pupils to touch themselves. 'Why are you afraid?' I ask, 'when each of you owns a skull and skeleton. We all carry death within us.' They feel themselves, and they say: 'Yes it's true, we too are made of bones.'

Death in Mexico is usually personified as a woman. Often we portray her humorously, with scant respect. We show her as a sugar skull, and we eat her clean away. We show her as a skeleton, dressed in black and carrying a scythe. Or we show her dancing, in accordance with our sense of fun and jollity. We like to see her as someone from everyday life, someone who belongs to the Mexican people. We clothe her in every conceivable way, in modern jeans and old-style frocks. This is our way of showing that we love her, that we are not afraid of her. She is with us from the moment of our birth; sooner or later, we will know her intimately.

Halloween, by contrast, distorts the image of death. I regard it as an invasion, as something that doesn't belong to us. Halloween is truly frightening for children, because it focuses on witches and witchcraft, sorcerers and devils. It deforms the imagination, and threatens our indigenous traditions. In the City of Puebla, however, it has gained little ground. A few schools observe both festivals, because they don't want to seem old fashioned. But La Secretaría de Educación Pública and La Casa de la Cultura are working to protect local customs and the *ofrenda*. Most people honour the beliefs of their forebears; in this city you will find *ofrendas* in roughly eighty-five percent of homes. In the countryside and in working-class areas of the city these are usually positioned on a shelf or table by the wall. The middle classes, however, prefer to use the dining-room table. It offers greater comfort and seems more appropriate: it

121. **Pair of polychrome painted pottery figures in the form of skeletons.** H (approx.) 35 cms

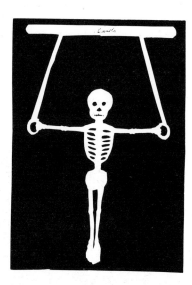

122. Paper silhouettes in the form of skeletons cut out using scissors by Victor Manuel Cuellar. Puebla City. Average H 10.5 cms

suggests that the living are sharing their lives with the departed. When I was a child I learnt to receive the dead this way, and I do so still.

This year I decided to exhibit my family *ofrenda* in La Casa de la Cultura, so that people could see a traditional version. It was dedicated to my mother and father, my *nana* (nursemaid) whom I looked on as a second mother, my sister, a baby, my niece, and two *profesores* (teachers) who were friends of the family. *Ofrendas* are for those one loves and misses. Each guest has his or her own place-setting at the table. The living never sit down with the dead – that wouldn't be respectful.

As with most *ofrendas*, pre-Hispanic and

Spanish elements merge. We always burn incense, because it purifies; when it rises, it carries our prayers to heaven. There is also a cross, because Christ must be present in all *ofrendas*, and candles. Flowers have been important since pre-Conquest times: *cempasúchil* flowers are like the sun; they guide the souls of the dead back to earth. *Mano de león*, by contrast, was probably introduced by Spanish settlers; I believe it was favoured in the houses of the rich, while the poor could afford only *cempasúchil*.[1]

When the dead return it's like a fiesta. In Puebla we always serve *mole* with chicken or turkey during celebrations, so this is what we offer our departed. This year I also prepared pork in green *mole* sauce with *chayotes*. It's not really a meal – more an assortment of dishes: we offer our friends and relatives the things they most enjoyed in life. Some, like my mother, had a sweet tooth; for her I prepare crystallised fruits. We love sweets and puddings in Puebla, and we hope these will guarantee the dead a sweeter and a more agreeable life in the next world. When we share sugar and salt with the dead, we are symbolically sharing the sweet and bitter things of life. Many *ofrendas* include guavas, mandarin oranges, pumpkin or *tejocotes* (choke-cherries) in sweet syrup. My nursemaid had other preferences; to her I give fruit, *tamales* and *pulque*. Sometimes people offer their dead *aguardiente* or beer.

Many of these drinks and foods are indigenous to Mexico, but some were introduced after the Conquest. Wheat flour came to us from Spain, and today you will find sweet breads in every *ofrenda*. Several regional variations have been lost – *pan de agua* (water bread) is no longer made. But others, like the *hojaldra*, are still popular. Highly stylised in shape, it has a central bump and four raised sections. These, so it is said, are paths or cardinal directions; they lead the dead to the *ofrenda* which is symbolised by the bump at its heart. *Hojaldras* are also patterned with raised tears. In many houses you can find additional bread styles;

some are smooth, while others display simulated bones.

In this way we share bread and salt with the dead. Salt, so it is said, is especially important for children who die before baptism. Our offerings are served as daintily and as lovingly as possible, as if the dead were living guests. No effort is spared; we would never give stale or badly prepared food to flesh-and-blood guests – still less to dead ones. We want our visitors to be happy when they depart. We imagine them as embarking once again upon a journey: they need to eat and drink well, because the *ofrenda* must last them a full year.

It is the spirit, or the essence, that the dead extract. I've never noticed a change in food, but we always offer water and, do you know, the level really does go down! This can't be evaporation because there's no heat – just the flames of the candles. If we put out a full glass of water, it is often half full next day. This tells you how thirsty our visitors are! I remember, as a child, being forbidden to taste a crumb of food or a drop of water from the *ofrenda*. That would have been sacrilege! Only when the dead have finished can it be shared out among the living.

Dead people never change their habits or their tastes. My *ofrenda*, as I have said, paid homage to two *profesores*. One was Professor Zamítiz, a musician who composed many fine

123. Painted breadshop window showing a skull eating an *hojaldra* (bread for the dead) in the City of Puebla.

huapangos;[2] here in Puebla we sometimes entertain the dead with music, so I played him old recordings of his songs. The other teacher was Professor Mora. 'You've forgotten his cigarettes!', exclaimed a friend, who immediately rushed off, returning with a packet of *Raleigh*, Professor Mora's favourite brand. Such gestures are a symbol of our affection. We are saying: 'You liked this when you were alive; now here it is.'

Sometimes the dead are offered their belongings. Each guest has his or her own place-setting, with cutlery, a plate and glass; nearby, on the table or on a chair, we lay the treasured possessions of each loved one. Perhaps this is a pre-Hispanic trait. We imagine our dead arriving tired, with their clothing tattered and soiled after a year of use. My family is middle class, so I give my mother her *mantilla*, her missal and her rosary; when she was alive she was a keen church-goer, and these things meant a lot to her. My father has his hat and cane, and my niece her doll. She was twenty when she died, but she loved it as a child. I also lay out the dress she wore near the end of her life in a procession of *carros alegóricos* (floats depicting Biblical themes).

In working-class homes the dead may be offered their old tools: the carpenter is reunited with his hammer, and the shoemaker with his last. When they leave, the dead take with them the essence of their possessions. These objects help us retain an intimacy with our loved ones. When we offer them, we are saying: 'I haven't forgotten you. Only see, I've kept your belongings. I love and cherish the things you loved.'

The dead start to arrive on 28 October. This day belongs to *los accidentados* and to *los ahogados* (those who died by drowning). The 29th is for those in limbo, who died without baptism. On the 29th, too, small outdoor *ofrendas* begin to appear in the streets; there, where a loved one was run over or carried off by sudden illness, relatives place water and a cross with flowers. Dead children visit their homes on 31 October, and depart on 1 November, All Saints' Day. Dead adults arrive at midnight on the night of the 1st, and leave between noon and 3pm on the afternoon of the 2nd. Some dishes, especially sweet ones, can be prepared in advance; others are cooked on the day they are needed. We change the food frequently; sweets and puddings last a while, but savoury ones deteriorate fast.

This year, to my great surprise, I witnessed the departure of the adult dead. My son and I were with our *ofrenda* in La Casa de la Cultura. The space was free of drafts and the flames of our candles had been burning steadily. Then, around noon on 2 November, all the flames started leaning to the north. My son, who is young and free of superstition, assumed the onlookers were causing a breeze. 'Only marathon-runners could cause a breeze this strong,' I told him. By 1pm the flames were almost horizontal. An old woman, who had been watching, came up to me. 'This is the hour,' she told me, 'when the souls of the dead withdraw. Your *ofrenda* is dedicated to real people, people who really lived. You summoned them with your prayers, your love and your offerings. They came, and now they are leaving. The candle flames are wavering to signal their departure.'

Some people say it is possible to talk with the dead. No one I know has ever tried, yet I have sometimes been aware of my father's presence. He died of heart failure in Mexico City, so we never saw him at the last. We mourned him terribly. Then we began to hear knocking sounds around the house; if we looked, we found no one there. The last time this happened I was with my fiancé before my wedding. There came a knocking at the window, yet no one appeared. I like to think my father was with me during those moments.

The dead feel sad if they're not remembered. There is a story in these parts about the Day of the Dead. I've heard several versions, but this is the most usual. In a village near Puebla City there lived a recently married woman. When 1 November arrived, she asked her husband for money to make an *ofrenda*. 'This is mere foolishness', he said. 'I provide you with enough to eat, but I'm not prepared to waste money on lies.' 'What about our parents?' she asked. 'They will grieve if we offer them nothing.' 'If you believe in superstition, give them wild flowers and water', he told her angrily. Then he went to work in the fields. The young wife did the best she could. She put water in a chipped jug and burned sweet-smelling *ocote* wood; she killed their only chicken, made a few *tamales*, and laid these paltry offerings on palm leaves because she had no cloth. When night fell, she prayed and finally went to bed.

Her husband, meanwhile, had finished his day's work. His return route took him past the local cemetery; as he reached it, he saw a candlelit procession coming towards him, and he stood back to let it pass. Each member carried flowers, sweet breads, a basket of fruit and a candle. Some even had maize cobs or a plump turkey. Everyone was happy and singing. Then, at the rear of the procession, he saw a small group of people. Dragging their feet in sadness, they carried *ocote* wood, wild flowers and a few meagre *tamales*. His heart sank for he recognised his own parents and those of his wife. At first he thought they were flesh-and-blood, then he remembered they were dead. In fear and trembling he ran home. 'Did you disobey me? Did you make an *ofrenda*?' he asked his wife. 'Yes', she replied. 'I believe the dead return each year to see us. If we make no *ofrenda*, they know they have been forgotten and they grieve.' 'What did you offer them?' he asked. She listed all the things he'd seen, so he told her about the procession and promised never to be so mean again. Each year, for the rest of their lives, they welcomed their loved ones with a profusion of offerings. Never again did their parents return to the graveyard in sorrow.

The Day of the Dead is commemorated in legends such as these; sometimes we laugh and call them old wives' tales, yet deep down we think they may be true. We want to be sure, like the wife in the story, that our dead don't depart with empty hands. The Catholic Church doesn't like everything we do, but it chooses to turn a blind eye: some traditions are too deeply engrained to be uprooted. Passed down from generation to generation, they are at the core of our being. If we behave respectfully and prudently, the Church will not oppose us. Yet many Church leaders see us as fanatical and idolatrous. In an orthodox world, the living would express their attachment to the dead through prayer, masses, rosaries and visits to the cemetery. If priests couldn't bury our pyramids, however, they'll never eradicate our beliefs about death. We, the people of Mexico, have our own way of remembering the dead. While the living honour their memory, the dead can never truly die. They die only if we forget them.

124. Competition *ofrenda* in the style of Xochitlán from the highlands of Puebla State. La Casa de la Cultura, Puebla City.

Arsacio Vanegas Arroyo

(Mexico City)

During the last part of the nineteenth and the early part of the twentieth century, Antonio Vanegas Arroyo published the work of both Manuel Manilla (approx. 1830–90) and José Guadalupe Posada (1852–1913).[1] His grandson, Arsacio Vanegas Arroyo, still prints their work, using many of the original blocks. Born in 1922 in a popular barrio, *or quarter, of Mexico City, he has lived in the same house all his life; his umbilical cord lies buried in the yard. For many years he worked as a wrestler under the names 'Kid Vanegas' and 'El Indio Vanegas'. He helped to train Che Guevara and Fidel Castro in the art of wrestling and self-defence in 1955–6, when they lived in Mexico; the First and Second Cuban Manifestos were printed on the family press.*

125. Arsacio Vanegas Arroyo. Mexico City.

126. *Calavera,* **or broadsheet, published in 1907 in self-mockery by Antonio Vanegas Arroyo (the printer) with an engraving by José Guadalupe Posada. Printed before the Day of the Dead,** *calaveras* **carry satirical epitaphs for the living.**

It is often said that Mexicans have a special relationship with death, because we perceive ourselves in life as the skeletons and skulls we really are. Many of our best poets and songwriters have written about death. It commands awe and respect, yet different people view it in different ways. For some death is a termination; it signifies everything we will never experience or see. For others it is joyous; life is understood – as it was in the poetry of the Aztecs – to be fleeting and ephemeral, whereas death takes us into the beyond, to eternity.

In Mexico death is often personified as a woman. This is not logical, because men and women are both destined for death: when we die, our bones are sexless. But we speak of *la muerte* or *la calaca* (death) in the feminine gender. Our language is remarkably rich in terms which evoke death and dying. We say 'se estiró la pata' ('he stretched out his legs'); 'tiró los tenis' ('he threw away his trainers'); or 'va por delante' ('he's going ahead').

Since Aztec times and beyond we have been surrounded by images of death. After the Conquest the Spaniards imposed their culture. Like the Aztecs, they had special days for honouring the dead, but they changed the face of death in Mexico. European engravings offered a different perspective; they centred on Death the Reaper. Today we have our own unique vision.

The influence of José Guadalupe Posada has

been immense. He worked closely with my grandfather, who inspired many of his engravings. Perhaps they knew the poetry of Jorge Manrique, who wrote meditative verses on the death of kings, viceroys and other powerful figures of the Colonial period.[2] Manrique was later followed by the engraver Santiago Hernández. He was the first person to print illustrated verses, or *calaveras*.[3] Very little of his work survives today.

My grandfather, Antonio Vanegas Arroyo, founded his publishing house in 1880 with the help of my grandmother, Doña Carmen Rubí, who came from Toluca. He had been born in the City of Puebla in 1852 – which, coincidentally, was also the year of Posada's birth. They met and married in Mexico City, and settled eventually in *la Calle de la Perpetua*. In the early days his chief artist was Manuel Manilla, who died around 1890.[4] His technique was to engrave on lead alloy. According to my father, Manilla had been born in Mexico City in 1830 into a family of *dulceros* (sweetmakers). Manilla also knew how to make sugar skulls, so perhaps he was a precursor in this field as well!

Posada was born in Aguascalientes, where he received a thorough grounding in printmaking techniques. In 1872 he moved to León in the state of Guanajuato, but left in 1888 after floods had devastated the town. In Mexico City he began to work for my grandfather, and contin-

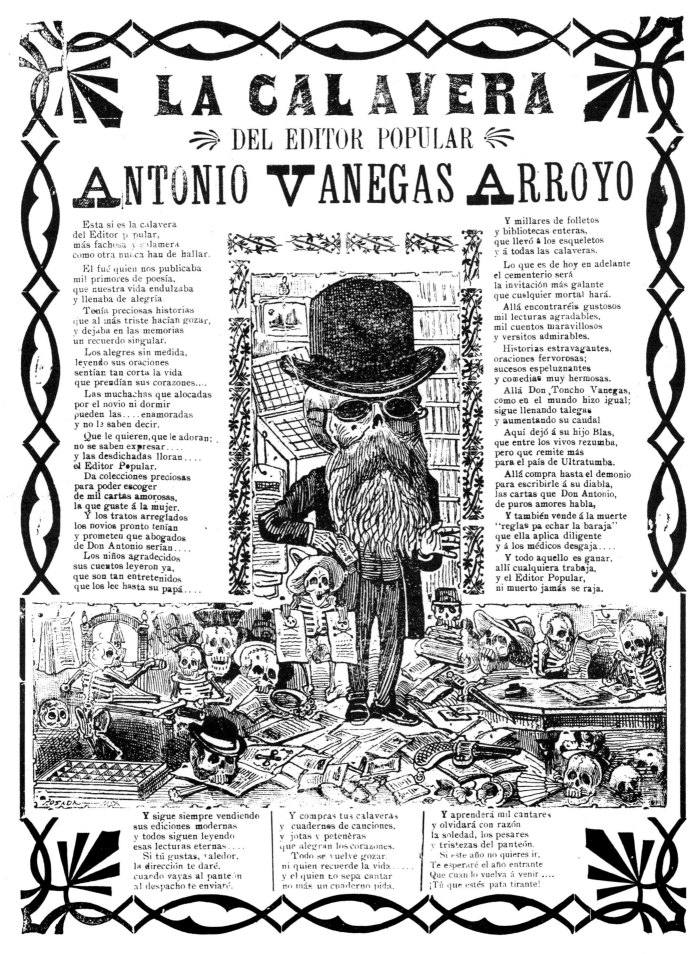

LA CALAVERA
≈ DEL EDITOR POPULAR ≈
ANTONIO VANEGAS ARROYO

Esta si es la calavera
del Editor popular,
más fachosa y salamera
como otra nunca han de hallar.

El fué quien nos publicaba
mil primores de poesía,
que nuestra vida endulzaba
y llenaba de alegría.

Tenía preciosas historias
que al más triste hacían gozar,
y dejaba en las memorias
un recuerdo singular.

Los alegres sin medida,
leyendo sus oraciones
sentían tan corta la vida
que prendían sus corazones....

Las muchachas que alocadas
por el novio ni dormir
pueden las....enamoradas
y no lo saben decir.

Que le quieren, que le adoran;
no se saben expresar....
y las desdichadas lloran....
el Editor Popular.

Da colecciones preciosas
para poder escoger
de mil cartas amorosas,
la que guste á la mujer.

Y los tratos arreglados
los novios pronto tenían
y prometen que abogados
de Don Antonio serían....

Los niños agradecidos
sus cuentos leyeron ya,
que son tan entretenidos
que los lee hasta su papá....

Y millares de folletos
y bibliotecas enteras,
que llevó á los esqueletos
y á todas las calaveras.

Lo que es de hoy en adelante
el cementerio será
la invitación más galante
que cualquier mortal hará.

Allá encontraréis gustosos
mil lecturas agradables,
mil cuentos maravillosos
y versitos admirables.

Historias estravagantes,
oraciones fervorosas;
sucesos espeluznantes
y comedias muy hermosas.

Allá Don Toncho Vanegas,
como en el mundo hizo igual;
sigue llenando talegas
y aumentando su caudal

Aquí dejó á su hijo Blas,
que entre los vivos rezumba,
pero que remite más
para el país de Ultratumba.

Allá compra hasta el demonio
para escribirle á su diabla,
las cartas que Don Antonio,
de puros amores habla,

Y también vende á la muerte
"reglas pa echar la baraja"
que ella aplica diligente
y á los médicos desgaja....

Y todo aquello es ganar,
allí cualquiera trabaja,
y el Editor Popular,
ni muerto jamás se raja.

Y sigue siempre vendiendo
sus ediciones modernas
y todos siguen leyendo
esas lecturas eternas....
    Si tú gustas, valedor,
la dirección te daré,
cuando vayas al panteón
al despacho te enviaré.

Y compras tus calaveras
y cuadernos de canciones,
y jotas y petenéras
que alegran los corazones.
    Todo se vuelve gozar,
ni quien recuerde la vida....
y el quien no sepa cantar
no más un cuaderno pida.

Y aprenderá mil cantares
y olvidará con razón
la soledad, los pesares
y tristezas del panteón.
    Si este año no quieres ir,
Te esperaré el año entrante
Que cuando vuelva á venir....
¡Tú que estés pata tirante!

125

ued working with him until his death in 1913. Don Antonio's publications had a vast circulation; they reached most of Mexico and parts of North America. Posada would have known about my grandfather's publishing house from the illustrated broadsheets and chap-books[5] that were peddled in village squares and fairs. He would also have been familiar with Manilla's work.

My father, Blas Vanegas Arroyo, used to help my grandfather with his business. Sometimes Don Antonio would give him verses to take to Posada. 'Give Don Lupe this', he would say, 'and tell him to do me an engraving of such-and-such a size.' Most had fairly standard measurements. Posada's earliest work for my grandfather was done on lead alloy – with this technique the burin (engraver's chisel) leaves furrows; after the block has been inked, these print white. Later he went over almost totally to relief etching on zinc. Posada would draw directly on to zinc plate, using a special pen and greasy ink; then he would give the plate an acid bath, and the lines of the image would be left in relief.

This was the method used by Posada for the print which is known today as *la calavera catrina* (the *calavera* of the fashionable lady). In fact she started out as *la cucaracha*, to illustrate the song of that name. Don Antonio had apparently asked Posada to portray a high society woman. Later, as he occasionally did, he re-published this image, using it to parody lower-class women who ape their social superiors, maids who dress up in their mistress' cast off finery.

127. *La Catrina*. Today the most popular of José Guadalupe Posada's many engravings, she is widely associated with the Mexican Day of the Dead. Her image appears frequently in the work of artists and craftworkers.

In medieval engravings the dead were generally depicted with bare bones. Posada's skeletons were dressed like true Mexicans, however. He personalised them. He portrayed Madero with a *sarape*, a tall *sombrero* and a bottle of Parras *aguardiente*. Most often his *calaveras* featured common people. He showed lovers, or women who sold chickens, *tamales*, vegetables and *petates*, and he showed them fully clothed with all their wares. He was deeply rooted in the popular traditions of his day.

There is a tendency to think of Posada solely as an engraver of *calaveras*, yet he covered many other subjects. He portrayed national events, miracles and saints; he illustrated songbooks, parlour games, plays, cookery books and children's stories – these were often hand-coloured with stencils. Another popular misconception concerns the text. Posada was an illustrator, not a writer of verses. These were composed mostly by professional writers or by my grandfather, although some, of course, were popular songs which belonged to the people.

Posada didn't work solely for my grandfather. He worked for other publishers too, and eventually made quite a name for himself, although he never won the acclaim he deserved. Often he worked for short-lived periodicals, like *El Diablito Rojo* (The Little Red Devil). Some of these only lasted for a few issues. After his death, Posada was largely forgotten. My father went on printing and selling his work, but no one was interested in the identity of the artist. It was Jean Charlot in the early twenties who really rediscovered Posada.[6] Diego Rivera and Clemente Orozco were also admirers of his work.[7] In 1930 my father, Frances Toor and Pablo O'Higgins edited a *Monografía* of Posada's work;[8] then in 1943 my father and I mounted an enormous Posada exhibition at the Palacio de Bellas Artes in Mexico City.

As a child I was fascinated by the engravings of Manilla and Posada. They were my introduction to the graphic arts. When I was very small I used to play with the letters in the printing trays; later I learnt how to assemble booklets, to fold pages and to print. My father used to sell broadsheets, religious pamphlets, *oraciones* (prayersheets) and popular songbooks – many illustrated by Posada – at country fairs, and I loved going with him. In Veracruz near Catemaco, where there is a lot of witchcraft, we would sell incantations for lovers or for casting good and bad spells.

When I became a wrestler I began to carry

Posada's prints with me on my travels. I organised an exhibition of Posada's work in Peru when I went there to fight. Another time, I remember, I had to go to a town in Chiapas. I went to the authorities to ask if I could show Posada's work, but they had never heard of him and they refused. All the prints were mounted, so next day I pinned them up in the arcades of the main square. More and more people came to see them, and the local newspaper ran an article criticising the authorities. They apologised, and offered me a hall, but I turned them down.

Today Posada is a world figure. In Mexico he has motivated many artists and craftworkers. Take the Linares – the inspiration for many of their papier mâché figures comes directly from Posada.[9] Other artists, working with different materials, are also exploring the theme of death. I don't think they are laughing at death. I don't imagine that Posada was laughing at death! I am sure Mexican artists fear death as do the rest of us, but they make death a part of their creation. They have a profound respect for death, because death is a part of life.

The Festival of the Dead, and the weeks which precede it, are a beautiful time. We believe the dead will grieve if we don't provide them with offerings. They might think that we look down on them, or imagine that we don't want them visiting us and troubling us here on earth. The dead feel sad if we don't receive them joyfully, but they love it when we welcome them with music. Male friends and relatives often like to be offered booze, although female guests might prefer a more sober reception!

Because the dead are here for a short time only, you must make the most of it. Dead children arrive on 1 November; they come at midday, and leave at three in the afternoon. They are with us for just a few hours. Dead adults arrive on 2 November; they, too, come at midday and leave at three.

Preparations start a day or even a week ahead. Most *ofrendas* are arranged on two or – more rarely – three levels, like you get in churches. Usually this is a table with a smaller raised area at the back. There will be one or more photographs of the deceased, flowers, and a picture of the Virgin Mary – the Virgin of Guadalupe or a different one. We light candles, and many people burn oil. This is to illuminate the path the dead will take. We also burn *copal*, as in pre-Hispanic times, and provide water for purification.

In our house we like to offer a lot of food, so

that the dead can eat as much as they want. We provide sweet breads, and seasonal fruits such as bananas, apples and oranges. We give them pumpkin cooked in sugar, and *tejocote* fruits in syrup; we make sweets using *camote* and *biznaga*. And we prepare dishes of *mole*. You can put out whatever the departed liked in life – or you put out any food, regardless! Some people offer *pulque*, or bottles of *tequila*. Others put out cigarettes: popular brands would be *Alas* or *Faros* – never a posh one like *Raleigh*! This is the way we do things in the City of Mexico. People offer what they can afford. Today, however, rising prices are undermining all our traditions. It costs a lot to receive the dead.

We have a duty to visit the cemetery on 1 or 2 November. Some people go on 31 October to tidy graves, but in Mexico City advance visits

128. Portrait of Madero by José Guadalupe Posada from *Calaveras del montón* (Skeletons on the heap), 1910. A wealthy lawyer from the north of Mexico, Francisco I. Madero opposed the reelection of Porfirio Díaz, and became President of Mexico in 1911.

are unusual. The Panteón de Dolores, the Panteón Jardín and all the other cemeteries are full on the 1st, and even fuller on the 2nd! By nine in the morning everything is in full swing. In the Panteón de Dolores people often sing and play guitars among the graves.

Beliefs and customs vary from region to region. For many people the dead have a very real presence. In parts of Michoacán, on 1 November, it is usual to spend the whole night in the cemetery, and to share food and drink with the dead. Once, in Tzintzuntzan, I saw a beautifully decorated grave. A woman was tending it and arranging flowers. Later, my friends told me to return to this grave. The woman had lifted up her skirts: she was lying on the earth of the grave, and she was going through the sexual motions . . .

I remember too, long ago, visiting an elderly woman in the City of Puebla. It was 1 November, and I was shown into the dining room. She was sitting alone at the table, where a large meal had been served. 'Make yourself at home', said her daughter. 'She'll be with you in a moment.' To my surprise the old woman seemed to be communing with invisible guests. Later her daughter explained that she had been receiving the dead.

Few people today would think of sitting down to eat with the spirits. Myself, I find the idea quite spooky. I have no desire to talk to the dead – that's something for spiritualists! I remember, also, witnessing a *peyote* ceremony at Real del Catorce with some Huichol friends.[10] They wept, and told me afterwards that they had seen and talked with their dead. But this sort of thing bears no relation to the Festival of the Dead. Nor do the incantations and spells invoking death that are sometimes used by sorcerers and healers. Printed prayersheets, of the kind we used to sell at Catemaco, can be used for good or evil.[11] There are two or three which call on *La Santísima Muerte* (Most Holy Death). For a *limpia* (ritual cleansing),[12] some people employ a carved skeleton of bone; they may also use powdered bones, prepared when the moon is full. The Sonora Market, here in the city, always has an array of magic powders, potions and differently coloured candles, which honour *La Santísima Muerte*.

Children in Mexico grow up with death.

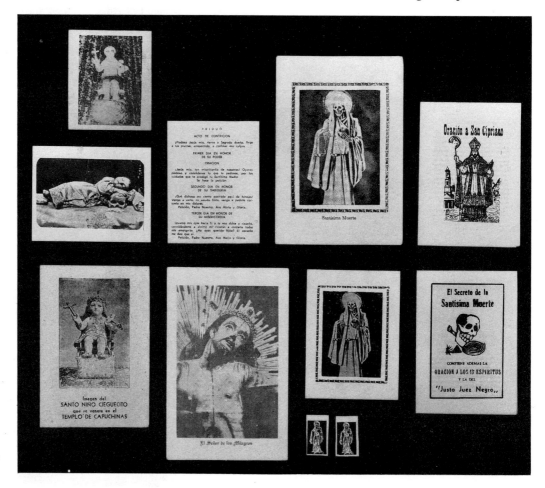

129. Prayer sheets (*oraciones*) and religious images, some for *La Santísima Muerte* (Most Holy Death). Mexico City. H 3 to 13 cms

View of the cemetery at San Gabriel Chilac, Puebla, showing a family mausoleum and graves. In the foreground are wooden crosses ornamented with stylised rays of light; the names of the deceased are painted upon plaques in the form of hearts, flowers and open missals.

PLATE 25

a. Maurilio Rojas (left) and family holding papercuts they produce for sale at the time of the Day of Dead. San Salvador Huixcolotla, Puebla.

b. Traditional sweet for the Day of the Dead in the form of a heart made from *dulce de pepita* (paste made of sugar and squash seeds) decorated with a hand holding a bunch of roses. Toluca region, State of Mexico. L 18 cms

PLATE 26

Painted pottery candelabrum in the form of a
'Tree of Life' decorated with an angel, skulls,
birds and flowers. In the style of Aurelio Flores.
Izúcar de Matamoros, Puebla. H 65 cms

Papier mâché figure of *La Catrina*, a character made famous by the engraver
José Guadalupe Posada in the late nineteenth century. The figure of *La Catrina* is
today much identified with the celebration of the Day of the Dead. Made by the
Linares family, Mexico City. H 129 cms

PLATE 27

PLATE 28 *overleaf*

Figures of skeletal newspaper
vendors made from painted
wire and papier mâché by the
artist Saulo Moreno. H 43 cms

previous page PLATE 29
**Male *Xantolo* dancers dressed as women during celebra-
tions for the Day of the Dead in Zapotitla, Hidalgo.**   PLATE 30

Procession for the Day of the Dead in San Juan Bautista, California U.S.A.

PLATE 31   **The performers are from the *Teatro Campesino* (Rural Theatre Group).**

**Children in the Nahua village of Atla, Puebla, making a path of *cempasúchil*
petals to lead the souls back to the cemetery after the Day of the Dead.**   PLATE 32

Even their toys teach them about mortality. When death is made of sugar, they eat it. When it is made of chocolate, it tastes even nicer! As a child I too played with death. Before the festival my father bought me market toys of pottery, cardboard, paper and wood. There were two toys that I particularly liked. One was a skeleton on a stick; it had arms and legs which vibrated on springs. The other was an articulated skeleton with movable hands and feet on threads. You could also buy pottery skulls with jaws that opened and closed if you pulled a string, and painted skull masks of papier mâché. These masks were sold again during *Carnaval*. I still have one somewhere – it must be over fifty years old! There were also sugar figures in abundance, shaped in all the ways that they are today; these we bought in the sweet market of Ampudia, just off the main market of La Merced.

It was customary, at this time of the year, to ask for donations. As a small boy, I would say '*Calavera* . . . Give me my *calavera*.'[13] We made holes in cardboard boxes and lit candles inside; then we would walk through the streets, asking passers by for money. With the proceeds we bought sweets and small toys. In the old days everyone asked for their *calavera*, and my grandfather printed delightful rhyming requests. Shoe-cleaners, roadsweepers, barbers, bath-house attendants . . . , all used to ask for their *calavera*. They would hand you a printed verse, and expect a coin.

Children today still ask for money, but many now put their candle in a hollowed-out pumpkin, with holes for nose, eyes and mouth.[14] No longer do they ask for their *calavera*; instead they want money for Halloween! The United States is a close neighbour, and attitudes here in Mexico are changing. Children are growing up with the idea of Halloween. On 31 October young people flock to fancy dress Halloween balls. All this is culturally alien, and it is part of a much wider problem.

We are being infiltrated by North American values: our roots are being attacked by business interests, and our heritage is being undermined by advertising and television. American-style stores, such as Woolworth and Sanborns, are

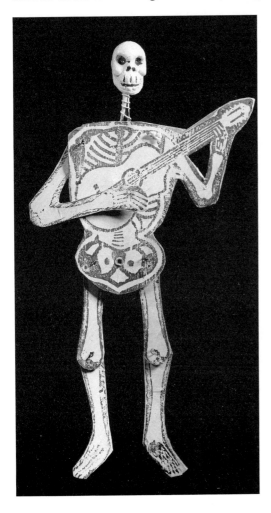

130. Toy puppet of printed card with a pottery head. Mexico City. H (approx.) 27 cms

131. Metallic papercut with a full-figure representation of *La catrina*. San Salvador Huixcolotla, Puebla. H 40 cms

129

promoting Halloween in an effort to increase sales, and many Mexicans are being seduced. This process starts with the well-off, who prefer North American and European culture to their own. But the effect spreads.

If we don't take care of our traditions, they will die. Sadly, our government is not doing enough to preserve them. Sometimes you will see 'official' *ofrendas* in schools and government buildings, but these often include witches and goblins! Mexican festivities and Halloween are being muddled up together in a totally incoherent way. It's the same at Christmas. You get Mexican nativity scenes, but you also get Christmas trees and Father Christmas. These have long been popular in North America; now they're taking up residence here! In the heart of this city, in the Alameda Park, children are photographed each year with smiling Father Christmases. Imagine how confusing this could be. Mexican children are losing touch with their

traditions, and this will be a terrible loss for future generations. We will become like the people of Costa Rica, who live and think like North Americans! In parts of northern Mexico this is already happening. If we want to hold on to our customs and beliefs, we must make an effort, and the government must lead the way. We must keep stressing that Halloween is not Mexican, that it is alien to the Mexican sensibility.

I hope, after my death, to be welcomed in time-honoured fashion by my relatives and friends. I hope the Festival of the Dead will never die. Sometimes, if I think about my own death, I feel afraid. Many of those I have loved have died in my arms. Who knows what awaits us. When I die I want there to be music, I want people to dance, to get drunk and to feel no sadness. I think it will be beautiful to die and to journey into the unknown.

132. Toy masks of papier mâché from Celaya, Guanajuato. H (approx.) 21 cms

Víctor Fosado Vázquez

(formerly Mexico City)

Víctor Fosado Vázquez is a distinguished jeweller. Born in Mexico City, he now runs a small gallery in Cancún. In 1974 he was one of several advisors on 'La Muerte: Expresiones mexicanas de un enigma' ('Death: Mexican Expressions of an Enigma'), a major exhibition hosted by the Universidad Nacional Autónoma de México. His love and deep understanding of popular art were acquired at an early age. Víctor's father, Víctor Fosado Contreras, was the founder of 'Víctor: Artes Populares Mexicanas', a specialist shop committed to selling only the finest examples of popular art. Old Don Víctor was among the first to commission work from Roberto Ruiz, Pedro Linares, Saulo Moreno and others who today are acclaimed artists in their field.[1]

In Mexico, our sense of death is absorbed as if by osmosis. It is shared by farmers, factory-workers, doctors and artists, and it finds expression during the Days of the Dead in toy funeral processions, sugar skulls, and skeletons painted on breadshop windows. It even appears in children's songs. The other day I heard a small child singing:

At six o'clock the skeletons cut their cake
At seven o'clock the skeletons go to bed
At eight o'clock the skeletons are all asleep.

This verse is about the daily events in a child's life, yet it takes the form of a *calavera*. When children sing it, they are visualising themselves as little skeletons, and accepting the idea of death in a healthy and natural way. Non-Mexicans, of course, might consider this attitude unnatural. Imagine the furore in Switzerland, for example, if a breadshop were to paint skeletons on its windows, or if a sweetshop were to sell sugar skeletons to children! Such events would be regarded as macabre and strange in any country where the prevailing view of death is different from our own.

Nothing remains static, however. North American influence, especially on city children, is growing. Although they celebrate the Days of the Dead, they are surrounded by the imagery of Halloween. This is the reality of life in

133. Víctor Fosado Vázquez at home in Cancún, near the north-eastern tip of the Yucatán Peninsula.

Mexico City or Monterrey. Yet Mexican children seem able, as our ancestors were in the wake of Conquest, to reconcile apparently conflicting notions. They retain the Mexican view of death, yet adopt the most attractive features of Halloween. They may enjoy dressing up as death – death in this case being cheerful, not spooky – yet also buy skulls and skeletons of sugar.

Contemporary craftworkers often mingle old and new styles in a similar way. Plastics, metallic paper and acrylic paint offer new creative possibilities. Alongside traditional toys you'll find plastic skull-masks and skeletons of rubber, twentieth-century skeletons driving cars, and cardboard skeletons with Batman painted on their chests. Workers in papier mâché now make Halloween masks of witches and monsters, while continuing to produce skull-masks with brightly coloured eye sockets and flower-painted cheeks.

This fusion of traditions has given rise to wonderful things in the field of popular art. Think of the 'trees of life' of Metepec. They illustrate, in a highly elaborate narrative form, the fusion which has taken place over centuries.

Themes vary according to the season. Sometimes they show the Creation, or Noah with his ark, because Mexicans are drawn to the exuberance of nature. During the Days of the Dead, they may offer a vision of Hell. Works such as these, shaped in a spirit of enthusiasm and enjoyment, are true expressions of popular culture. The Linares family in Mexico City or the Soteno family in Metepec have absorbed a range of influences.[2] So too have many indigenous artists – the Huichol,[3] for example, remain within a native tradition, while adopting traits from outside their own culture.

Artisans in Mexico rarely study their calling in a school or college. They learn their skills from parents or neighbours, and express their emotions and beliefs through their creations. They are on the same level as people who buy their Judas figures at Easter, or their flower-vases and candlesticks for the dead. Traditionally, makers and purchasers have shared a common culture. This balance is changing, however. Production is increasing, the market is widening, and the imagination of our artisans is growing.

Mexico's escalating population is a crucial factor. Twenty years ago villages were smaller: where there were once twenty artisans, there may now be fifty. With this proliferation comes a new competitive spirit. Individual craftworkers are competing with one another to produce the best figure or the best candlestick. This sense of rivalry can also affect communities. During the Days of the Dead villages near Xochimilco, in the Valley of Mexico, strive to have the best decorated graves and the most ornate *ofrendas*.[4] Sometimes this determination leads to scenic displays of theatricality – to rock-and-roll bands dressed as skeletons, and neon-lit displays in the cemetery.

By definition, 'popular art' means that something is both 'art' and 'popular'. Changing circumstances throw up certain paradoxes, however. Arts once considered 'minor' are increasingly accepted as 'major', and many artisans now expect just recognition for their achievements. They sign their work and raise their prices. Their output, beyond the price range of the average Mexican, is increasingly aimed at collectors from outside the community. Their work will be exhibited in art galleries, or museums of 'folk' art around the world, and bought by people with money who want to decorate their homes. It has transcended the term 'popular', yet, confusingly, it is still 'popular art'.

134. 'War': papier mâché figure representing one of the Four Horsemen of the Apocalypse. Made by the Linares Family of Mexico City, it forms part of a much larger ensemble. H (approx.) 210 cms

Víctor Fosado Vázquez

This transition will have negative results. As artisans change their intentions and their audience, they run the risk of losing those qualities which originally shaped their work. Words which spring to mind are 'ingenuousness' and 'freshness', but I prefer 'authenticity'. It is right and proper that artisans should improve their status and their way of life, but they and their children may lose the ability to create naturally. Each generation will be driven to surpass the one before, to be famous and appear on television. The harder they push themselves, the further they will travel from the context of function and ritual which once determined their effects and ideas.

Fortunately Mexico still has 'everyday popular art' for use in the community, made by 'authentic' artisans without number. Some may raise their prices, and acquire a colour television, a breezeblock house or more comfortable chairs – this is their right. The outward form of their lives may change, yet their chosen form of expression remains their own. Maybe their children won't all follow in their footsteps – some may go to university and become professional people. Maybe their way of working differs from that of their predecessors, but their output remains 'authentic'. The vitality and dynamism of popular culture must not be lost.

This situation is parallelled by contemporary celebrations for the dead. *Ofrenda* is a collective term for the foods, fruits, flowers, photographs and decorations which we offer our deceased during their brief time on earth. Some people prefer the term *altar de muertos* (altar for the dead), but I think they are wrong. An altar is used during a religious ceremony, yet these offerings do not in themselves constitute a ceremony. I suggest, therefore, that 'offering' is a more accurate term. Today *ofrendas* in city homes are often 'sophisticated', with elements of invention. Less and less do they adhere to the traditions of a given region. What matters most, however, is the underlying motivation. If families feel an urge to make an *ofrenda*, then they are faithful to the spirit of the festival. By remembering their dead each year, they are honouring an ancient custom.

I'm sometimes asked to compare the attitudes of Indians and rural Mestizos. Predictably, celebrations for the dead reflect major differences in their ways of life. Indians have a profound respect for the dead. Through their *ofrendas* they offer everything they have, everything the earth provides. Mestizos, as the term

135. Pedro Linares surrounded by papier mâché figures. Mexico City.

136. Roberto Ruiz and his wife beside his work table. Ciudad Nezahualcoyotl, Distrito Federal.

137. Oscar Soteno with a newly fired pottery 'tree of life' commissioned by the British Museum. Metepec, State of Mexico.

133

implies, have a mixed heritage from Colonial or more recent times. They tend to imitate foreign, never Indian, ways. When they decorate their homes, they are drawn most often to foreign styles. This is the nature of *mestizaje*, and it is apparent in their *ofrendas*. Instead of home-woven *servilletas*, you may see a plastic cloth imitating lace. Instead of handmade beeswax candles, there may be factory-produced candles of paraffin wax, or mould-made candles with angels. Instead of earthenware, there may be white porcelain. When offering food and drink, Mestizos use the best cups and plates available. Sometimes these are newly made by a Mexican firm such as Ánfora; more rarely, if the family had European connections, they may be inherited Delft. Despite these and other outward differences, Indians and Mestizos share a common cause: they are offering their best to the departed. In Indian homes the dead are given locally grown *cacao*, ground on a *metate*; in Mestizo homes they are offered factory made chocolate bars with well known Mexican or North American brand names. The intention remains the same. For Indians and Mestizos alike, this festival is sacred yet festive. Both are engaged in making an offering, an *ofrenda*.

Among 'educated' city-dwellers, this sense of the 'sacred' has diminished, and intimacy with death has lessened. The dead are still remembered, but communication with them becomes more difficult; the dead are honoured, yet increasingly they become marginalised. Although this process seems inevitable, I respect Government attempts to reinforce our traditions. If organisations like the DIF[5] show support for the Day of the Dead and for popular culture in general, then I think this is positive.

Why, you may ask, should the Government worry about our traditions? I think this is clear: the goal is social and political stability. The DIF was formed to foster family values and family well-being. In Mexico the family is still a powerful force. Understandably therefore, the Government encourages loyalty to one's family, one's region and one's traditions. It would be optimistic to imagine that everyone now upholding tradition is doing so out of deep conviction. There is a strong element of snobbery and affectation, and many people are merely following the official line. Some, I have

138. Detail of a recent *ofrenda* organised in honour of Diego Rivera by Dolores Olmedo. Staged in the Anahuacalli (the Rivera museum), it takes a different form each year and attracts large numbers of visitors. Mexico City.

no doubt, use their *ofrendas* to impress their neighbours, decking them out like Christmas trees with fairy lights. Nevertheless, I'm glad that interest is being maintained. With or without feeling, for the right or the wrong reasons, our traditions are being promoted and perpetuated.

I want, in passing, to mention the public *ofrenda* dedicated each year by Dolores Olmedo to Diego Rivera.[6] Like the artisans I have mentioned, she uses all the means at her disposal. Flowers in abundance, skeletons of papier mâché, colourful papercuts, painted pottery figures – traditional and non-traditional elements – are freely combined. Of course it's an eclectic creation, of course it's theatrical invention! But what matters is her sincerity, and the fact that innumerable visitors share in her *ofrenda*. By ensuring social contact, it is fulfilling one of the most important functions of all *ofrendas*. Indians and Mestizos visit the *ofrendas* of relatives and friends in the countryside; Doña Lola's *ofrenda* is visited by the inhabitants of Mexico City. So, although purists may complain that her *ofrenda*, and others like it, are pretentious and elitist, I think they are as valid as more traditional kinds.

Offerings, in pre-Hispanic times, were buried with the dead. Today they are set out at home on tables, or even, in some places, displayed on the top of graves. The continuity is clear, yet post-Conquest history is shrouded in mystery and speculation. Those who make *ofrendas* today know little of these distant origins. If asked, they may reply: 'This is the way our parents made them', or 'This is the way we honour our dead'. We can explain why we make *ofrendas*, but not how the custom evolved. And yet, whether we live in small villages or in neon-lit cities, we are sure of one thing: our pre-Hispanic past is with us still. Like our forebears, we are living with death.

139. Miniature figure of carved bone showing a skeleton bride in nineteenth-century dress. Made by Roberto Ruiz. Ciudad Nezahualcoyotl, Distrito Federal. H 7.7 cms

140. Skeleton figure of a
widow with pottery head
and arms; her clothes are
of black crêpe paper.
Oaxaca City. H (approx.)
18 cms

141. Figure of *La Catrina*
with skeletons and flowers,
carved from bone by
Roberto Ruiz, the
celebrated miniaturist.
Ciudad Nezahualcoyotl,
Distrito Federal. Shown
actual size.

Appendix

142. Poster advertising Day of the Dead celebrations in Mixquic, Distrito Federal, which annually attracts increasing numbers of visitors.

The following is an extract from an essay on the subject of the Day of the Dead in Mixquic, especially written for this book by Dr Elizabeth Baquedano Meza. There is unfortunately not space to include her description of the archaeological history of Mixquic. Dr Baquedano is a Mexican resident in London and author of a thesis with the title Aztec Death Sculpture *(Baquedano: 1989).*

The Day of the Dead in Mixquic

Mixquic is a town on the outskirts of Mexico City. It has a long tradition of celebrations in honour of the dead. What follows is a description of the events there at the time of *Todos Santos* drawn from observations during the past three years and incorporating information from local informants.

Mixquic is located on Lake Chalco. It depends upon the traditional highly productive *chinampa*[1] system of cultivation. Important for this reason since pre-Hispanic times, it is today

also a centre for recreation: boats take people along the canal system between the *chinampa* beds.

Mixquic has long been one of the most renowned centres in Mexico because of the manner in which the people of the town celebrate their dead: with music, with competitions for the best-decorated boat and for the best 'offering' within the houses.

At the time of *Todos Santos*, the women cook all kinds of food for their relatives, their guests and for their dead. On the lake, the owners paint their boats and make them ready for special tours around the lake and canals. Market-gardeners are busy gathering flowers from their fields to take to the market or to sell outside the cemetery.

The cemetery in Mixquic is the focal point of the celebrations. The graves are cleaned before 31 October, and the families bring candlesticks and vases for flowers. The streets of the town which lead to the graveyard and to the central square, where many activities take place, are also specially cleaned. The civic authorities make arrangements for temporary parking

Mixquic

areas, and the whole community is involved in the preparations for the festival. The *Delegado* (local mayor) inaugurates the exhibitions, presides over the competitions and takes a share in the preparation of special events.

Everyone makes ready to receive the souls of their deceased relatives. In some nearby villages people erect arches of flowers around the doorways of their houses to welcome the arriving souls. The images of saints attached to the outer walls of houses are cleaned; some houses have instead tenoned stone skulls of pre-Hispanic date by way of decoration. Sometimes one sees an elderly person with an incense burner seated by a house entrance to guide the souls to the place where the offering has been set out. The souls of the dead come to take an active part in the life of the household where they once lived. The families try to please the souls, who have almost the status of saints and can intercede on the family's behalf in times of physical or economic hardship. Many of these practices are obviously of ancient origin, such as the making of chocolate for the dead, which was also an important part of offerings to the dead in pre-Hispanic times.

The Days of the Dead: Sacred and Profane

Death among the people of Mixquic embraces two concepts. On one hand, the act of dying (the end of life) and on the other, the personification of death as an omnipresent force. In Mixquic, death seems one aspect of life. It is the object and subject of jokes. If there is a fear of death, it has been masked and in modern Mexico, appears in the guise of entertainment. The Day of the Dead in Mixquic is both a fiesta and a day of mourning.

First, at midday on 31 October the church bell tolls twelve times. This is taken as the signal for the arrival of the souls of dead children. Some local people imagine the event to be as if the children were coming out of school, happy and smiling, gathered in a group to meet their loved ones for a brief twenty-four hours. At home their relatives have an offering ready: a table ornamented with white flowers, glasses containing water and a dish of salt. There is a candle to symbolise each dead child of the household. There are pottery figurines and toys for the children to play with. When the bell tolls, the families light the candles and the incense burners containing *copal* resin (*bursera*

143. Grave with decorations for the Day of the Dead in the cemetery at Mixquic, Distrito Federal.

139

jorullensis) and incense. After seven o'clock in the evening, the children are 'fed' with *atole*[2], chocolate and sweets.

On 1 November (All Saints' Day), between eight and nine in the morning the souls of the children are served breakfast: they are given *atole*, chocolate, bread and fruits. At twelve o'clock the church bell tolls again to announce the departure of the children. Again the bell tolls twelve times signalling the arrival of the souls of the adults. They are greeted with marigold and carnation flowers.

Marigolds are known by the Náhuatl name of *cempoalxochitl* (*Tagetes erecta*), meaning 'flower of twenty petals'. In present-day Mexico this flower is synonymous with the celebrations of the Day of the Dead and it abounds in the graveyard and upon every household altar.

During 1 November, frequent visits are paid to godparents, godchildren and relatives in general. These social gatherings are an extremely important part of the Day of the Dead celebrations, as a means of maintaining social relationships among the members of the community.

In the evening the residents of Mixquic carry round a coffin containing a cardboard skeleton. There are four bearers who also carry candles; people dressed as mourners pretend to be crying but in such a way as to make people laugh. The purpose of this procession is the collection of alms from the householders in the form of food or fruit. One person carries a bell and a candle, another collects the alms in a large sack. A small group of choristers sing whenever the group are admitted to a house. First they place the coffin on the floor, then kneel down to say a prayer which is followed with a song. The person carrying the bell rings it and they ask for a *tamal*[3]. All the gifts of food are kept in the sack and are distributed among the members of the group at the end of the evening.

Other events are organised by the young 'bell-ringers' (*campaneros*), such as asking for a *cerita* (little candle): they knock at doors and ask for the candles which are later taken to the local church; these days they may be given fruit instead.

The Day of the Dead (2 November) is so important in Mexico that people make great efforts and go to enormous expense in its celebration. Women and children put on new clothes for their visits to the graveyard. The church bells toll at four in the afternoon. The inhabitants of Mixquic hurry to the cemetery to

worship with their relatives and friends. In Mixquic, there is a particular way of doing this. People carrying large bunches of flowers, candles, candlesticks and wooden crosses, all head towards the graveyard. This is known as going to 'light-up' (*ir a iluminar*), since in the evening candles are lit next to the graves. All the families go to the cemetery to keep company with the souls of their dead. Members of the family may take turns in watching at the graveside, but someone must be present at all times. People pray, chat, eat and even listen to music which is played outside the church. Musicians willingly play there. Some of the instruments they use are the same as those of Aztec times, for example the upright drum, an instrument that was played before important rituals. The chief importance of all these events is the way in which they keep the community together.

In the evenings, thousands of people gather both in the cemetery and in the market which is open throughout the night, selling food and drinks, sweets, amaranth seed and chocolate skulls. There is a profusion of smells from the incense, food and flowers. There are dancing skeletons, T-shirts, brooches with death imagery as well as fluorescent skulls shining in the dark. The main square, the market and the cemetery are packed with both locals and visitors. There are cameras, television crews and spectators attending one of the evening's events: the judging of the competition for skeletons, or the play of *Don Juan Tenorio*, a play traditionally performed at this time.

The tourists are allowed to enter the houses to see the offerings, take photographs and enjoy the hospitality of the householders. Tradition has it that it makes the dead very happy to see so many people visiting their homes and the offerings dedicated to them.

Domestic Offerings

When a person dies he or she retains a special place in the home. On the domestic altar is an offering which will vary in quantity according to how much time has passed since the death.

From time to time the deceased will be offered a glass of tequila, beer or whatever he enjoyed drinking when alive. Food will also be placed on the offering in his memory. All the dead relatives are honoured and have offerings made to them.

The modern altar for the dead consists of the

following: a table adorned with an embroidered white tablecloth for the souls of the children. At the centre is an image of the patron saint of the family next to a photograph of the deceased. A glass of water is always put out for children but may be replaced with a glass of wine or beer for adults. The altar is then decorated with candles and flowers. In some houses flowers are laid upon the floor in the form a path which leads from the entrance of the house to the offering; it is believed that this guides the souls to their *ofrenda*.

Next to the altar is placed a smaller table on which the offering will be set out. This consists of a tablecloth or sheet decorated with flowers and candles. Bread of all shapes, different kinds of fruit, pumpkin preserved in sugar-syrup and all the dishes that the dead person enjoyed when alive. Beer or other favourite drinks, cigarettes and other goods are included. Incense burners filled with *copal* are placed on the floor. The altar and the offering are arranged by members of the family and are usually in the main room of the house, or a room facing onto the street. The room itself is decorated with paper decorations and paper representations of mountains or the sky. Living plants are added to the decorations. Some households have images of saints or wooden crosses placed upon the most prominent part of the altar, and some have real coffins which are usually hired from funeral shops.

The photograph of the deceased is always part of the *ofrenda*, as are a dish of salt, bread and water that has been blessed. A glass of wine and some rice flour are also set out representing spiritual food. The salt is a symbol of baptism, but has other meanings too: as a seasoning, it represents the savour of life. Biographical details of the deceased, such as the dates of birth and death are written up and displayed; the relatives sometimes write letters or poems dedicated to the deceased. These customs are universal.

In some households a bedroom is cleaned and prepared so that the soul can rest and pass the night in his or her former bedroom; when this is done, no one else uses room. Among other variants, there may be the playing of music for the dead.

It is customary to exchange the foods on the offering with relatives who will take some of the fruit or bread, the wine or soft drinks. Everyone stays up all night and the following day all go to the cemetery to take flowers, candles and sometimes food to the graves. Few people pray in the graveyard since they have already said prayers in the home. The graves are sprinkled with holy water and decorated with flower petals laid out in the form of crosses. Incense burners are lighted at the graveside.

144. *Calavera*, or illustrated broadsheet, signed by J. Cortés (active from about 1900 to 1910). It shows a stall selling candles of pure wax. Vendor and customers are portrayed as skeletons. Entitled *Calavera Comercial* (The Salesman's Epitaph), it opens with the rhyme: 'Here are epitaphs for all vendors, because they were deceitful and dishonest the real thing came to them at last!'

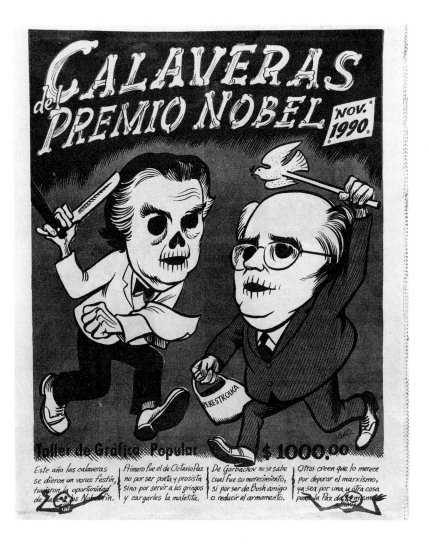

CALAVERAS del PREMIO NOBEL NOV. 1990.

Taller de Gráfica Popular $ 1000.00

Este año las calaveras se dieron un voraz festín, tuvieron la oportunidad de ganarse los Nobel fin.

Primero fue el de Octavio Paz no por ser poeta y prosista sino por servir a los gringos y cargarles la maletita.

De Gorbachov no se sabe cual fue su merecimiento, si por ser de Bush amigo o reducir el armamento.

Otros creen que lo merece por depurar el marxismo, ya sea por una y otra cosa para la Paz de sí mismo.

145. Example of a modern *calavera* for the Day of the Dead, published by the Taller de Gráfica Popular (1990). It shows the celebrated author, Octavio Paz, and President Mikhail Gorbachev in the year both had received a Nobel prize.

there is *pulque*, a drink made from fermented agave juice as well as pumpkin preserved in sugar-syrup and *golletes* (doughnut-shaped biscuits covered with pink sugar).

Amaranth seeds (*alegría*) are a high protein crop grown in this area and used in a variety of ways: to produce an oil, make sweets and as an ingredient in a drink with milk and flavourings. Amaranth seeds and marigold flowers are essential to the offerings for the Day of the Dead.

The contest is an important event in the life of Mixquic. It provides an opportunity for the local people to show the local food specialties; one can even sample them, since some of the boats have charcoal stoves and tables set up where one can eat.

Calaverear

Calaverear is the communal act of sharing offerings and prayers. On 1 November, around ten at night the people of Mixquic gather to go round collecting alms in the form of some part of the food set out on the offerings. The food collected is to be offered to the souls of those who no longer have living relatives. Tradition has it that these souls arrive at ten o'clock and leave again at two on the morning of 2 November. The offering is accompanied by singing and prayers. The official representatives of the church go to gather in the offerings.

The Trajinera Contest

At about five in the evening all attention is centred around the lakeside area. The local people prepare their *trajineras* (shallow boats) for a contest. At the moorings the owners adorn them with flowers and set up an offering on the boat; the offering may be traditional in style with the usual contents as described above or may be more 'imaginative' or fanciful.

The boats decorated with traditional offerings do not often win the contest: typically some special and unusual feature decides the winner. For example in 1990, the winner made up an *ofrenda* using all the traditional products of Mixquic: the *ajolotes* (tadpoles) which locally are made into a filling for *tamales* (*tamales de pescado* or *tlapiques*). There were dishes of the local sauce, *chiles criollos*, and the boat was decorated with all the kitchen utensils needed for the preparation of the foods: *metates* (grinding stones), *comales* (griddles). On some offerings

The Midnight Contest of Skeletons

When all the other activities are over, the main square of the town is filled with visitors who have come to see the 'Skeleton Contest'. This activity is organised by the local authorities. Those who wish to participate have to enrol a few days before the event. Anyone can join in but the contestants are usually craftsmen. The skeletons are made of wood and cardboard and the theme is death, although reference is sometimes made to events of social or political importance: the death of a politician, a train crash, the second marriage of a widower, among others. The scenes set up are usually accompanied by the figure of a skeleton holding broadsheets or pamphlets which make some satirical comment upon death.

Again the winner is usually the most innovative or perhaps the maker of the most realistic skeleton, whether of wood or papier-mâché. Some entries feature life-size skeletons, some, small puppets. One can see boxers, a bull-ring scene or whole orchestras of skeletons playing every kind of musical instrument. There is a judge who decides which work is the most original and which contestant has made the most imaginative use of the materials at his disposal. The prizes which the judge gives out are donated by local shopkeepers, and usually consist of bottles of rum and tequila or baskets of tinned food. This is one of the most popular events in Mixquic, and each year seems to attract more and more contestants.

Don Juan Tenorio

This is the title of a nineteenth-century play written by the poet and dramatist José Zorilla y Moral in 1844. The play, first performed on the Day of the Dead in 1864, found immediate favour with Mexican audiences. Ever since, the play has been performed at this time each year and has become part of the tradition of the Day of the Dead. It is a mixture of religiosity and enjoyment that coincides with the typically Mexican treatment of death. The actors dress in period costume to play out the theme of the seducer Don Juan who courts many women only to leave them. This is a theme which is in accord with the *macho* mentality of many Mexicans. In the nineteenth century, the middle and upper classes enjoyed the verse, and the less well educated enjoyed the broad themes of the play. It remains popular to this day when it is sometimes used as a vehicle for political comment. In Zorilla's version of this story, Don Juan is not damned, but is saved by the love of a true woman, Doña Inés. In Mixquic, the play is usually performed by students.

The ancient Mexicans had belief in an afterlife as is well represented in their sculptures, architecture and pottery and also in their poetry. In Mixquic such a belief was modified by the introduction of Spanish Catholic religion. Today during the festival of the Day of the Dead it is evident that the dead are remembered and everything done to please them. In their turn, because of their status as near-saints, the dead look after their living relatives and intercede before God to ensure good harvests, protection from sickness and the overcoming of misfortune. The souls of the dead 'speak' to their relatives, offering them guidance and advice; occasionally they may also be seen. In Mixquic the souls of the dead come to join the living.

Only for very devout Catholics is this a time of mourning. There is no need to fear death in Mexico where the tendency is towards necrophilia rather than necrophobia. In Mixquic one finds the fusion of two worlds: 'pagan'-Indian and Spanish Catholic customs come together in honouring the souls of the dead.

146. The figure of Don Juan Tenorio from a *calavera* **illustrated by José Guadalupe Posada (1913). José Zorilla y Moral's nineteenth-century play about Don Juan Tenorio is still widely performed in Mexico around the time of** *Todos Santos.*

147. Horn comb with
figure of skeleton and
skull. San Antonio de
la Isla, State of Mexico.
H 12.5 cms

Notes to Part I

Introduction

1. *Cempasúchil*: the Náhuatl name of this flower is romanised in many ways in the literature. This form has been chosen as being the easiest to read that still comes close to the sound of the name. Readers will find *cempoalxochitl*, *zempoalxochitl*, *sempasuchil* and numerous other variations. All refer to the marigold flower of *Tagetes* spp., several of which are native to Mexico. This is the 'flower of the dead', grown for use on the Day of the Dead either in the yards close to houses for personal use or on a commercial scale to send to market. Heyden (1987) quotes the Mexican botanist Gloria Andrade as having identified the species concerned as *Tagetes erecta* and *Tagetes lucida*, a closely related species. Those most commonly used resemble in appearance the African Marigolds of our own gardens. Many grown on a commercial scale are probably hybrids. All have the characteristic 'marigold' scent.

2. Line from a popular song, *La Valentina*: 'Si me han de matar mañana, que me maten de una vez.'

The Day of the Dead

1. Copal is a term applied to many scented resins used as incense in pre-Hispanic Mesoamerica. According to Carmen Cook de Leonard, it comes 'from several trees of the Burseraceae family ... The species mostly used in Mexico for ceremonial copal today are *Elaphrium jorulense* [sic] (H.B.K.) ... and *E. aleoxylon* (Schiede)' (Cook de Leonard: 1971).

Tozzer quotes the *Relaciones de Yucatan* of Mama: 'There is a tree which the Indians call *pom* ... it distills from itself a resin-like turpentine ... The Spaniards call it copal, and it smells very good and has many virtues ... The natives use this fume a great deal, for they offered it as a sacrifice to their gods' (Tozzer: 1941). He also quotes Roys (1931) that in the *Chumayel* MS 'It is called the super odor of the center of heaven ... and the brains of heaven.'

Incense burners are known in Mesoamerica from pre-Classic times, and are still in use today. The early Spanish commentaries, such as the writings of Sahagún, abound in references to the use of incense in religious ceremonial.

2. Although *Todos Santos* means 'All Saints', it is used in Mexico to refer collectively to the two main dates upon which the dead are honoured – 1 and 2 November, the Days of All Saints' and All Souls'. As well as *Día de Muertos* the festival will be found described as *Día de los Muertos* (or abbreviated simply as *Muertos*), *Días de los Muertos*, *Día de los Difuntos* or *Fieles Difuntos*: 'Day of the Departed' or 'Day of the Faithful Departed', or *Día de las Ánimas Benditas*, 'Day of the Blessed Souls'.

3. There is an interesting custom at the time of *Todos Santos* among the Cora, for example, of the western Sierra Madre (States of Jalisco and Nayarit), a people who have retained much of the indigenous religion although they celebrate some Catholic feasts (Grimes and Hinton: 1969). The Cora take 'messages' to the church, (along with an offering) to be delivered to God by the saints. These consist of petitions written on circular pieces of cotton attached to a spray of flowers which are placed about the figures of the saints near the coffin-shaped altar for the dead. The 'messages' request good health and successful harvests. During this ceremony, a group of men (chosen by the 'governor') represent the dead; they are transformed by being covered, both bodies and heads, with unfolded tunics and cloths. So dressed, they visit the houses to gather alms from the household offerings. An account of this is given in Herrasti and Vargas: 1985.

4. For example Madsen, writing of the people of San Francisco Tecospa (Milpa Alta, Federal District) notes that the part of 'heaven' devoted to the adult dead is 'much like Tecospa: people live in the same houses they had on earth, wear the same clothes, work in the fields and keep their dogs, burros [donkeys] and chickens, turkeys, sheep, bulls, and cows' (Madsen: 1960a).

5. For a full consideration of the Spanish-Catholic components of *Todos Santos*, see Nutini: 1988. For descriptions of rural Spanish celebrations of the festivals of All Saints' and All Souls' in modern times, see Foster: 1960; Hoyos Sáinz: 1945; Hoyos Sáinz, Hoyos Sancho: 1947.

6. The dancers perform to music with a particular pulsing beat typical of music for the Day of the Dead. One of the dancers is a man dressed as a woman with his face disguised by ribbons hanging from the brim of 'his' hat. Such transvestite dancers often appear in the dances of *Todos Santos*, especially in the Huasteca (Veracruz). In towns there are large so-called *xantolo* dances with long lines of couples – both male, but with one partner masked and dressed as a woman. The urban 'women' dress in outrageous versions of the current fashions, whereas in rural areas more typical dresses are donned.

7. Stanley Brandes (1988), gives a description of *La Noche de Muertos* (The Night of the Dead) at Tzintzuntzan. It forms part of an interesting analysis of the effects state promotion of tourism has upon the celebration of *Todos Santos*.

8. See Glossary.

9. Other of the many popular names for this flower, a purplish-red amaranth are *pata de león* (lion's paw), *moco de pavo* (turkey crest) and *la terciopelada* (the velvet one). Probably all are of the species *Amaranthus hypochondriacus* (Nutini: 1988). Ornamental amaranths were probably introduced from Europe. In pre-Hispanic religion, the seeds of native amaranths were used in the preparation of a dough from which figures representing gods were made and eaten as part of ritual. Such usage was discouraged by the Catholic Church; possibly the ornamental species were substituted for this reason (Leyenaar: 1980). The seeds are still used today to make a sweet called *alegría* (happiness).

10. The breads of Mexico are of such astonishing variety that there are monographs on the subject. For the Day of the Dead in rural areas, they are often shaped into animal and human figures ('souls'). Some of the anthropomorphic forms have small heads of pottery or paste inserted into them. Many are sprinkled with vivid pink sugar or painted with pink dye. Some have very elaborate geometric and floral patterns marked out in paler dough. The typical city form is the *hojaldra*, a round bread with stylised 'bones' on the upper surface. As well as breads, many forms of biscuits and small cakes will be added to the *ofrenda*.

11. For the different types of candle used in Tlaxcala see Nutini: 1988. Different kinds of candles include candles of beeswax or paraffin wax, of various sizes, some with decorations; cone-shaped candles or those in glass containers.

12. The precise dates and times at which the various categories of souls arrive and depart varies from place to place; apart from such special categories as those who die violently or in accidents, all other souls arrive between 31 October and 2 November.

13. *Mole* is a thick sauce made from many ingredients including chilis and sesame seeds, herbs and spices, and, to add to the richness, chocolate or fruit. There are several types of *mole* with different recipes; some are referred to according to the colour of the sauce, green *mole* or black *mole* etc., others according to the particular recipe or ingredient that gives it its character: *mole de pipián* (pumpkin seeds), *mole de guajolote* (turkey *mole*), *mole prieto* (pork and maize *mole*), to name but a few.

14. *Tortillas* are the thin flat pancakes of unleavened maize flour that have been the 'bread' of Mexico since pre-Hispanic times. In the home they are prepared on a *comal* or griddle of pottery or metal. In the special bakeries (*tortilleras*) that produce them on a commercial scale, they are made and baked in a machine. The patting sound of *tortillas* being formed by hand in rural homes is an indispensable part of the *Todos Santos* vigil. So many are needed to satisfy family and guests that the women continue to make and bake them throughout the night of 1 November.

15. At the Anahuacalli Museum in one of the homes of the painter Diego Rivera, there is each year an *ofrenda*, prepared under the guidance of Señora Dolores Olmedo. It takes a whole gallery and, using the artefacts associated with the Day of the Dead from many regions and papier mâché figures which are specially commissioned, an offering in honour of Diego Rivera is set out. These

represent perhaps the pinnacle of this style of offering, and the *ofrendas* at the Anahuacalli Museum are much visited.

16. This was prepared by COLLHI the *Grupo de Taller de Teatro del Colegio de Lingüística y Literatura Hispánica de la Escuela de Filosofía y Letras, Universidad Autónoma de Puebla.*

17. It transpired that the costumes had actually been worn at a dance held the day before the *ofrenda* was set up. After the dance, the costumes were arranged in the quiet of this inner courtyard beneath a fine Colonial arch. At the dance there had been cross-dressing with women wearing male costumes and vice versa. This perhaps made reference to the transvestite figures of men dressed as women in the *xantolo* dances performed for the Day of the Dead in some rural areas.

The Pre-Hispanic Background

1. Lines from a Náhuatl poem.

2. Náhuatl is the language of the Aztecs, which was spoken extensively in pre-Hispanic Mexico with many regional variations.

3. In Aztec cosmogony there had been several worlds or 'suns'. The sources do not always agree as to the number of creations or the means by which they were successively destroyed. Typically, the present universe is the fifth 'sun', which the Aztecs believed would be destroyed by earthquakes. Of the four creations before our own, the first was destroyed by jaguars (symbolising the element 'earth'), the second by winds, the third in a rain of fire and the fourth in a great deluge. See Nicholson: 1971.

4. Bierhorst: 1974.

5. The Spaniards made records of Aztec history and mythology etc. in both Spanish and romanised Náhuatl. The Aztecs themselves made their records on deer-skin or bark-paper, using a combination of pictographs and glyphs, but had no fully developed writing system.

6. The most useful translation of this creation story appears in Bierhorst: 1974. This short summary is, in part, based upon Bierhorst's version. The original Náhuatl texts relating to Quetzalcoatl are fragmentary, this section coming from the *Leyenda de los Soles* (Legend of the Suns), preserved in the *Codex Chimalpopocatl*, now in the National Museum of Anthropology in Mexico City.

Bierhorst favours the romanisation Mictlanteuctli for the name of the Lord of the Underworld; the more widespread Mictlantecuhtli is used here.

Quail are birds associated with the underworld elsewhere in Mesoamerican literature, see also Bierhorst: 1974.

7. For a fuller description of Aztec religious beliefs and concepts of the universe see Nicholson: 1971, from which the present account is largely drawn. Also León-Portilla: 1963 and Pasztory: 1983.

8. Some sources note nine or eleven as the number of heavenly regions.

9. The Mesoamerican cultural region comprises the modern countries of Mexico, Guatemala, Belize and the western fringes of El Salvador and Honduras.

10. Diego de Durán, *Historia de las Indias de Nueva España y Islas de Tierra firme*, Mexico, 1867–80. León-Portilla (1963) quotes from Father Durán's *History*: 'The need of a temple to commemorate all of the idols worshipped in the land seems to have been felt by King Motecuhzoma. Motivated by religious enthusiasm, he ordered that it be built within the temple of Huitzilopochtli ... They call it *Coateocalli*, which means temple of many gods, because within it, in one room, were located the countless gods of many peoples ... Whoever has passed by ... has surely noticed that great was the number of these gods, of many kinds, faces and workmanship, for they are now strewn all about.'

11. Fray Bernardino de Sahagún (*c.* 1499–1590), a Franciscan friar, arrived in Mexico in 1529, some ten years following the Conquest. He learned the Náhuatl language and compiled a vast body of information concerning every aspect of Aztec lore, belief and observation of the natural world. His informants were the Aztec themselves. His life's work then became the formidable task of transcribing, collating and translating the vast body of accumulated data. The *General History of the Things of New Spain* (*Historia general de las cosas de Nueva España*) forms a part of this work, and along with his other manuscripts is the preeminent source for the study of Aztec life at the time of the Conquest. See Anderson & Dibble: 1950–82; Edmonson: 1974.

12. Heyden and Villaseñor: 1984.

13. Many examples can be cited: Madsen's studies in Tecospa in the Valley of Mexico revealed belief in a heaven where the souls arrived at 'God's jail' which was 'just like the one in Xochimilco' (a nearby town, now virtually a suburb of Mexico City), but also a belief that women who die in childbirth and men who die in battle go directly to the sky world to live 'regardless of their sins' (Madsen: 1960b). The Tzotzils of Chiapas believe that the souls of dead infants go to an afterworld where a tree has leaves that become breasts to give them sustenance (Sepúlveda: 1983).

14. In the *Codex Magliabechiano*, these two feasts are known as *Miccailhuitl* (Feast of the Dead), and *Hueymiccailhuitl* (Great Feast of the Dead). As Elizabeth Boone remarks in her edition of this codex, 'It is apparent that the series of eighteen feasts continues to pose intricate problems for the student of Meso-american culture.' She makes reference to some of the considerable literature that attempts to disentangle the various references to them in the early source material (Boone: 1983).

15. In the modern celebrations for the Day of the Dead, men dressed as women feature in many *xantolo* dances.

16. For a further description and interpretation of this feast, see Graulich: 1989. He suggests an interpretation of the dough figure at the top of the pole as a rendering of a funerary bundle (as it is shown in, for example, *Codex Borbonicus*) with the mask of Otontecuhtli, so that the 'fruit' of the tree could be 'a victim representing Otontecuhtli, or a funerary bundle, or a many-coloured bird,' etc. Any of these representations could be associated with the idea of the dead warrior 'who usually was burned in effigy and became a star during the night, and a colourful bird in the afternoon.' He quotes sources which testify that the 'effigies of warriors who had died on the battlefield were adorned with the attributes of Otontecuhtli, the god who was a prototype of the heroic warrior, "who had been transformed by fire and divinized ..."'

17. Hugo G. Nutini in his *Todos Santos in Rural Tlaxcala* (1988) gives a most useful account of the various early Colonial sources with translations of relevant sections. He notes that the 'interpreter of this codex [*Telleriano-Remensis*], José Corona Nuñez, goes on to say that this celebration of the dead is similar to the feast of the dead among contemporary Mexican Indians, but unfortunately, he does not identify the contemporary Indians, nor does he specify what the similarities are.'

18. Sandstrom and Sandstrom: 1986. This is an excellent account of the use of paper figures among the contemporary Nahua and Otomí. See also Christensen: 1942; Dow: 1973, 1975, 1982; Galinier: 1976 a & b, 1987; Williams García: 1963.

19. Writing of the sugar and squash seed figures sold in modern markets, Leyenaar suggests that they are 'reminiscent of the small figures made in honour of the gods in the pre-Columbian period. These figures were made of *tzoalli*, a paste prepared from *Amaranthus retroflexus*. This plant ... was used at many religious celebrations. This explains why cultivation of the purplish-red amaranth was discouraged by the Catholic Church and perhaps for this reason was replaced by the reddish-purple cockscomb (genus *Celosia*)' (Leyenaar: 1987).

Madsen writes: 'Aztec communion consisted of eating dough images of pagan gods and the flesh of sacrificial victims. An image of Huizilipochtli made from wild amaranth seeds was eaten every year by unmarried men at the festival of Panquetzaliztli ... Bachelors who ate pieces of the image obligated themselves to serve in a temple for one year and to pay a large tribute to the temple priests (Sahagún: 1932, 120–22). Motolinía (1950, 46) wrote that the Aztecs believed the dough images of Tezcatlipoca turned into the flesh of Tezcatlipoca' (Madsen: 1960a).

20. See also Bierhorst: 1985 for an interesting discussion of the *volador* 'dances' and their connection with the 'ghost songs' of Náhuatl poetry.

21. Bierhorst: 1985 has an interesting account of the survival of pre-Hispanic religious practice at the time after the Conquest when a period of 'revitalization' took place, manifest for example in the spectacular dance of the *voladores*. This was performed as a spectacle for the delight of the Spaniards, but 'from time to time suspicions were aroused,

and on more than one occasion the *volador* was actually banned.'

22. There are too many instances to cite, but for example, the Otomí of the Sierra de Puebla and the Nahua of the Huasteca still have strong beliefs in agricultural and other deities, and make offerings to them which include figures of the deities cut from paper. In San Pablito (Sierra de Puebla), this has become something also of a tourist trade, wherein 'books' describing the rites and ceremonies of the native gods are sold to tourists and to Mexico City craft shops. In the area around Chicontepec in the Huasteca however, there still exist Casas de Costumbres (Houses of the Customs), where there is no commercialisation, and the paper figures of the gods are produced and used in ceremonial by the villagers. For many other examples of the survival of pre-Hispanic religious customs, the volumes of the *Handbook of Middle American Indians* may be consulted as an introduction. (HMAI, vols.7 & 8).

23. For a fuller consideration of this subject see Eduardo Matos Moctezuma, numerous publications, especially *Muerte a Filo de Obsidiana*, 1978.

24. For many publications on death in pre-Hispanic Mexico, the works of Eduardo Matos Moctezuma should be consulted. A useful resource are the Dumbarton Oaks conference publications (see Benson: 1975 and Boone: 1983), not least for the bibliographical information they provide. The as yet unpublished doctoral thesis of Elizabeth Baquedano Meza on *Aztec Death Sculpture* (University of London, 1989) gives a very complete analysis of some 400 sculptures, and a summary and assessment of the manuscript and published literature on the subject.

The Spanish Conquest

1. Part of a Náhuatl poem.
2. There is an edition in English of Cortés' letters from Mexico: *Hernán Cortés: Letters from Mexico*, translated and edited by A.R. Pagden, Oxford, 1972. *The True History of the Conquest of New Spain* by Bernal Díaz del Castillo, exists in a 5-volume edition translated by A.P. Maudslay for the Hakluyt Society, 2nd series, nos 23–5, 30, 40, London, 1908–16.
3. The best accounts of these writings are by Miguel León-Portilla. Nigel Davies also makes extensive use of the native accounts in his *The Aztecs: a history*, London, 1973.
4. Hernán Cortés, *Cartas de Relación*, 10th ed., Mexico City, 1978
5. Fourth Letter from Mexico, Pagden: 1971
6. The Franciscan Fray Toribio de Benavente (Motolinía), one of the so-called 'Twelve Apostles', the group of Franciscan friars who landed in Mexico in 1524 to commence the work of methodical evangelisation.
7. For a description of the pageant, *mascarada* and other events in the celebration of the *Glories of Querétaro* held in 1680, see Leonard: 1959.

8. Ricard (1966) writes: 'There is no doubt that the missionaries caused the disappearance of a great number of native antiquities. In 1525 Fray Martín de la Coruña destroyed all temples and all idols in Tzintzuntzan, the holy city of Michoacán. Pedro de Gante, in his letter of ... 1529, stated that one of the great preoccupations of his pupils was to cast down idols and destroy temples under his direction. He wrote again, [in] ... 1532, that for the past six years he had been busy, among other things, in destroying idols.' He gives further examples culminating in the destruction of the manuscripts.

9. Anita Brenner was commissioned to undertake an investigation of Mexican art for the National University of Mexico, and worked with the photographers Edward Weston and Tina Modotti. *Idols Behind Altars* is a fascinating series of essays anecdotal and poetic in style.

Travellers' Tales

1. For general reading and extensive additional references, the following works included in the bibliography of this volume will provide an introduction to the subject of life in Colonial Mexico: Gibson: 1964 & 1966; Elliott: 1989; Meyer & Sherman: 1979; Simpson: 1967; MacLachlan & Rodriguez: 1980 (contains a useful bibliographical essay with literature concerning Colonial Mexico considered under topical headings); Leonard: 1959. These are English language works, but all give references to the equally enormous body of Spanish language sources.
2. Gage renounced Catholicism in 1642. For a complete account of his religious career and life see Thompson: 1958.
3. *The English-American his Travail by Sea and Land ... By the true and painfull endeavours of Thomas Gage, now Preacher of the Word of God at Acris in the County of Kent, Anno Dom. 1648.* See Thompson: 1958.
4. For a full description of sweets see Zolla: 1988; for a complete listing of the sweets and preserves offered at the Day of the Dead in Tlaxcala, see Nutini: 1988. For descriptions of sugar figure and sugar skull making, see pp.108–16 of this volume.
5. See Zolla: 1988.
6. It seems likely that *carnero* here has the meaning 'sheep' or 'ram' or maybe even 'deer', rather than the more common meaning of 'cemetery', 'charnel-house' or 'burying place'.
7. Revelations 7: 'After this I beheld, and, lo, a great multitude, which no man could number, of all nations, and kindreds, and people, and tongues, stood before the throne, and before the Lamb, clothed with white robes, and palms in their hands; and cried with a loud voice, saying, Salvation to our God which sitteth upon the throne, and unto the Lamb. And all the angels stood round about the throne, and about the elders and the four beasts, and fell before the throne on their faces, and worshipped God, saying, Amen: Blessing, and glory, and wisdom, and thanksgiving, and honour, and power, and might, be unto our God for ever and ever.

Amen. And one of the elders answered, saying unto me, Which are these which are arrayed in white robes? and whence came they? And I said unto him, Sir, thou knowest. And he said to me, These are they which came out of great tribulation, and have washed their robes, and made them white in the blood of the Lamb. Therefore are they before the throne of God, and serve him day and night in nshis temple: and he that sitteth on the throne shall dwell among them. They shall hunger no more, neither thirst any more; neither shall the sun light on them, nor any heat. For the Lamb which is in the midst of the throne shall feed them, and shall lead them unto living fountains of waters: and God shall wipe away all tears from their eyes.'

8. This may have been local festive music, however, on the night of 1 November it could also have been the singing of hymns (*alabanzas*). There is a style of singing in Veracruz that includes high nasal tones on the part of male singers.
9. A number of nineteenth-century sugar ornaments have miraculously survived in the Starr collection. These include two sugar skulls, one of which is now sadly in a fragmentary state; the second, a small skull, is intact. See Starr: 1898.
10. *Incidents of Travel in Yucatan*, John L. Stephens, 2 vols., 1843. The account of their first journey was: *Incidents of Travel in Central America, Chiapas and Yucatan*, also in two volumes, 1842.
11. Prescott: 1873.
12. By 1862, after turbulent years of civil war, in which the Church and powerful landowners were pitted against the middle-class, the Mestizos and the Indian population, the economy of Mexico was in ruins. The government of Benito Juárez declared a suspension of the payment of all foreign debts. The European creditors found this unacceptable. Soldiers representing Spain, France and England were sent to take control. The French Emperor Napoleon III conceived the plan of installing as Emperor of Mexico, Ferdinand Maximilian (1832–67), the second son of Ferdinand I, Emperor of Austria. He, and his wife Charlotte (Carlota) of Belgium, went from their castle of Miramar at Trieste to Mexico, where Maximilian sincerely tried to understand and rule the troubled land he found. He was executed by firing squad at the Hill of Bells, Querétaro, on 19 June 1867 at the hands of the Juarista Liberals.

The Here and Now

1. There are many excellent accounts of Mexican history. A volume which supplies good bibliographies of both Spanish and English language sources in addition to a useful text is Meyer and Sherman: 1979.
2. *La Portentosa Vida de la Muerte* by Fray Joaquín Bolaños, 1792, was a work illustrated with engravings of skeleton figures, which like those on the catafalques are 'alive', i.e. they move and act as mortals do.
3. President Porfirio Díaz held office between 1876 and 1880 and again from 1884

to 1911. The latter period became known as the *Porfiriato*. Díaz 'developed his country at the expense of his countrymen' (Meyer and Sherman: 1979). A wealthy middle-class flourished, but the poor of the cities and rural areas suffered deeply. Wealthy taste inclined towards French manners, customs and cuisine. There was plenty for the satirists to tilt at in this society.

4. Esta alegre calavera
   hoy invita a los mortales
   para ir a visitar las regiones infernales.
   Habrá trenes especiales
   para recreo de este viaje
   y no habrá necessidad
   de ponerse nuevo traje.

5. Mira Muerte, no seas inhumana.
   No vuelvas mañana,
   déjame vivir.
   Recordando que el día de mañana,
   clarín de campaña
   nos llame a pelear.

The *corridos* or popular songs of Mexico took on new life at the time of the Revolution, as chronicles recounting the bravery, and the sadness of the times. 'Para saber quién es quién, hay que escuchar los corridos ...' (popular saying meaning 'To know who's who, you must listen to the *corridos* ... ').

6. Dr Atl (1875-1964), the landscape painter Gerardo Murillo Cornadó. *Atl* is the Náhuatl word for water. Dr Atl was an important figure in the revival of interest in national art in Mexico. He joined the revolutionary movement against Victoriano Huerta, and was forced to leave Mexico because of his political activities. Following his return in 1920 he pursued his long career as author and painter.

7. Rockets are set off upon all religious and festive occasions in Mexico; their noise punctuates all ceremonial, marking the completion of each stage of the event.

8. Childs and Altman (1982) quoting Hoyos Sáinz note that this custom also existed in Spain. 'Until the mid-nineteenth century, householders arranged a bed with its richest covers and left it vacant all night to allow the dead to rest during their annual visit' (Hoyos Sáinz: 1945, 46–7).

Frederick Starr (1898) also records an interesting Mexican custom concerning beds: he writes that at Jiménez for 'Nov. 2nd. People go out into the churchyard, carrying their household ornaments and the bed or bedstead on which the dead died; this is ornamented with lace and curtains, white for children, black for grown persons. Those who have no beds take tables and place them over the grave. These they adorn with strips of paper, gold and silver paper stars, paper flowers etc. The churchyard is crowded with smiling, gossiping people, who seem quite careless. Candles are burned at the graves. All sorts of refreshments are sold at the gates.'

Notes to Part II

Introduction

1. According to the National Census of 1980, there are currently 1,317,001 speakers of Náhuatl; together they constitute Mexico's largest indigenous group. The Nahua, who speak the ancient Aztec language with minor dialect differences, live chiefly in the States of Puebla, Veracruz, Hidalgo, Guerrero, San Luis Potosí, Tlaxcala, Morelos, the State of Mexico and the Federal District. Smaller groups also live in Oaxaca, Jalisco, Michoacán, Nayarit and Tabasco.

Fredy Méndez

1. Although the archaeological site is meant here, El Tajín is also the name of the modern-day Totonac settlement nearby. For a description of the archaeological site see p. 83.

2. For additional information about the Totonac and celebrations for *Todos Santos* see p. 61.

3. The *nichos* mentioned here are specially commissioned wooden display-cases; they house locally carved wooden saints, factory-produced pottery saints, and holy pictures printed on card or paper. *Nichos* are often made with highly decorated tops by skilled carpenters in Totonac communities such as Cazuelas.

4. Víctor Fosado explains on p. 133 why he prefers the term *ofrenda* to *altar*. In El Tajín and Huaquechula, however, informants employ both terms, and their choice of words has been respected here. They speak of the *ofrenda* when referring to the offerings, but use the word *altar* to denote the underlying structure.

5. The Aztec solar calendar was divided into eighteen twenty-day months and a five-day 'unlucky' period; the names of the months related to crops and indicated the agricultural origin of this time count. This system was combined with a ritual 260-day calendar based on twenty day names and thirteen numerals. The combination of both calendars permitted the numbering of years in fifty-two year cycles. See also p. 28.

6. Fredy Méndez admires the beauty of the archaeological site, but Candido Méndez, his father, is less impressed. At this point in the conversation, he gave his own point of view: 'The pyramids are pretty but they bring us no profit. Tourists come, it is true, but they pass through, taking their money with them. We need schools, roads, bridges, and other things besides. It's a pity that our community draws so little benefit from the ruins on our doorstep.'

7. The term 'Protestant' is used in a general sense to describe the numerous evangelical sects currently working in Mexico. Froylan Martínez Cuenca and Luis Vivanco also refer to evangelism.

8. Throughout this region tissue-paper cut-outs of varying complexity are widely found. In some homes, however, opaque paper is patterned to show churches and other pictorial devices. Each sheet is then glued on to a second sheet of a contrasting colour. (See fig. 15).

9. La Vigilia (eccles.) eve (of a religious festivity).

10. The *tepejilote* palm (*Chamaedorea tepejilote* Liebm.) derives its name from the Náhuatl words *tepetl* (hill) and *xilotl* (jilote). This small, reedy palm provides leaf blades up to 1.2 m in length.

11. The *palma de coyol* (*Acrocomia mexicana* Karw.) derives its name from the Náhuatl word *coyolli*. This palm produces edible fruits.

12. See *The Day of the Dead*, note 1, p. 145.

13. This is a reference to *espiritualistas* or to *espiritistas*: Spiritualists and Spiritists are two quite distinct movements. Both cure sickness, but Spiritists specialise in curing those who have been 'bewitched'. Spiritism first appeared in Mexico during the 1860s. William and Claudia Madsen (1969) write, 'Men who die by violence materialize in Spiritist temples whenever their spirits are called down to cure the sick ... Spirits of light are supposed to help the Spiritist curer in his efforts to combat the dark spirits, who work for Satanic witches. Nevertheless, Mexican Spiritists are often suspected of collaborating with dark spirits ... Our informants seemed totally unaware of the official conflict between Spiritism and Catholicism.'

14. According to Totonac anthropologist, Crescencio García Ramos (1983), a dead-musician or a dead dancer may be offered the musical instruments or dance costumes that belonged to him in life; these will be placed by the side of the *ofrenda*.

15. It is generally agreed that this outside altar is for *las ánimas solas* (*limaxqanín*). Those who have no living relatives to care for them are given their own *ofrenda*, and denied entry to the house. Other informants, including Filamón Santiago Tiburcio of El Remolino, say that this altar also serves orphans, those who have been murdered, those who have died through drowning, those who have mysteriously died away from home, and those who have committed evil deeds.

Crescencio García Ramos, however, identifies many of these categories with the Day of San Lucas, on 18 October. He writes (1983): 'This day is really the beginning of celebrations for the dead. San Lucas is the patron saint of those who die a violent death: those who are murdered or drowned, and those who die from strange diseases, are guided by evil or by the female deity of water and of rivers (*aktsín*); they are identified as *los malos aires* (harmful winds) which bring sickness.' He makes no mention of food being offered to these visitors on the Day of San Lucas, but confirms that *las ánimas solas* are received during *Todos Santos* as Fredy has described.

16. The *octava* or *ochavario* (eighth day) is celebrated in many areas of Veracruz including the *Huasteca*. In the community of Tancoco, for example, Huastec villagers visit the graveyard on this day; they build *arcos* of leaves and offer food and drink, while dancers perform among the graves. Near Papantla, according to Crescencio García Ramos (1983), the dead have still not withdrawn completely. 'It is believed that on this day they will finally return to the world of the dead; people therefore visit the cemetery, and take an *ofrenda* to guide them on their way, for they will not return until the following year.' He makes no mention of the Day of San Andrés.

17. A man who is *de calzón* wears white cotton drawers. In lowland Veracruz most young Totonac men prefer to wear trousers in their everyday lives.

18. In Mexico the institution of *compadrazgo* extends strong kinlike ties beyond the family. Non-kinsmen may be invited to serve as godparents to children; parents and godparents then become baptismal *compadres* and *comadres*. This relationship is close, intimate but respectful, and involves mutual support. In the *Handbook of Middle American Indians*, H. R. Harvey and Isabel Kelly (1969) describe the formalised ties adopted by the Totonac. 'Close friends may become ritual kin. Between *compadres*, there is great "respect", exchange of gifts, and considerable economic assistance ... In highland Eloxochitlan *compadres* are acquired for certain church rites: baptism, confirmation, first communion, and marriage ... There is also an impressive array of *compadres* in the lowlands. Those associated with church rites are substantially the same as in the Sierra. In addition, if a visiting saint comes to Tajín and a family decides to give a festival in his honour, the host seeks *compadres* to help with the expenses. There are also *compadres* of the cross, which is set up in the graveyard 80 days after death. If one goes to the coast for his first bath in the waters of the Gulf, he seeks a *compadre*. Sometimes a new cane crusher or a new fishing net has such sponsorship.' Fredy is referring here to marriage *compadres*, although later in the interview he explains that his father will be a *compadre de la cruz* (godfather of the cross).

19. The *acamaya* derives its name from the Náhuatl words *acatl* (reed) and *mayatl* (beetle). In parts of Veracruz and Hidalgo, however, the term is used to describe small freshwater crustaceans which are regarded as a delicacy.

20. In Totonac cemeteries, the dead are generally buried with their heads and their wooden crosses to the west. Headstones are rare.

21. The Ceremony of the Cross, which we attended, was in fact held exactly one year after death. In the dead woman's home two tables stood side by side against the wall; the first was for the saints, while the second was for *la difunta* (the dead woman). The new cross, inscribed with the dead woman's name, was placed in front of her *ofrenda*. Two *rezanderos* were present.

Jean Simbrón

1. See *Fredy Méndez*, note 5, p. 148.

2. The archaeologist S. Jeffrey K. Wilkerson writes (1980): 'Weighing the archaeological and ethno-historical evidence, I am convinced that El Tajín's people were of Huastec stock, cousins of the Maya.' 'El Tajín probably was never entirely vacated, but by the 15th century it seems to have become Mictlan, or "place of the dead", referred to in Indian documents.' '... today the ruined city is in possession of the Totonac, who consider it to have been built in the time of their "grandfathers", and still to be the abode of powerful, sacred forces.' Michael D. Coe (1984) prefers when discussing El Tajín archaeology to talk only of a distinctive 'Classic Veracruz' style. 'The tribal name "Totonac" has often been inappropriately applied to these carvings; while it is true that the Totonac now occupy most of the zone in which such remains are found, it may or may not have been they who made them. Archaeologists prefer caution in these matters.'

3. Almanac published in Mexico.

4. Today the ancient buildings of El Tajín are often referred to as *las ruinas*. Out of habit, Juan Simbrón uses the term *ruina* to describe the Pyramid of the Niches when newly built.

5. Juan Simbrón recorded this interview in Spanish, although his first language is Totonac. This translation gives the word 'son', assuming a reference to Jesus Christ. However genders are confused at this point, so Juan Simbrón could actually have intended to say 'daughter'.

6. During the Dance of the *Guaguas* four men climb on to a revolving frame of wood; the weight of their bodies turns the frame like a giant catherine wheel. During the *Voladores*, or Flyers' Dance, five men climb to the top of a tall pole measuring as much as a hundred feet. While one plays a drum and a reed-pipe on a tiny platform at the very top, the other four 'fly' towards the ground, suspended on ropes. Each flyer circles the pole thirteen times before reaching the ground, making a total of fifty-two turns. Before the Conquest, time was calculated in fifty-two-year cycles. Both dances are performed in Papantla during the festival of Corpus Christi; in remote communities they may be performed on holy days to honour a patron saint. For further information on the *Voladores* see p. 33.

7. Maize, beans and squash remain the three staple foods of Mesoamerica. Twenty miles from El Tajín, at Santa Luisa, large-scale irrigation works and hillside farming terraces have been unearthed. Before the Conquest these enabled the people of Santa Luisa to produce an abundance of crops, such as maize, beans, squash, cotton and *cacao*. S. Jeffrey K. Wilkerson (1980) suggests that these crops were probably exported, perhaps as tribute, to the overlords at El Tajín.

8. *Pulque* is an intoxicating drink made by fermenting the sweet sap of the *maguey* plant (*Agave atrovirens* Karw. and other species). S.

Jeffrey K. Wilkerson (1980) notes that *pulque* was central to a pattern of beliefs at El Tajín. The *pulque* cult, imported from highland Mexico, inspired an important sequence of carvings in the South Ball Court; these show 'a sacrificed warrior, in death a semidivinity, asking the gods for pulque. The setting is the Mountain of Foam, mythical source of pulque in the realm of the rain god.'

9. The *tlacuache*, or opossum, is a marsupial of the family Didelphidae.

10. El Tajín is more usually associated with lightning and thunder. According to Michael D. Coe (1984), 'The site derives its name from the belief of the modern Totonac that twelve old men called Tajín live in the ruins and are lords of the thunderstorm ...' S. Jeffrey K. Wilkerson (1980) writes: 'In the heart of El Tajín rises the Temple of the Niches, a shrine to the wind and rain deities, the focus of Tajín religion.' 'In the language of present-day Totonac, the name Tajín (or Taxim) means "lightning" or "place of the invisible beings".'

11. Juan Simbrón refers here to *las ánimas solas* (see note 15 on p. 148). He uses the word *pobres* (poor), presumably in the sense of 'wretched'.

12. Among the lowland Totonac chocolate is an important feature of the *ofrenda* for *Todos Santos* (see also p. 77-8). Interestingly S. Jeffrey K. Wilkerson's description of carvings from the pre-Hispanic site of El Tajín includes a reference to a *cacao*-cult ritual.

13. For an alternative version of this story, as told in Puebla City, see p. 122. This same story is also mentioned by Luis Vivanco of San Salvador Huixcolotla on p. 105. Another version (not included here) was also told to us by Froylan Martínez Cuenca of Huaquechula.

Froylan Martínez Cuenca

1. For additional information on the *ofrendas* of Huaquechula, see p. 66.

2. See *Introduction*, note 1, p. 145.

3. For Totonac attitudes to the *ánima sola* see p. 81.

4. In 1989 we saw an *ofrenda nueva* in the nearby hamlet of La Venta. Built in the Huaquechula style by the family concerned, it was for a dead man; included among the offerings was his revolver.

5. The term *ixcatles* is derived from the Náhuatl words *ichtli* (*ixtle*, or agave fibre) and *cactli* (*cacles*, or sandals). Although such sandals are used for the dead in Huaquechula, they are worn by Nahua women in several villages in the State of Morelos. Made locally in San Felipe Ixcatlán, and in the State of Puebla in the village of Tepemaxalco, they are reminiscent of archaeological examples from the Tehuacán Valley and other regions. Tepemaxalco lies near to Huaquechula, so this may be the community of sandal-makers and firewood-sellers referred to here.

6. Writing about the Nahua, William Madsen (1969) notes: 'Death is the climax of life and requires the most elaborate ritual. The corpse is draped in a shroud and placed on a table. In Ocotepec a cross of lime is placed

under the table to absorb contaminating air from the corpse.' 'In the Sierra Norte de Puebla a cross of sacred marigolds is placed beneath the coffin table ... An all-night wake is held at the dead man's home on the night after his death ... The corpse is buried with food and drink for his journey to the afterworld. Wakes are held every night until a series of nine has been completed. On the ninth night after death the shadow soul in the coffin is supposed to leave the corpse and go to heaven. Various local ceremonies are held to help raise the shadow soul and make sure it gets to its proper destination without returning to haunt its old home.'

7. As mentioned above, many men from Huaquechula go to work in the USA. If they die, their bodies are returned to their relatives. Despite the accompanying death certificates, written in English, families are often left with unanswered questions about the circumstances surrounding these deaths. In 1988 we saw two altars for sons who had died in the USA. One had been shot in Los Angeles; the other had died of a sudden illness in New York.

8. Many rural communities in Mexico have lay-preachers. The role of the *rezandero* in Totonac society is described on p. 76 and pp. 81–2.

Luis Vivanco

1. *Fierritos* are small iron chisels with shaped points. Some artisans in San Salvador Huixcolotla now work with a hundred or more. Varying numbers of paper or polythene sheets are perforated simultaneously, but it can take a whole day to complete a single design.

2. Honoured each year on 12 December, the Virgin of Guadalupe is the Patron Saint of Mexico. Her image is reproduced by countless craftworkers.

3. Luis Vivanco still sells work to the shop 'Víctor: Artes Populares Mexicanas', founded in 1931 and still run by the Fosado family.

4. *La Catrina*, by José Guadalupe Posada, is shown in fig. 127.

5. *Las fiestas patrias* take place on Independence Day on 16 September.

6. In Mexico Mestizo parents usually celebrate a daughter's fifteenth birthday with a mass followed by a party. Its importance is equivalent to a 21st birthday in the UK.

7. This reference to dogs and a river echoes pre-Hispanic beliefs (see p. 27). S. Jeffrey K. Wilkerson (1980) writes: 'At Santa Luisa we found children buried outside the walls of temple precincts. Frequently dogs were placed with them to guide them through the underworld labyrinth.'

8. In San Salvador Huixcolotla, as in other places, various types of bread are produced for *Todos Santos* by local bakers. These include *pan colorado*, literally bread with red colouring, and *pezuñas* (hooves), so called because their shape is reminiscent of the cloven hooves of donkeys or asses. Additional bread forms include *rosquetes* and *hojaldras*.

9. *Memelas* is the local word for *gorditas*. Made from maize dough, they are shaped to contain various fillings.

10. For two complete versions of this same story, see pp. 87 and 122.

Consuelo García Urrutia

1. See *Travellers' Tales* for information on eighteenth and nineteenth-century Mexican sugar figures. As Wenceslao Rívas Contreras remarks in the following interview, the making of sugar lambs and similar figures is a European legacy.

2. In contemporary Mexico *pápalo* is also known as *pápaloquelite*. According to Francisco J. Santamaría (1959) this delicious and aromatic plant is eaten raw. Known to botanists as *Prophyllum coloratum* DC., it derives its name from the Náhuatl words *papalotl* (butterfly) and *quilitl* (vegetable, edible herb). Santamaría states that *chautle* or *chaucle* (spelt *chautl* in the text, in keeping with local pronunciation) is derived from the Náhuatl word *tzaucli*; he refers to a glue, or paste, made by Indians from the root of the *Blettia campanulata* Llave & Lej.

3. *Pateador* is an invented word derived from *pata* (leg).

Wenceslao Rívas Contreras

1. 'Trees of life' are pottery candelabra of an often gigantic size (see plate 7, fig. 137). The Soteno family and others have become famous for the complexity of their work. Trees of life in Metepec portray the Garden of Eden and other Biblical or historical themes. Metepec is also open to modern trends: in 1989 Oscar Soteno peopled several trees of life with characters from 'Batman'.

2. See *Arsacio Vanegas Arroyo*, note 3, p. 150.

3. In the previous interview, Consuelo García Urrutia referred with some alarm to the quantity of sugar skulls offered for sale during the *feria del alfeñique*; here Wenceslao shows a comparable lack of enthusiasm for her craft. There is clearly a degree of rivalry in Toluca between the makers of skulls and the makers of lambs and similar figures.

María Antonieta Sánchez de Escamilla

1. The *cempasúchil* (*Tagetes erecta*), often referred to simply as *la flor de muerto* (the flower of the dead), is discussed in *Introduction*, note 1, p. 145. Cockscomb (*Celosia argentea* L), belongs to the Amaranthaceae family. In Mexico, where it is cultivated for ornament, it is known by several regional names including *mano de león* (lion's paw) and *la terciopelada* (the velvet one). Generally a dark pinkish-red, it may also be beige. (See note 9, p. 145).

2. The term *el son*, which literally means 'a sweet sound', covers an immense and extremely varied category of Mestizo music. Profane and festive, it comprises many regional sub-genres. *El son huasteco* (from the Huasteca region), or *huapango*, is played by three male musicians on the violin, the *jarana* (five stringed guitar) and the *huapanguera* (large eight-stringed guitar). Verses are sung, often in falsetto.

Arsacio Vanegas Arroyo

1. Very little is known about the life of José Guadalupe Posada and still less about that of Manuel Manilla. Their fame today is due in large part to the generation of artists who changed the direction of Mexican art after the Revolution, and who hailed Posada in particular as a forgotten genius and a source of inspiration. The French artist Jean Charlot was one of the first to recognise the importance of Mexican print-making traditions and to signal the important role played by Antonio Vanegas Arroyo. He wrote (1939): '[Print making] ... is narrowly linked to the penny pamphlet, the rhymed "corrido" or the prose "relato" which it illustrates. In Colonial times Mexico received such sheets from Spain, of which a collection dated 1736 exists in the National Museum. But the mestizo did transform such models, as he had already put Spanish santos to somewhat heathenish use. This Mexican style came to maturity with Don Antonio Vanegas Arroyo, circa 1880, when his staff of reporters, poets and artists, published works so homogeneous in style, so beautifully attuned to race and land, as to be almost immediately classified as anonymous.'

2. Jorge Manrique (1440–79) was born into an aristocratic family in Castile. Often described as a warrior-poet, his verses were an adjunct to his military exploits. His most famous work, *Coplas por la muerte de su padre* ('Couplets on the Death of his Father'), offers a vision of Death the Leveller, bringing young end and old, rich and poor alike to a common end. Not an elegy in the strict sense of the term, it exhorts the reader to heed the power of death and the importance of the exemplary life as symbolised by his father, Rodrigo Manrique.

3. The literal meaning of *calavera* is 'skull' or, by extension, 'skeleton'. In Mexico the term is applied to prints which show skeletons miming the activities of everyday life. Published for 2 November, *calaveras* serve as witty epitaphs for the living, and provide an opportunity for political satire and comment. The historical antecedents are described on p. 58. During the government of Porfirio Díaz, José Guadalupe Posada became the master of the *calavera*. Personalities and professions of the time were portrayed as skeletons and accompanied by humorous verses.

4. Very little is known about the life of Manuel Manilla. Jean Charlot (1939) paid homage to the work of Manuel Manilla and offered some rare biographical details: 'One of his [Don Antonio Vanegas Arroyo's] first draftsmen and relief-cut makers was M. Manila (*sic passim*), native of Mexico City. Their collaboration, started in 1882, resulted in some 500 prints. Manila carved on metal, with the whites scooped out as in wood ... We find reflected in his prints Mexican characteristics.' These include 'the chumming with death', and 'women wrapped in

rebozos, tradesmen surrounded by their wares, workers and their tools ... For ten years his art did service through tens of thousands of penny sheets, peddled through fields and cities. In 1892 he stopped working with Arroyo, shifted probably to another manual trade, little dreaming that print-making differs in kind from carpenter or mason's work. He died in '95, a victim of the typhus plague.' By Charlot's time only a few of the original blocks were left. Many had been 'smoothed into nothingness through excessive printing.' Others had been looted during 'political raids aimed at wrecking Arroyo's outspoken presses.' Art historians are still trying to identify Manilla's surviving prints, many of which had been wrongly attributed to other artists including Posada.

5. Chap-books, widely sold in nineteenth-century Mexico by itinerant vendors, were small pamphlets containing popular tales, songs and verses.

6. Two important essays, in which Jean Charlot paid tribute to José Guadalupe Posada, have recently been re-published in Rothenstein: 1989. They are *José Guadalupe Posada: Printmaker to the Mexican People* and *Posada's Dance of Death*.

7. Diego Rivera portrayed Posada in his murals for the monumental stairway in the National Palace in 1929-30. He also incorporated *la calavera catrina* into his 1947 Hotel del Prado mural; converted into a full-length figure, she was shown arm in arm with Posada himself. *José Guadalupe Posada*, a short essay by Diego Rivera, appears in Rothenstein: 1989.

8. Toor, Frances, Pablo O'Higgins and Blas Vanegas Arroyo: *Monografía: las obras de José Guadalupe Posada, grabador mexicano.* Mexican Folkways, Mexico City, 1930.

9. Behind the bustling Sonora market in Mexico City, three generations of the Linares family currently make figures of papier mâché. In his youth Pedro Linares, now a great-grandfather, made seasonal items for different festivals. These included toys for the Days of the Dead, masks for *Carnaval*, 'Judas' figures for Holy Week, and Christmas *piñatas*. Using traditional production methods he also started to make fantastical and brightly painted creatures which he calls *alebrijes*. Skulls and skeletons, inspired by the engravings of José Guadalupe Posada, also joined his repertoire. Today his sons, Felipe and Miguel, continue to make *alebrijes* and *muertos*. They, in turn, have been joined by their sons. In 1986 Felipe's son Leonardo was awarded the National Youth prize for Popular Art. The work of the Linares family can be seen in plates 16, 28; figs 19, 134, 135. In recent years a number of imitators, some trained by the Linares family, have also begun to create papier mâché figures and to forge distinctive styles of their own.

10. 49,519 Huichol speakers were registered in the National Census of 1980. Members of this Indian group live high up in the Sierra Madre, where the states of Jalisco and Nayarit meet. The Huichol have proved more resistant to outside pressure than most other Mexican groups; religious beliefs and ceremonies owe little to Christianity. *Peyote (Lophophora Williamsii)* is a small, spineless cactus with a high mescaline content. Ingested as an hallucinogen, it has the status of a god in Huichol society, and is identified with the deer and with maize. Wirikúta, the land where the sacred cactus grows, lies far outside Huichol territory in the high desert of San Luis Potosí. Once a year, at Real de Catorce, small bands of pilgrims gather *peyote*. This arduous quest is akin to a hunting ritual, for the tiny plants are initially shot with bows and arrows as if they were deer.

11. Lilian Scheffler (1985) discusses the importance of the *oraciones* (prayers) which reached Mexico after the Conquest. 'Many were truly Catholic and sanctioned by the Church, but others were an expression of Christian magic, since they combined elements which were both Catholic and magical ... Many prayers with a magical content became extremely popular during the Colonial era, despite strong opposition from the clergy; as time passed many of these *oraciones* were lost or transformed, while new ones evolved using ancient elements ... Prayers offer a means of increasing power to whoever desires to make contact with the supernatural ... [They] are recited in order to gain the intervention of supernatural beings in various matters; they may be used to regain lost health, to improve finances, to get out of a jam, to avoid danger and to attract or retain someone's love. Prayers of a profane kind which are still in use are dedicated to objects and beings of many kinds: stones with magical associations, herbs, animals, the souls of the dead or saints who are thought to possess a special power over the supernatural. The distribution and use of these *oraciones* is more frequent among Mestizos than among Indians. They are generally sold on printed sheets, which rarely carry the printer's name, in markets or on stalls which are set up outside churches on Sundays and feast days, next to orthodox Catholic prayers.' Lilian Scheffler lists several such prayers; they include *Oración al Brazo Poderoso* (Prayer to the Powerful Arm), *Oración a las nueve velas* (Prayer to the Nine Candles) and *Oración de la Herradura* (Prayer of the Horseshoe).

12. 'The practices of the curers of today are a fusion of Mexican indigenous and European folk methods – massaging, bleeding, cupping, sucking, spitting, sweating, prayers and offerings to pagan gods and Christian saints, as well as to good and evil spirits. Practically all curers use magic, herbs, and mineral and other objects; many perform magic rites.' This brief introduction to an extremely complex subject, written by Frances Toor in 1947, in *A Treasury of Mexican Folkways*, still applies today.

13. The word *calavera* can also mean, as here, a gift or gratuity given during the Festival of the Dead; *calaverear* is to ask for treats. The Mexican custom of asking for donations was described by Frederick Starr (1899). Notes for the town of Aguascalientes state: 'Boys cut out skulls in cloth and attach them to a second piece, square and the size of the hand. With these they stamp designs in flour or chalk on backs. Others are pinned on to coats ... Children ask for "deaths".'

14. Although the hollowed-out pumpkin is generally associated with Halloween celebrations in North America, its use was not uncommon in Spain. Luis de Hoyos Sáinz and Nieves de Hoyos Sancho (1947) observe: 'The small [Spanish] town of Huete is not the only place where small lamps are placed inside a pumpkin, so as to simulate a skull positioned in the open windows of houses, as a more public offering than that which shines in the living room or the kitchen of dwellings ...'.

Víctor Fosado Vázquez

1. For information on Pedro Linares, his family and his followers, see note 9, this page. Saulo Moreno, who works with wire and papier mâché, has forged a unique style (see plate 30). Roberto Ruiz carves miniatures of bone; in 1988 he was awarded the prestigious *Premio Nacional de Ciencias y Artes* in the category *Artes y Tradiciones*. All three artists have been inspired by the theme of death.

2. For information on the Soteno family and the 'trees of life' of Metepec, see *Wenceslao Rivas Contreras*, note 1, p. 150.

3. For information on the Huichol, see note 10, this page.

4. For a description of graveyards and *ofrendas* in Mixquic, in the State of Mexico, see Appendix.

5. The DIF (Desarollo Integral de la Familia, or Family Development Agency) is a government organisation. The DIF often organises *concursos* (contests) of *ofrendas* during the Festival of the Dead.

6. Dolores ('Lola') Olmedo was a patron and a close friend of Diego Rivera; she is the Director of the Museo Frida Kahlo and the Museo Diego Rivera-Anahuacalli. Each year she organises a large and impressive *ofrenda* in Rivera's honour.

Appendix

1. In *chinampa* cultivation, layers of vegetation and mud are piled up in shallow areas of the lake waters to form long beds surrounded by water on at least three sides. This highly productive system of cultivation was used in pre-Hispanic times to grow maize, beans and squash, chili, amaranth, *chía (salvia chian)*, and innumerable other vegetables and flowers.

2. A drink made of maize meal flavoured with fruit or chocolate.

3. Steamed 'cakes' of maize dough filled with chicken or pork in a chili sauce.

Glossary

accidentados those who die in accidents.

aguardiente literally, firewater. Alcoholic drink made by distilling sugarcane juice.

alabanza Catholic hymn of praise.

alfeñique sugar paste.

angelito literally, little angel; here the term refers to the soul of a dead child.

ánima soul, generally of the dead.

ánima sola soul in purgatory; soul without living relatives to welcome it during *Todos Santos*. Granted permission to leave purgatory, such souls rely on the generosity of strangers, who sometimes leave them a small *ofrenda*.

barandal literally, railing or balustrade. In the town of Huaquechula in the State of Puebla, the term refers to the borders of hand-punched card that are used to adorn *ofrendas*.

biznaga also spelt *visnaga*. Species of the *Ferocactus*, which gives a fruit with viscous juice and seeds. In Mexico the candied pulp of this fruit is a popular sweetmeat. From the Náhuatl *huitznahuac*, literally 'surrounded by prickles', composed of *huitztli* (thorn or prickle) and *nahuac* (near).

cacao a tropical tree (*Theobroma Cacao* L.); the seeds are used to produce chocolate.

calavera literally, skull. By extension, this term is applied to satirical broadsheets featuring mock epitaphs for the living; these are circulated during *Todos Santos*. The term has a further meaning: at this time of the year children (and adults in the past) ask for *calaveras*, or gifts of money. In some rural areas people visit the houses of their neighbours and ask for a share of the *ofrenda* on behalf of *las ánimas solas*. This custom is called *calaverear*.

camote sweet potato (*Ipomoea batatas*). From the Náhuatl *camotli*.

cempasúchil a marigold often referred to in Mexico as 'the flower of the dead'. Although this is the spelling favoured by Francisco J. Santamaría, there are several other modern variants. From the Náhuatl *cempoalxochitl*, composed of *cempoalli* (twenty) and *xochitl* (flower), because each plant produces many flowers.

chayote green spiny or smooth-skinned relative of the squash. Eaten as a vegetable, fruits of the *Sechium edule* Swartz may be boiled, fried or stuffed.

compadres godparents in relation to the parents of a child. The institution of *compadrazgo* extends strong kinlike ties beyond the family. As described in note 18 on page 149, *compadrazgo* may include a range of other social relationships between non-relatives.

copal scented resin used as incense. Such resins are extracted from trees of the Burseraceae family. From the Náhuatl *copalli*.

feria fair; market.

fieles difuntos faithful departed.

fiesta festival; celebration; social gathering.

hojaldra sweet bread made with eggs for the Festival of the Dead.

ikat method for tie-dyeing yarn before it is woven.

jícama woody vine (*Exogonium bracteatum*); the roots, which are large, watery and sweet, are often eaten raw as a vegetable.

Judas Judas Iscariot. By extension, the term describes papier mâché figures which sometimes take the form of devils and skeletons. Traditionally Judases were decked out with fireworks: these were ignited on Easter Saturday, known in Mexico as the Saturday of Glory.

llorón tearful person. In the town of Huaquechula in the State of Puebla, pottery figures of weeping children (*llorones*) are often used to adorn altars for the Day of the Dead.

mano de león literally, lion's paw. Cockscomb (*Celosia argentea* L).

mestizaje crossbreeding.

Mestizo Mexican of mixed European and Indian descent.

metate grinding stone. From the Náhuatl *metlatl*.

mezcal also spelt *mescal* in English-language dictionaries. Generic term for the hard liquor which is distilled from the *piña*, or heart, of plants belonging to the genus Agave. Roasted *piñas* are crushed; the juice is transferred to fermentation tanks, then to stills.

mole thick and spicy sauce. *Moles* play a pre-eminent role in Mexican cooking; there are many varieties. Dark *mole* is made from chili peppers, *cacao*, sesame seeds and many other ingredients which vary regionally; it is usually eaten with turkey meat. Green *mole*, made with green chili peppers and *tomatillos* (green tomatoes), contains no *cacao*. From the Náhuatl *molli* (sauce or stew).

Náhuatl language spoken by the Aztec and, with minor variations, by the modern-day Nahua. From the Náhuatl verb *nahuati* (to sound clearly like a bell).

nicho niche; the term is also used to describe glass-fronted boxes for saints.

ninin Totonac term for the Days of the Dead.

nixtamal maize kernels soaked in water with slaked lime (calcium hydroxide) for grinding into *masa* (maize dough) for *tortillas* or *tamales*. From the Náhuatl *nextamalli*, composed of *nexatl* (bleach or lye) and *tamalli* (*tamal*).

ocote wood from conifers of the Pinaceae family. Used for burning, it is often sweet-smelling. In English *ocote* is generally referred to as torch-pine or pitch-pine. From the Náhuatl *ocotl* (torch or firelighter).

octava (also *ochavario*) octave, or eighth day of a festival.

ofrenda collective term for the offerings set out for the returning souls during All Saints' and All Souls'. An *ofrenda nueva* is for those who have died during the preceding year.

oración literally, prayer; by extension, this term often refers to printed prayer-sheets.

peso Mexican unit of currency.

panela coarse brown cane sugar.

petate mat of palm or rushes, which serves as a bed in many homes. In some Indian communities the dead are buried in *petates*.

pipián red or green spicy sauce thickened with ground pumpkin seeds and flavoured with chili peppers.

pulque intoxicating drink made by fermenting the sweet sap of the *maguey* plant (*Agave atrovirens* and other large species).

refresco factory-produced soft drink, usually fizzy.

rezandero prayer-maker.

rosquete sweet bread for the Festival of the Dead.

sarape blanket, often with an opening for the head.

servilleta cloth, often used for ceremonial purposes or to cover food.

sombrero hat.

tamal steamed cake of maize dough and lard, wrapped in maize husks or green banana leaves. Recipes vary from region to region. Savoury *tamales* may contain meat, cheese, *mole*, chili peppers, beans and other vegetables. Sweet *tamales* often contain fruit. From the Náhuatl *tamalli*.

tejocote small orange-yellow, bitter-sweet fruit which grows on shrubs or small trees of the genus Crataegus. In the USA it is known as a choke-cherry. From the Náhuatl *texocotl*, composed of *tetl* (stone or hard object) and *xocotl* (sharp-tasting fruit).

tequila regional variant of *mezcal* made from *Agave tequilana* near the town of Tequila in the State of Jalisco.

Todos Santos All Saints' Day. By extension, the term often refers to All Souls' Day as well.

tortilla cooked flat cake made from unleavened maize dough.

totopo crispy *tortilla* made from maize dough, lard, cane sugar and other ingredients. From the Náhuatl *totopochtic* (toasted or fried).

xantolo term used for the Days of the Dead in parts of the Huasteca (States of Veracruz and Hidalgo).

Bibliography

The following, as well as including all works to which mention is made in this book, is a selection of texts which have good descriptions of the Day of the Dead in Mexico as well as dealing with the wider topics of death, wakes, and funerary practices.

Aceves Piña, Gutierre. 1988. *Transito de Angelitos: Iconografía Funeraria Infantil*, catalogue of exhibition in Museo de San Carlos, Mexico

Ades, Dawn. 1989. *Art in Latin America: the Modern Era, 1820–1980*. Catalogue of exhibition at the South Bank Centre, London

Ajofrín, Francisco de. 1958. *Diario del Viaje ... hizo a la América Septentrional en el siglo XVIII*, Madrid. (Mexican edition with introduction, selection and notes by Heriberto Moreno, Mexico, 1986.)

Alarcón, Hernando Ruiz de. *see* Andrews, Hassig: 1984

Álvarez Boada, Manuel. 1985. *La Musica Popular en la Huasteca Veracruzana*, Mexico

Anderson, Arthur J. O. and Dibble, Charles E. (trans and eds). 1950–82. *Florentine Codex: General History of the Things of New Spain [by] Fray Bernardino de Sahagún*, 13 parts, Santa Fe

Andrews, J. Richard and Hassig, Ross (trans and eds). 1984. *Treatise on the heathen superstitions and customs that today live among the Indians native to this New Spain, 1629*, by Hernando Ruiz de Alarcón, Norman

Anguiano, Marina, et al. 1987. *Las Tradiciones de Día de Muertos en México*, Mexico

Ariès, Phillipe. 1981. *The Hour of our Death*, London (paperback 1983)

1985. *Images of Man and Death*, Cambridge, Mass. and London

Artes de México: various numbers, particularly no. 145, 1971

Bailey, Joyce Wadell. 1979. 'The Penny Press' in Ron Tyler (ed.) *Posada's Mexico*, Fort Worth. (Quoted in Ades: 1989)

Baquedano Meza, Celia Elizabeth. 1989. *Aztec Death Sculpture*, unpublished doctoral thesis, University of London

Barlow, R. H. 1952. 'Decree of Philip III, November 14, 1613, Concerning the Knowledge of Native Languages by the Clergy' in *Tlalocan*, 3, 3

Bauer, A. J. (ed.). 1986. *La Iglesia en la economía de América Latina: siglos XVI al XIX*, Mexico

Beals, Ralph L. 1946. *Cherán: a Sierra Tarascan village*, Washington, D.C.

1951. 'Ethnology of the Western Mixe' in *University of California publications in American Archaeology and Ethnology*, XLII, Berkeley and Los Angeles

Benson, Elizabeth P. (ed.). 1975. *Death and the Afterlife in Pre-Columbian America*, Washington, D.C.

Berlin, Heinrich; Balsalobre, Gonzalo de; Hevia y Valdés, Diego de. 1988. *Idolatría y Superstición entre los Indios de Oaxaca*, Mexico

Bierhorst, John. 1985. *Cantares Mexicanos: Songs of the Aztecs*, Stanford

Bierhorst, John (trans. and ed.). 1974. *Four Masterworks of American Indian Literature*, New York

Billeter, Erika (ed.). 1987. *Images of Mexico: the Contribution of Mexico to 20th Century Art*, catalogue of exhibition at Schirn Kunsthalle, Frankfurt

Bloch, Maurice and Parry, Jonathan (eds). 1982. *Death and the regeneration of life*, Cambridge

Boase, T. S. R. 1972. *Death in the Middle Ages*, London

Boone, Elizabeth Hill. 1983. *The Codex Magliabechiano*, 2 vols, Berkeley

Boone, Elizabeth Hill (ed.). 1982. *The Art and Iconography of Late Post-Classic Central Mexico*, Washington, D.C.

1984. *Ritual Human Sacrifice in Mesoamerica*, Washington, D.C.

1987. *The Aztec Templo Mayor*, Washington, D.C.

Brandes, Stanley. 1988. *Power and Persuasion: Fiestas and SocialControl in Rural Mexico*, Philadelphia

Brenner, Anita. 1929. *Idols Behind Altars*, New York

Brocklehurst, Thomas Unett. 1883. *Mexico To-Day*, London

Brown, Peter. 1981. *The Cult of the Saints*, London

Brundage, Burr Cartwright. 1979. *The Fifth Sun: Aztec gods, Aztec World*, Austin

Calderón de la Barca, Frances. 1843. *Life in Mexico*, London. (Paperback edition, London, Berkeley and Los Angeles, 1982.)

Carrasco, David. 1982. *Quetzalcoatl and the Irony of Empire: Myths and Prophecies in the Aztec Tradition*, Chicago and London

Carson, W. E. 1909. *Mexico: the Wonderland of the South*, New York

Caso, Alfonso. 1967. *Los Calendarios Prehispánicos*, Mexico

Cervantes, Fernando. 1991. *The Idea of the Devil and the Problem of the Indian: the case of Mexico in the sixteenth century*, London

Charlot, Jean. 1939. *Art from the Mayans to Disney*, New York and London

Chase, Stuart. 1931. *Mexico, A Study of Two Americas*, New York

Childs, Robert V. and Altman, Patricia B. 1982. *Vive tu Recuerdo: Living Traditions in the Mexican Days of the Dead*, Los Angeles

Christensen, Bodil. 1942. 'Notas sobre la fabricación del papel indígena y su empleo para 'brujerías' en la Sierra Norte de Puebla, México' in *Revista mexicana de estudios antropológicos*, 6, 1–2, Mexico

Christian, William A., Jr. 1981a. *Apparitions in Late Medieval and Renaissance Spain*, Princeton (paperback 1989)

1981b. *Local Religion in Sixteenth Century Spain*, Princeton (paperback 1989)

Chumayel, Chilam Balam de, see Roys: 1933

Clendinnen, Inga. 1987. *Ambivalent Conquests: Maya and Spaniard in Yucatan, 1517–1570*, Cambridge

Codex Chimalpopocatl (MS). Museo Nacional de Antropología,Mexico. (For published facsimile see Velázquez: 1945.)

Coe, Michael D. 1984. *Mexico* (rev. and enlarged ed.), London

Cook de Leonard, Carmen. 1971. 'Minor Arts of the Classic Period' in Wauchope, Ekholm, Bernal: 1971

Cortés, Hernán *see* Pagden: 1972

Cortés Ruiz, Efraín; Gomez Poncet, Jorge; Oliver Vega, Beatriz M.; Villanueva Peredo, Plácido. 1988. *Barro, Pan y Recuerdo: Ofrendas a los Muertos*, Catalogue of exhibition in Museo Nacional de Antropología, Mexico

Covarrubias, Miguel. 1947. *Mexico South*, New York

Craine, Eugene R. and Reindorp, Reginald C. (trans and eds). 1970. *The Chronicles of Michoacan*, Norman

Dibble, Charles E. 1974. 'The Nahuatlization of Christianity' in Munro S: Edmonson (ed.), *Sixteenth Century Mexico*, Albuquerque

Dow, James W. 1973. 'Saints and Survival: the function of religion in Central American Indian society'. Ph.D dissertation, Brandeis University, Waltham

1975. *The Otomi of the Northern Sierra de Puebla*, East Lansing

1982. 'Las figuras de papel y el concepto del alma entre los Otomís de la sierra' in *América Indígena*, 42, 4

Durán, Diego *see* Horcasitas, Heyden: 1964, 1971

Edmonson, Munro S. (ed.). 1974. *Sixteenth-century Mexico: the work of Sahagún*, Albuquerque

El Guindi, Fadwa. 1977. 'Lore and Structure; Todos Santos in the Zapotec System' in *Journal of Latin American Lore*, 3, 1, Los Angeles

Elliott, J. H. 1989. *Spain and its World 1500-1700, Selected Essays*, New Haven and London

Epton, Nina. 1968. *Spanish Fiestas*, London

Farb Hernández, Joanne and Hernández, Samuel R. 1979. *The Day of the Dead: tradition and change in contemporary Mexico*. Catalogue of exhibition in Triton Museum of Art, [Santa Clara]

Flanet, Véronique. 1982. *La Maîtresse Mort, violence au Mexique*, Paris

Florentine Codex (MS). Biblioteca Medicea-Laurenziana, Florence. See Anderson, Dibble: 1950–82

Foster, George M. 1945. *Sierra Popoluca Folklore and Beliefs*, Berkeley

1960. *Culture and Conquest: America's Spanish Heritage*, New York

Fuente, Beatriz de la. 1987. 'El amor a la vida en las ofrendas a la muerte' in Noelle: 1987

Gage, Thomas, *The English-American* 1648 *see* Thompson: 1958

Galinier, Jacques. 1976a. 'Les frontières culturelles actuelles des Otomís de la Huasteca méridionale' in *Sociedad Mexicana de Antropología*. Mesa redonda 14:185–90.

1976b. 'La grande vie: représentation de la mort et practiques funéraires chez les indiens Otomís (Mexique)' in *Cahiers du Centre d'Etudes et de Recherches Ethnologiques*, 2, 4, Bordeaux

1987. *Pueblos de la Sierra Madre: Etnografía de la Comunidad Otomí*, Mexico. Spanish translation by M. Sánchez Ventura and P. Chéron of *n'yuhu: les indiens otomis*.

García Cubas, Antonio. 1945. 'La Verbena del Día de Muertos' in Alvarez and Alvarez de la Cadena (eds), *México, Leyendas y Costumbres Trajes y Danzas*, Mexico

García García, Domingo; García Ramos, Crescencio. 1983. *Ninin*, Papantla

García Ramos, Crescencio. 1983. 'Puchaw: la ofrenda totonaca' in *Boletín informativo del Instituto de Antropología*, 2, Xalapa

Garibay K., Ángel María. 1948. 'Sahagún: Relación breve de las fiestas de los dioses' in *Tlalocan*, 2, 4

1964–8. *Poesía Náhuatl*, 3 vols., Mexico

Gibson, Charles. 1964. *The Aztecs Under Spanish Rule*, Stanford

1966. *Spain in America*, New York

Gomez de Orozco, Federico. 1945. 'Costumbres, Fiestas, Enterramientos y Diversas Formas de Proceder de los Indios de Nueva España' in *Tlalocan*, 2, 1

Gooch, Fanny Chambers. 1887. *Face to Face with the Mexicans*, New York

Gossen, Gary H. 1984. *Chamulas in the World of the Sun*, Prospect Heights

Graulich, Michel. 1989. 'Miccailhuitl: The Aztec Festivals of the Deceased' in *Numen*, 36, 1

Green, Judith Strupp. 1969. *Laughing Souls: the Days of the Dead in Oaxaca, Mexico*, San Diego

Greenberg, James B. 1981. *Santiago's Sword: Chatino Peasant Religion and Economics*, Berkeley, Los Angeles, London

Grimes, Joseph E. and Hinton, Thomas B. 1969. 'The Huichol and Cora' in Wauchope, Vogt: 1969

Gruzinski, Serge. 1989. *Man-Gods in the Mexican Highlands*, Stanford

Guerrero Guerrero, Raúl. 1987. *Toneucáyotl: El pan nuestro de cada día*, Mexico

Harvey, H. R. and Kelly, Isabel. 1969. 'The Totonac' in Wauchope, Vogt: 1969

Herrasti, Lourdes and Vargas, Enrique. 1985. 'Día de Muertos entre los Coras' in *México Indígena*, 7

Heyden, Doris. 1987. 'Symbolism of Ceramics from the Templo Mayor' in Boone: 1987

Heyden, Doris and Villaseñor, Luis Francisco. 1984. *The Great Temple and the Aztec Gods*, Mexico

HMAI. *Handbook of Middle American Indians* see below, entries under Wauchope

Horcasitas, Fernando. 1979. *The Aztecs Then and Now*, Mexico

Horcasitas, Fernando and Heyden, Doris (trans and eds). 1964. *The Aztecs: The history of the Indies of New Spain*, New York. English translation of part of Diego Durán, *Historia de las Indias de Nueva España y Islas de Tierra Firme*

1971. *Book of the Gods and Rites* and *The Ancient Calendar*, Norman. English translation of part of Diego Durán, *Historia de las Indias de Nueva España y Islas de Tierra Firme*

Hoyos Sáinz, Luis de. 1945. 'Folklore español del culto a los muertos' in *Revista de Dialectología y Tradiciones Populares*, I, Madrid

Hoyos Sáinz, Luis de and Hoyos Sancho, Nieves de. 1947. *Manual de folklore: la vida popular tradicional*, Madrid

Ichon, Alain. 1973. *La Religión de los Totonacas de la Sierra*, Mexico

Ingham, John M. 1986. *Mary, Michael, and Lucifer: Folk Catholicism in Central Mexico*, Austin

Jones, Barbara. 1967. *Design for Death*, London

Juárez, José. 1983. *Ofrenda*, Mexico. Introduction by Dolores Olmedo

Kolonitz, Paula. 1976. *Un viaje a México en 1864* (translated from 1868 Italian edition), Mexico (paperback 1984)

Krause, Anna. 1937. 'Jorge Manrique and the Cult of Death in the Cuatrocientos' in *Publications of the University of California at Los Angeles in Languages and Literature*, I, 3

La muerte, expresiones mexicanas de un enigma. 1975. Catalogue of an exhibition held in the Museo Universitario, Universidad Nacional Autónoma de México, Mexico

Lafaye, Jacques. 1974. *Quetzalcóatl et Guadalupe: la formation de la conscience nationale au Mexique (1531–1813)*, Paris

Landa, Diego de *see* Tozzer: 1941

Lane, Sarah and Turkovich, Marilyn. 1987. *Días de los muertos/Days of the Dead*, Chicago

Leander, Birgitta. 1972. *Herencia cultural del mundo náhuatl (a través de la lengua)*, Mexico

León, Imelda de (ed). 1988. *Calendario de Fiestas Populares*. 2nd ed., Mexico

León-Portilla, Miguel. 1963. *Aztec Thought and Culture: a study of the ancient nahuatl mind*, Norman

1969. *Pre-Columbian Literatures of Mexico*, Norman

1975. *Trece Poetas del Mundo Azteca*, 3rd. ed., Mexico

1985. *Los Franciscanos Vistos por el Hombre Náhuatl*, Mexico

León-Portilla, Miguel (ed.). 1966. *The Broken Spears: The Aztec Account of the Conquest of Mexico*, Boston (trans. of *Visión de los Vencidos*)

1980. *Native Mesoamerican Spirituality*, New York

Leonard, Irving A. 1959. *Baroque Times in Old Mexico*, Ann Arbor

Leyenaar, Th. J. J. 1980. 'The celebration of the Days of the Dead in Mexico' in van Gulik, W. R.; van der Straaten, H. S. and van Wengen, G. D. (eds), *From Fieldcase to Show-case*, Amsterdam, 1980

1987. 'The Days of the Dead – recurring reunion' in van Dongen, P. L. F.; Leyenaar, Th. J. J. and Vos, K. (eds). *The Seasons of Humankind*, catalogue of exhibition at the Rijksmuseum voor Volkenkunde, Leiden, 1987

Litvak King, Jaime and Castillo Tejero, Noemí (eds). 1972. *Religión en Mesoamerica*, proceedings of the XII Mesa Redonda of the Sociedad Mexicana de Antropología, Mexico

Lope Blanch, Juan M. 1963. *Vocabulario Mexicano Relativo a la Muerte*, Mexico

López Austin, Alfredo. 1973. *Hombre-Dios: religión y política en el mundo Náhuatl*, Mexico

Lyon, G. F. 1828. *Journal of a residence and tour in the Republic of Mexico in the year 1826*, London

MacLachlan, Colin M. and Rodriguez, Jaime E. 1980. *The forging of the cosmic race: a reinterpretation of Colonial Mexico*. Berkeley, Los Angeles, London

Madsen, William. 1960a. 'Christo-paganism: a study of Mexican religious syncretism' in *Nativism and Syncretism*, Middle American Research Institute, New Orleans.

1960b, *The Virgin's Children: Life in an Aztec Village Today*, New York, reprinted 1969

1967. 'Religious Syncretism' in Wauchope, Nash: 1967

1969. 'The Nahua' in Wauchope, Vogt: 1969

Madsen, William and Claudia. 1969. *A Guide to Mexican Witchcraft*, Mexico

Martínez, José Luis. 1972. *Nezahualcóyotl: Vida y Obra*, Mexico

Matos Moctezuma, Eduardo. 1986. *Muerte a filo de obsidiana*, Mexico

1987. *El Rostro de la Muerte en el México prehispánico*, Mexico

Matos Moctezuma, Eduardo, et al. 1971. 'Miccaihuitl: el Culto a la Muerte' [issue title of] *Artes de México*, 145

Mayer, Brantz. 1844. *Mexico as it was and as it is*, New York and London

Méndez, Leopoldo and Yampolsky, Mariana (eds). 1971. *Lo efímero y eterno del arte popular mexicano*, 2 vols, Mexico

Mendieta, Gerónimo. de. 1870. *Historia eclesiástica Indiana, obra escrita a fines del siglo XVI . . .*, Mexico

Merrill, William L. 1988. *Rarámuri Souls: Knowledge and Social Process in Northern Mexico*, Washington, D.C.

Metford, J.C.J. 1991. *The Christian Year*, London

México en el Arte: various numbers, especially no. 5, 1948

México Indígena: various numbers, especially no. 7, 1985

México Indígena: various numbers, particularly those issued in October 1979 and November-December 1985

Meyer, Michael C. and Sherman, William L. 1979. *The course of Mexican history*, New York

Michoacán, Relación de (MS) (Códice del Escorial), Real Biblioteca de El Escorial, Madrid *see* Crain, Reindorp: 1970

Monjarás-Ruiz, Jesús (ed.). 1987. *Mitos cosmogónicos del México indígena*, Mexico

Monsiváis, Carlos. 1970. *Días de guardar*, Mexico

1987. '"Look Death, Don't be Inhuman" Notes on a Traditional and Industrial Myth' introduction to Pomar: 1987

Motolinía, Fray Toribio. 1950. *The Indians of New Spain*. Berkeley

1971. *Memoriales, o libro de las cosas de la Nueva España y de los naturales de ella*, Mexico

Münch Galindo, Guido, 1983. *Etnología del Istmo Veracruzano*, Mexico

Navarrete, Carlos. 1982. *San Pascualito Rey y el Culto a la Muerte en Chiapas*, Mexico

Neuhart, John and Marilyn and Eames, Ray. 1989. *Eames design. The work of the office of Charles & Ray Eames*, London

Nicholson, Henry B. 1971. 'Religion in Pre-Hispanic Central Mexico' in Wauchope, Ekholm, Bernal: 1971

Noelle, Louise (ed.). 1987. *Arte Funerario*, 2 vols, Mexico

Nutini, Hugo G. 1988. *Todos Santos in Rural Tlaxcala: a Syncretic, Expressive, and Symbolic Analysis of the Cult of the Dead*, Princeton

O'Neill, John P. (ed.). 1990. *Mexico: Splendors of Thirty Centuries*, catalogue of exhibition at The Metropolitan Museum, New York

Ochoa, Lorenzo (ed.). 1989. *Huaxtecos y Totonacos, una antología histórico-cultural*, Mexico

Ochoa Zazueta, Jesús Ángel. 1974. *La muerte y los muertos*, Mexico

Oliver Vega, Beatriz et al. 1988. *Los Días de Muertos, una costumbre mexicana*, Mexico. Also published in English as *The Days of the Dead, a Mexican Tradition*.

Pagden, Anthony. 1990. *Spanish Imperialism and the Political Imagination*, New Haven

Pagden, Anthony (trans. and ed.). 1972. *Hernán Cortés: Letters from Mexico*, London (paperback New Haven and London, 1986)

Parsons, Elsie Clews. 1936. *Mitla Town of the Souls*, Chicago

Paz, Octavio. 1959. *El laberinto de la soledad*, 2nd ed., Mexico (paperback 1972). English translation: *The Labyrinth of Solitude*, London, 1967

1974. *Conjunctions and Disjunctions*, New York

1990. 'The Power of Ancient Mexican Art' in *The New York Review*, 6 December

Pelauzy, M. A. 1978. *Spanish Folk Crafts*, Barcelona

Pomar, Teresa. 1987. *El Día de los muertos, the life of the dead in Mexican folk art*, Fort Worth. Catalogue of an exhibition at the Fort Worth Art Museum also shown at the Serpentine Gallery, London, 1988

Posada, José Guadalupe. 1963. *José Guadalupe Posada: Ilustrador de la vida mexicana*, Mexico

1972. *Posada's Popular Mexican Prints*, New York. See also Rothenstein: 1989

Prescott, William Hickling. 1873. *History of the Conquest of Mexico*, Philadelphia

Quezada, Noemi. 1977. 'La Danza del Volador y Algunas Creencias de Tempoal en el Siglo XVIII' in *Tlalocan*, 7

Ramírez, Susan E. (ed.). 1989. *Indian-Religious Relations in Colonial Spanish America*, Syracuse

Redfield, Robert. 1930. *Tepoztlan, a Mexican village: a study of folk life*, Chicago and London

1941. *The folk culture of Yucatan*, Chicago

Redfield, Robert and Villa R., Alfonso. 1934. *Chan Kom: A Maya Village*, Washington, D.C.

Ricard, Robert. 1966. *The Spiritual Conquest of Mexico: an essay on the Apostolate and the evangelizing methods of the mendicant orders in New Spain, 1523–1572*, Berkeley

Romero Frizzi, María de los Angeles. 1973. 'Los Dias de Muertos en San Juan Atepec, Ixtlan, Oax.' in INAH, *Boletín*, 11, 7, Oct.-Dec.

Rothenstein, Julian (ed.). 1989. *J. G. Posada: Messenger of Mortality*, London

Roys, Ralph L. 1931. 'The ethno-botany of the Maya' in *Middle American Research Series*, 2, New Orleans

1933. *The Book of Chilam Balam of Chumayel*, Washington, D.C.

1943. *The Indian background of Colonial Yucatan*, Washington, D.C.

Sahagún, Bernardino de. *General History of the Things of New Spain*, (*Florentine Codex*) see Anderson & Dibble: 1950–82

1932. *A History of Ancient Mexico* (trans. Bandelier), Nashville

Salinas-Norman, Bobbi. 1988. *Folk Art Traditions II: A book of culturally-based, year-round activities with an emphasis on the Day of the Dead*, Oakland

Sandstrom, Alan R. and Pamela E. 1986. *Traditional Papermaking and paper cult figures of Mexico*, Norman

Santamaría, Francisco J. 1959. *Diccionario de mejicanismos*, Mexico

Sartorius, Carl. 1961. *Mexico about 1850*, Stuttgart. Reprint of *Mexico. Landscapes and Popular Sketches*, Darmstadt, London and New York, 1858

Sayer, Chloë. 1990a. *Arts and Crafts of Mexico*, London

1990b. (ed.) *Mexico: The Day of the Dead*, London

Scheffler, Lilian. 1985. *Magia y brujería en México*, Mexico

1989. *Grupos indígenas de México*, Mexico

Sebastián, Santiago. 1985. *Contrarreforma y Barroco*, 2nd ed., Mexico

Sepúlveda, María Teresa. 1973. 'Dias de Muertos en Iguala, Gro.' in INAH, *Boletín*, 11, 7, Oct.-Dec.

1983. *Magia, Brujería y Supersticiones en México*, Mexico

Serna, Jacinto de la. 1892. 'Manual de Ministros de Indios'. *Anales del Museo Nacional*, 6, Mexico

Simpson, Lesley Bird. 1967. *Many Mexicos*, 4th ed., Berkeley

Soustelle, Jaques. 1971. *The Four Suns* (trans. E. Ross), London

Spores, Ronald. 1984. *The Mixtecs in Ancient and Colonial Times*, Norman

Standley, Paul C. 1969. 'Trees and Shrubs of Mexico' in *Contributions from the United States National Herbarium*, 23, Washington, D.C.

Starr, Frederick. 1899. *Catalogue of a Collection of Objects illustrating the Folklore of Mexico*, London

1900, 1902. *Notes upon the Ethnography of Southern Mexico*, Parts I & II. Reprinted from *Proceedings of Davenport Academy of Natural Sciences*, 8 & 9, Davenport, Iowa

1908. *In Indian Mexico: A Narrative of Travel and Labor*, Chicago

Stephens, John L. 1842. *Incidents of Travel in Central America, Chiapas, and Yucatan*, new edition, 2 vols, London (paperback 1969)

1843. *Incidents of Travel in Yucatan*, 2 vols, New York (paperback 1963)

Tax, Sol (ed.). 1952. *Heritage of Conquest: the Ethnology of Middle America*, Glencoe

Thompson, J. Eric S. (ed.). 1958. *Thomas Gage's Travels in the new World*, ed with intro. by J. Eric S. Thompson, Norman

Todorov, Tzvetan. 1982. *La Conquête de l'Amérique: La Question de l'Autre*, Paris

Toor, Frances. 1947. *A Treasury of Mexican Folkways*, New York

Tozzer, Alfred M. (ed.). 1941. *Landa's Relación de las Cosas de Yucatan*, Cambridge, Mass.

Van Zantwijk, R. A. M. 1967. *Servants of the Saints: the Social and Cultural Identity of a Tarascan Community in Mexico*, Assen

Viqueira, Juan-Pedro. 1984. 'La Ilustracion y las fiestas religiosas populares en la Ciudad de mexico (1730–1821)' in *Cuicuilco*, 14–15, July-December, Mexico

Von Hagen, Victor W. 1943. *The Aztec and Maya Papermakers*, New York

Wauchope, Robert and Nash, Manning (eds). 1967. *Social Anthropology*, volume 6 of *Handbook of Middle American Indians*, Austin

Wauchope, Robert; Ekholm, Gordon F. and Bernal, Ignacio (eds). 1971. *Archaeology [sic] of Northern Mesoamerica, Part 1*, volume 10 of *Handbook of Middle American Indians*, Austin

Wauchope, Robert and Vogt, Evon Z. (eds). 1969. *Ethnology, Part 2*, volume 8 of *Handbook of Middle American Indians*, Austin

Weckman, Luis. 1984. *La Herencia Medieval de México*, 2 vols, Mexico

Weitlaner, Irmgard Johnson. 1971. 'Basketry and Textiles' in Wauchope, Ekhom, Bernal: 1971

Weitlaner, Roberto J. and Barlow, Roberto. 1955. 'Todos Santos y Otras Ceremonias en Chilacachapa, Gro.' in *El Mexico Antiguo*, 8

Westheim, Paul. 1985. *La Calavera*, Mexico

Wilkerson, S. Jeffrey K. 1980. 'Man's Eighty Centuries in Veracruz' in *National Geographic*, 158, 2

Williams García, Roberto. 1963. *Los Tepehuas*, Jalapa

1972. *Mitos Tepehuas*, Mexico

Zolla, Carlos. 1988. *Elogio del Dulce*, Mexico

List of Illustrations

All objects and photographs are copyright the Trustees of the British Museum with the exceptions noted below. Photographs indicated with s were taken by Chloë Sayer.

Colour plates

following page 32

1. Figure of a *cihuateteo*. Aztec. 1990 Am10 1
2. Cemetery in Michoacán. Copyright Louisa Buck.
3a. Feasting skeletons. Metepec, State of Mexico. 1989 Am12 467a-d
3b. Offering in the village of Atla, Puebla.
4. Pottery scene from Ocumicho, Michoacán. 1978 Am15 349
5. Offering table at Cazuelas, Veracruz.
6. Wedding trio. Mexico City. 1990 Am8 345
7. 'Tree of Life' representing the life cycle. Metepec, State of Mexico. 1990 Am8 42
8. Cemetery at San Gabriel Chilac, Puebla.

following page 64

9. Cemetery at San Pablito, Puebla.
10a. Truck with *cempasúchil* flowers. Atlixco, Puebla. s
10b. Candle-sellers. Tantoyuca, Veracruz.
11a. Market stall. La Merced, Mexico City.
11b. Sugar skulls. Toluca, State of Mexico. s
12. Papier mâché skull. Mexico City. 1990 Am8 366
13a. Miniature sugar coffins. Toluca, State of Mexico. 1990 Am8
13b. Miniature skeleton figures. Puebla and Morelos. Collection Chloë Sayer. Photo copyright David Lavender.
14a. Public offering for the Day of the Dead. Mexico City. s
14b & c. Sugar skulls of bride and groom. Toluca, State of Mexico. 1986 Am6 60 & 61
15. Mestizo *ofrenda*. Chicontepec, Veracruz. s
16. Lifesize papier mâché skeleton. Mexico City. 1990 Am8 2

following page 96

17. Model *ofrenda*. Oaxaca. 1986 Am6 3
18. Model catafalque. Oaxaca City. 1978 Am15 346
19. Offering in the town of Huaquechula, Puebla. s
20a. Totonac offering from El Tajín, Veracruz. s
20b. Adjacent Totonac altars for the saints and for the dead. Plan de Palmar, Veracruz. s
21. 'Tree of Life'. Izúcar de Matamoros, Puebla. 1990 Am8 33
22a. Otomí Indians from San Pablito, Puebla. Copyright Chloë Sayer.

22b. Cemetery at Hueyapan, Morelos. Copyright Ramón Penichet.
23a. *Xantolo* dancers at Zapotitla, Hidalgo. Copyright Chloë Sayer.
23b. Tissue paper banner from San Salvador Huixcolotla, Puebla. 1986 Am6 266
24. Death and the Devil dancing. Arrasola, Oaxaca. 1978 Am15 651

following page 128

25. Cemetery at San Gabriel Chilac, Puebla.
26a. Family with papercuts, San Salvador Huixcolotla, Puebla. s
26b. Sweet in the form of heart with flowers. Toluca region, State of Mexico. 1990 Am8 1248. Photo copyright David Lavender.
27. Painted pottery candelabrum. Izúcar de Matamoros, Puebla. 1989 Am12 411b
28. Figure of *La Catrina*. Mexico City. 1986 Am6 404
29. *Xantolo* dancers. Zapotitla, Hidalgo. Copyright Chloë Sayer.
30. Newspaper vendors. 1990 Am8 123
31. Procession in San Juan Bautista, California. Copyright Andy Jillings.
32. Making a path of flower petals. Atla, Puebla.

Front cover

Papier mâché figure of a bread-seller. Mexico City. 1990 Am8 346
Detail of an offering. Chicontepec, Veracruz. s

Back cover

Woman selling *cempasúchil*. Acaxochitlán, Hidalgo.

Black and white

Frontispiece: Detail of papier mâché figure of a skeleton with flowering branches. Mexico City. 1990 Am8 2
1. Papier mâché skeleton telephonist. Mexico City. 1989 Am12 382a & b
2. Two paper puppets. Toluca, State of Mexico. 1986 Am6 20, 21
3. Figure of Death on a wheeled dais. Yanhuitlán, Oaxaca. Copyright Ruth D. Lechuga.
4. 'El Grito'. Masked figure. Mexico City. Copyright Yolanda Andrade.
5. Sugar skulls. San Miguel de Allende, Guanajuato. Copyright Mariana Yampolsky.
6. Papier mâché skeleton with fireworks. Mexico City. 1986 Am6 207
7. Grave with food offering. Tancoco, Veracruz. s
8. Offering for the Day of the Dead. San Pablito, Puebla. Copyright Chloë Sayer.
9. The cemetery gate. San Gabriel Chilac, Puebla.
10. Men decorating graves. Xochitlán, Puebla. Copyright Marcos Ortiz.
11. Domestic pottery. Yecapixtla market, Morelos.
12. Papercut with skeletal animal design. San Salvador Huixcolotla, Puebla.

13. Chili peppers. Pahuatlán, Puebla. Copyright Chloë Sayer.
14. Totonac *ofrenda*. El Tajín, Veracruz.
15. Decorative paper for altar. Cerro del Carbón, Veracruz. 1986 Am6
16. Family *ofrenda*. Ixhuatlán de Madero, Veracruz.
17. Offering for dead children. La Venta, Veracruz. s
18. Decorated baker's shop window. Xochimilco, Distrito Federal.
19. Detail of papier mâché skeletons. Museo de Arte Moderno, Mexico City. s
20. Two papier mâché skulls. Mexico City. 1986 Am6 181 & 182
21. Competition altar. Atlixco, Puebla.
22. Detail of *La Última Movida*. Puebla City. s
23. Aztec death god. 1849 6-29 2
24. Page from *Codex Borgia*.
25. Detail from *Codex Laud*.
26. Page from *Codex Borbonicus*.
27. Detail of a skull-rack. Chichén Itzá, Yucatán. Copyright Chloë Sayer.
28. Page from *Codex Magliabecchiano*.
29. Carved stone from Izapa, Chiapas.
30. Pottery figurine head. Soyaltepec, Oaxaca.
31. Detail from a stone frieze. El Tajín, Veracruz
32. Stone carving of a skull. 8622
33. Stone panel with low relief carving of a skeletal figure. Benque Viejo, Belize. 1927 1-11 1
34. Low-relief stone carving of a skull.
35. Detail from frieze. El Tajín, Veracruz.
35. Pottery figure of a bishop. Metepec, State of Mexico. 1990 Am8 32
36. Pottery figure of a king. Metepec, State of Mexico. 1990 Am8 31
37. Illustration of Death from *La Portentosa Vida de la Muerte ...* (1792).
38. Painting of a dead nun. Museo Nacional del Virreinato, Tepotzotlán, State of Mexico.
39. Masked dancers. Petlacala, Guerrero. Copyright Ruth D. Lechuga.
40. Moors and Christians. Tepoztlán, Morelos. Copyright Chloë Sayer.
41. The Virgin of Guadalupe. Collection Chloë Sayer. Photo copyright David Lavender.
42. Stone cross. Huaquechula, Puebla.
43. Turquoise mosaic decorated skull. Aztec. St.401
44. Detail of skull rack. *Codex Borbonicus*.
45. Toy in form of church with skeleton. Oaxaca City. 1978 Am15 338
46. Engraving of the tomb of Carlos II. Coatepec, Puebla. AD1700.
47. *Gran Comelitón de Calaveras*. Engraving by José Guadalupe Posada.
48. Skull frieze (detail). José Guadalupe Posada.
49. Sugar animals. Toluca, State of Mexico; Huaquechula and Atlixco, Puebla. 1990 Am8
50. Market stall with toys. La Merced, Mexico City. Copyright Marcos Ortiz.
51. Three sugar skulls. Mexico City. 1978 Am15 318, 369-70. Photo copyright David Lavender.

Index

The page numbers in italics refer to the illustrations